The Reverse Discrimination Controversy

A MORAL AND LEGAL ANALYSIS

PHILOSOPHY AND SOCIETY SERIES

General Editor: MARSHALL COHEN

Also in this series:

The Reverse Discrimination Controversy

A MORAL AND LEGAL ANALYSIS

Robert K. Fullinwider

ROWMAN & ALLANHELD
Totowa, New Jersey

ROWMAN & ALLANHELD PUBLISHERS

Copyright © by Rowman and Littlefield, 1980

First published in the United States of America, 1980 by
Rowman and Littlefield, 81 Adams Drive, Totowa, New Jersey

LIBRARY OF CONGRESS CATALOGING IN PUBLICATION DATA

Fullinwider, Robert K   1942–
    The reverse discrimination controversy.

    (Philosophy and society)
    Bibliography: p.
    Includes index.
    1. Affirmative action programs—Law and
legislation—United States. 2. Discrimination
in employment—Law and legislation—United
States. 3. Discrimination—United States.
4. Affirmative action programs—United States.
5. Discrimination in employment—United States.
I.   Title. II.   Series.
KF3464.F84   344.73'01133   79-27344
ISBN 0-8476-6273-X
ISBN 0-8476-6901-7 (pbk.)

84 85 86 87 10 9 8 7 6 5 4 3

To Alan Shavzin—
Philosopher and Poet, Teacher and Friend

Contents

Preface

A healthy and democratic society must
bear in mind that although not all can
make social policy, all may judge it.[1]

The rights and wrongs of complex issues do not readily lend
themselves to fruitful popular debate. The din of public
controversy favors those who shout loudest and simplify
greatest. Nevertheless, a democratic society cannot avoid
popular debate on important matters of right and wrong
without yielding the ideal that informed and reasoned public
opinion will shape the direction of social policy.

This book is a contribution to the current controversy about
reverse discrimination, which has already produced its share of
"sound and fury." The reader should not expect in the
following chapters final and definitive solutions to the debate
about the proper (or improper) use of race (or gender) in social
policy. I am more successful at raising questions than answer-
ing them. This is partly because some of the normative issues in
this controversy are so intractable to solution. Nevertheless, I
believe there is a ground for establishing a reasoned public
consensus about reverse discrimination, and I try to show what
it is.

One way to contribute to public debate is to help clear away
confusions and misconceptions and point out blind alleys and

hopelessly bad arguments. This I attempt to do by surveying the main arguments and sub-arguments about reverse discrimination and examining the principles and concepts which give them life. This is a book of arguments, and arguments about arguments.

Another way to contribute to public debate is to inform, and I have tried to do that as well. If there is a particular failing of the democratic ideal in the present controversy, it is not so much the failure of public opinion to be reasoned as it is the failure of public opinion to shape social policy. Government policy on reverse discrimination has evolved in the past decade and a half largely through bureaucratic rule-making and judicial decision-making. It has not been shaped by the legislative process, through which public debate ought to inform and influence policy. Not only has this evolution of policy meant that popular debate has been somewhat sterile; it has also meant that the public has little understanding of what its government's policy is or why it is what it is. Thus, I devote nearly a third of this book to an examination of regulations, statutes, and case law bearing upon employment discrimination, an examination meant to be both informative and critical.

I conceive of this book as a stimulus to and resource for the reader's further thinking about the reverse discrimination controversy. By using the bibliography, the list of court cases, and the references to relevant statutes and regulations, the reader can explore further many sides of this complex controversy. Of the many arguments he will encounter in the following pages, the reader may find some unpersuasive or not to his liking; but they provide a framework, I hope, for him to reformulate them to his own satisfaction or to supply his own alternatives.

In writing this book, I have benefited greatly from the comments and encouragement of Josiah Gould, Steven Davis, and Carl Wellman, and I take this opportunity to publicly thank them. I am especially indebted to Carol Manning, who read every word of every draft. I should also acknowledge the helpful assistance of Richard Rimkunas and the efficient typing of Virginia Smith.

Parts of Chapters Three and Four incorporate materials from "Preferential Hiring and Compensation," *Social Theory and Practice,* 3 (Spring 1975), 307-320 (copyright © 1975 by *Social Theory and Practice,* Florida State University), and "On Preferential Hiring," in Mary Vetterling-Braggin, Frederick Elliston, and Jane English, eds., *Feminism and Philosophy* (Totowa, New Jersey: Littlefield, Adams and Company, 1977), 210-224 (copyright © 1977 by Littlefield, Adams and Company). I thank Littlefield, Adams and Company and *Social Theory and Practice* for permission to use those materials here. Initial work on this book was done under a grant from the State University of New York Research Foundation, for which I am grateful.

Center for Philosophy and Public Policy
University of Maryland, College Park

Abbreviations

C.F.R. (as in 41 C.R.F. 60)	Code of Federal Regulations
Cong. Rec. (as in 110 *Cong. Rec.* 6549)	Congressional Record
FEP (as in FEP 431:91)	Fair Employment Practices
FEP Cases (as in 13 FEP Cases 392)	Fair Employment Practices Cases
FR (as in 44 *FR* 4427)	Federal Register
F. 2d (as in 442 F. 2d 159)	Federal Reporter (Second Series)
F. Supp. (as in 356 F. Supp. 252)	Federal Supplement
LW (as in 47 LW 4650)	United States Law Week
P. 2d (as in 507 P. 2d 1169)	Pacific Reporter (Second Series)
S. Ct. (as in 96 S. Ct. 1251)	Supreme Court Reporter
Stat. (as in 91 *Stat.* 116)	U.S. Statutes at Large
U.S.C. (as in 42 U.S.C. 2000e)	United States Code
U.S. Code, Cong. & Ad. News	U.S. Code, Congressional and Administrative News
U.S. (as in 405 U.S. 330)	United States Reports

1

Introduction

In *The Washington Post*, June 12, 1977, there appeared an announcement for positions in the Department of Implementation of the School Committee of the City of Boston. The advertisement concluded with this stipulation:

Nominations for both acting and permanent positions cited will be made on the basis of one white person to one non-white person until at least 40 percent of the professional staff of the Department of Implementation is non-white. (p. K9.)

Will more and more job advertisements come to include similar stipulations? Can a policy of ratio hiring according to race be morally and legally justified?

* * *

In 1977, Congress passed legislation requiring that 10 per cent of all federal public works contracts go to minority-owned firms.[1] Is such legislation wise? Fair? Constitutional?

In 1973, Allan Bakke applied for admission to the Medical School of the University of California at Davis. He was denied admission to a class of one hundred. The Medical School had set aside 16 places in that class for minority students. Some of the minority students admitted had lesser scores than Bakke. He sued, claiming the University's admissions procedure unconstitutionally discriminated against him. On June 28, 1978, the United States Supreme Court ordered Bakke admitted to the Medical School. Was the University's admissions policy morally defensible? Was the Supreme Court's decision good law? How can it be illegal for the University of California to admit a certain number of blacks on the basis of their race and yet legal for the Boston School Committee to hire on the basis of color?

※   ※   ※

Suppose there were a law that limited the number of black students in a medical school class. Wouldn't such a law be attacked as racially discriminatory? Is not, then, a rule which limits the number of white students in a medical school class also racially discriminatory? Isn't this reverse discrimination? Surely, a law which set limits to the number of blacks who could hold a certain job would be viewed as racially discriminatory. Why isn't a law which places such limits on whites equally discriminatory? Isn't this reverse discrimination?

Some say: in giving preferences to blacks, we have instances of "benign" discrimination, discrimination designed to help include blacks in jobs and schools. Thus, the new discrimination is really different from the old discrimination and is not really discrimination at all.

Isn't this like arguing that a coin has only one side? If one person is discriminated "for," somebody else must be discriminated "against." The old discrimination was benign, too—benign to whites. There is nothing different about the new discrimination, it might be urged, except that the victims and the beneficiaries of discrimination have been reversed. That is why it is called reverse discrimination.

Some would reply that the fact that the victims and beneficiaries are reversed makes all the difference and makes the new discrimination justified. Others would respond that racial discrimination is racial discrimination and that if it is wrong to discriminate against a black on account of his race, then it is wrong to discriminate against a white on account of *his* race. It is as simple as that.

But nothing is as simple as that about this controversy.

ARGUING THE ISSUE

Reverse discrimination is a topic of intense public controversy and profound legal challenge. Affirmative action plans, affecting every sizable institution receiving federal contracts or assistance, have been accused of promulgating quota hiring. Busing children to schools according to race has occasioned public outcry and sometimes violent resistance. And programs giving minorities preferential admissions to law and medical schools have presented the Supreme Court with two of its most important constitutional cases of the decade—*DeFunis* v. *Odegaard* and *University of California* v. *Bakke*.[2]

What can one believe? On the one hand are charges that reverse discrimination is growing to a frightening magnitude. On the other are claims that there isn't any reverse discrimination at all, that it is a myth propagated by a racist elite.[3] A person trying to sort his way through the controversy will encounter confusing and contradictory arguments, disputes about the facts, conflicting interpretations of the law, appeals to the same principles in support of opposed conclusions, charges of bad faith and racism. Lawyers, jurists, moralists, philosophers, union leaders, educators, civil rights leaders, legislators, government officials, clergymen, and editorialists vehemently disagree about the justifiability, the effects, the meaning, and even the existence of reverse discrimination. This is amply enough illustrated in the recent *Bakke* case:

Item: An unprecedented number of organizations submitted legal briefs to the Supreme Court as "friends of the court." Former allies in the civil rights struggles of the 1950s and 1960s found themselves divided against one another in support of or in opposition to preferential admissions for minorities.

Item: The dean of the University of Michigan Law School publicly supported racial preferences in admissions to medical and law schools as moral and lawful. The dean of Indiana University Law School was equally certain in print that reverse discrimination in admissions was immoral and illegal.[4]

Item: Headline in *The Washington Post,* November 28, 1977: "Temporary 'Reverse Bias' Endorsed by 90 Professors." The story quoted a statement released by the American Civil Liberties Union, in response to the *Bakke* case, in which ninety professors said that "special programs for minorities are temporarily necessary to make up for 'deeply entrenched discriminatory patterns' of the past." (p. A15.)

Item: What some professors support, others can oppose. On February 9, 1978, *The New York Times* carried this story: "One hundred and twenty-five college and university professors have opposed a statement last November by 90 other university professors that special hiring and admissions programs for minorities were temporarily necessary to make up for discriminatory patterns of the past." (p. A16.)

Item: Kenneth Tollett, a frequent commentator on *Bakke* as it was awaiting decision by the Supreme Court, said in early 1978: "the affirmance of Bakke would mean the reversal of affirmative action; it would be an officially sanctioned signal to turn against blacks in this country. . . . Opposition to special minority admissions programs and affirmative action is anti-black."[5]

Item: In *The New York Times* and *The Washington Post* for June 29, 1978, several civil rights leaders provided a somewhat calmer assessment of the Supreme Court's actual order to admit Bakke. Jack Greenberg, Director of the NAACP Legal Defense Fund, said the Court's decision "means that the sort of affirmative-action programs that most schools have are constitutional and gives a solid basis upon which such programs can be sustained."[6] It was not the end of affirmative action and nobody detected a signal to turn against blacks.

A person who is confused by the competing charges and claims will not likely resolve his doubts by attending to the public debate. Arguments on either side are often little more than gut reactions, though they are usually rooted in widely accepted moral beliefs: that compensation ought to be made for wrongs done; that past imbalances in treatment ought to be redressed; that unjust advantage ought to be rectified; that there is a pressing social need to improve the economic and educational level of minorities; that the burden of social reforms should be spread fairly; that race is an undesirable basis for distributing benefits and burdens; that equal opportunity requires (forbids) racial preferences; that people's basic rights cannot be violated even to secure important social goods.

Although appealing to widely accepted moral intuitions, the arguments constructed on these appeals are usually imprecise, indecisive, and incomplete even when they are moderate and careful. Opponents talk past one another, never coming to grips. Catch-phrases and slogans substitute for analysis and criticism. The issues remain unfocused, unrefined, and no progress is made toward bringing a full understanding of the moral and legal questions in dispute.

What are the arguments? Proponents of preferential treatment for blacks urge it as a way of making up for centuries of racial injustice. We are told we must as a matter of justice rectify a present situation where whites have an unfair competitive advantage. Moreover, it is socially imperative that blacks be integrated into all segments of society and that racial division be diminished. It is true that some whites will be discriminated against by policies that prefer blacks, but some interests must be disappointed by any social policy. Both justice and the public interest favor preferential treatment of blacks for the short run.

Opponents charge that preferential treatment lowers the quality of workers and students and creates inefficiency, that it imposes an unfair burden on some whites, and that it violates the merit principle of selection. It involves the use of a racial criterion and this is morally vicious and legally unconstitutional.

Confronted with such a sketchy preliminary survey, a puzzled bystander might like to address several questions to both proponents and opponents of preferential treatment. To the proponents:

1. What is the principle of compensation to which you appeal? Is it related to the moral-legal principles that apply to other aspects of our dealings with one another? How could it justify broad preferences for blacks (and others) in employment and education? Does it matter who has to bear the burden of such compensation?

2. Might not individuals (whites) have rights that stand in the way of preferential treatment for blacks? Can individual rights be overriden to promote social good or greater equality or deserved compensation? Always? Sometimes? When?

3. Although it is indeed true that some people must be hurt by nearly any social policy, surely you recognize some limitation on involuntary individual sacrifices for the public good. Surely there are some sacrifices that society cannot legitimately extract from individuals no matter how much is to be gained. What are the limits to what society may do to individuals in pursuit of its policies? Why, specifically, may society diminish a white's job opportunities in order to benefit blacks but may not diminish his political liberties?

To the opponents of reverse discrimination:

1. Why is it always wrong to employ a racial criterion? What moral or political principle entails this absolute prohibition?

2. Preferential treatment of blacks imposes special burdens on some whites, to be sure, but why is this unfair? Desirable and acceptable policies often place burdens unevenly. Why is it unfair in the present case?

3. What gives the merit principle its standing? Why is it sacrosanct? Why must it always take precedence over other considerations? Why may not efficiency be sacrificed for compelling reasons of justice or even charity?

4. What rights do individuals have which would be violated by preferring minorities in employment and education? What constitutional grounds are there for denying to government a possibly useful tool in promoting racial equality?

Behind these questions lie yet others: What is equal opportunity? What is affirmative action? What is the difference between racial goals and racial quotas? What are qualifications and how are they to be ascertained?

PREVIEW

These and other questions are taken up in this book. I offer answers to them, but not always with confidence. In fact, I believe there are not many decisive answers to be found in this controversy. The quarrel about the rights and wrongs of reverse discrimination may ultimately prove intractable. It is one of the underlying themes of this book that persons of good will, fully informed and considering all the arguments, can still reasonably disagree about the moral and legal merits of racially preferential treatment. There are two reasons for this which are discussed in following chapters. The first is the incompleteness of our knowledge about the future effects of alternative social policies and, beyond that, the absence of a common and uniform way of weighing those effects. The second reason lies in the vagueness and indeterminacy inherent in the broad principles of justice to which we must appeal. The controversy about reverse discrimination raises the deepest questions about social justice and tests our principles in a way few controversies have.

In this respect, the debate about reverse racial discrimination differs from the earlier movement against racial segregation and subordination. The earlier patterns of racial discrimination and oppression in our nation were so egregiously offensive that people could unite in condemning them without being forced to formulate with precision the principles upon which their condemnation rested. We need not look far into our moral beliefs, whatever they are, to find grounds to condemn lynching, to despise bullying, to denounce hatred and hypocrisy, and to decry the denial of elementary liberties. Our system of racial segregation offended against every civilized mortality, whether utilitarian or Kantian, Christian or Jewish, absolutist or situationalist. Thus, we could unite to fight against segregation and for racial justice without being forced to notice that at the level of deepest principles there might be considerable disagreement among us and deep puzzlement about how to resolve those differences.

The controversy surrounding reverse discrimination brings out the deeper differences because it demands that we articulate and defend answers to some of the most basic questions about social justice and human rights. About these answers there is much disagreement, disagreement which need not derive from ill-will, or truculence, or mental laziness, or hypocrisy. There is sufficient source for it in the fact that we are driven to our intellectual frontiers, where it is difficult to achieve precision without arbitrariness and where archimedian foundations are elusive.

This book explores those frontiers and the disputes that lead us there. I explore the philosophical, moral, and legal sides to reverse discrimination and examine the various arguments for and against it, detailing their weakness and strengths, exhibiting their hidden assumptions, speculating about their theoretical foundations. I am first of all concerned to identify and probe the principles upon which the various arguments rest. I want to know if reverse discrimination violates the basic rights of individuals or offends against one or more basic moral principles. If it does violate rights or transgress basic principles, we may conclude that reverse discrimination is morally unacceptable. If it does not, then we may conclude that the rightness of reverse discrimination will depend upon the good it does. And the conclusion to be drawn might be that it does little good at great cost. Whether this is true, or whether the reverse is true, takes us beyond the bounds of this book. I discuss in later chapters some of the goods and bads that might be expected from the use of racial preferences, but this discussion is cursory and does not constitute the kind of exhaustive marshalling of facts and well-founded projections which would be needed to establish a strong case in support of one or the other conclusion.

In order to simplify the exposition that follows, I shall concentrate on one specific form of alleged reverse discrimination, namely *preferential hiring*. Much of what I say about preferential hiring will, of course, apply to other forms of preferential treatment, but not always. Moreover, in order to simplify the discussion, I will speak about preferential hiring of *blacks*. Controversy about reverse discrimination extends, of course, to proposals to give preferences to women and to some ethnic minorities such as Puerto Ricans and Mexican-Americans. Nevertheless, I will focus mostly upon the issue of racial preferences. Again, much of what I say about reverse racial discrimination will readily transfer to other forms, but not always.

The arguments for and against preferential hiring of blacks are versions of the arguments already sketched. They will be considered in detail in the next several chapters. I will consider arguments that appeal to principles of compensation or reparations, principles of social utility, and principles of distributive justice. I will pass on to a discussion of equal opportunity, the nature of rights, and a number of other topics raised by the preceding arguments. In the middle portions of the book I discuss the law and affirmative action. I end by looking at constitutional principles and by returning to the search for moral conclusions.

But first, we must define terms.

TERMS

Before we can begin to assess arguments we must be clear about words. The terms involved in the reverse discrimination controversy are especially treacherous, including foremost the phrase "reverse discrimination" itself. It is often disputed whether a certain practice really is reverse discrimination and we must be careful not to beg any questions of substance by playing upon controversial words.

What is discrimination? The dictionary says that to discriminate is to note or observe a difference; or (more appropriately for our purposes) to make a distinction as in favor of or against a person or thing.[7] But we would fail to understand the force of our current political discourse if we understood no more than this. "Discrimination" has become a word of opprobrium, used as a term of condemnation or complaint. It is used to refer to those distinctions-in-favor-of-or-against which the speaker feels is unjustified. It derives this use from instances of differential treatment based on race, sex, wealth, religion, or other bases of differentiation widely thought to be inappropriate or unacceptable. Thus, commonly enough, to say that a practice discriminates is at the same time to condemn it, all the more so if it is in connection with race.

Now, there is nothing about the bare idea of making a distinction in favor of or against a person which implies that such distinguishing is wrong or undesirable. So the dictionary meaning of discrimination is morally neutral, not saying anything one way or another about the rightness or wrongness of a particular discrimination or of discrimination in general. In this neutral sense, we discriminate all the time. When a teacher gives one student an "A" and another a "D", he is discriminating between good work and inferior work. When a child gives a birthday present to his mother but not to his neighbor, it discriminates. Voters discriminate between Republican and Democratic candidates. Such discrimination is not only pervasive in human life, most of it is perfectly justified and much of it morally required. (A father who failed to discriminate between his own and other children in the disposal of his income has failed to meet his paternal obligations.)

The dictionary sense of "discrimination" is neutral while the current political use of the term is frequently non-neutral, perjorative. With both a neutral and a non-neutral use of the word having currency, the opportunity for confusion in arguments about racial discrimination and reverse racial discrimination is enormously multiplied. For some, it may be enough that a practice is called discriminatory for them to judge it wrong. Others may be mystified that the first group condemns the practice without further argument or inquiry.

Many may be led to the false sense that they have actually made a moral argument by showing that the practice discriminates (distinguishes in favor of or against). The temptation is to move from "X distinguishes in favor of or against" to "X discriminates" to "X is wrong" without being aware of the equivocation involved.[8]

If one takes "discrimination" as including wrongful or unjustified treatment as part of its meaning, then "reverse discrimination" must likewise imply wrongness since reverse-direction wrongness is still wrongness. As a consequence, one who uses the non-neutral sense of "discrimination" and who favors selecting blacks for jobs wholly or partly on account of their race will want vigorously to resist calling this reverse discrimination.[9] To call it such is, for him, to condemn it.

On the other hand, a person might concede that selecting blacks on account of their race is reverse discrimination but claim that nevertheless it is justified. This person must be using "discrimination" in a neutral way. An argument between the first person and the second over whether selecting blacks because of their race is really reverse discrimination would be a purely verbal dispute. Both would approve of preferential selection, disagreeing only about what name to call it.

My concern in this book is with the merits of certain substantive policies and not with what they are called. Since the phrase "reverse discrimination" is a source of mischief, I will avoid using it and "discrimination" as much as I can, although in later chapters where I examine statutes and court cases, avoidance will be impossible. I shall not, in any case, judge something to be wrong merely because it is labeled "discrimination" or "reverse discrimination." Unless the context of my remarks plainly indicate otherwise, I shall use these phrases in a neutral, descriptive way.

For the most part, I shall be talking about preferential hiring (and other forms of preferential treatment). Now, strictly speaking, all hiring is preferential, since all hiring involves selection of the basis of some quality or qualities valued ("preferred") by the employer. When I talk about preferential hiring, I will be talking about a situation where a person is hired because he or she is black, a woman, a veteran, an Indian, etc., and where these characteristics are irrelevant to job performance. It is this kind of situation which stimulates charges of discrimination and reverse discrimination. My discussion will be confined primarily to preferential hiring of blacks.

By calling such hiring "preferential" I intend only to label it, not to evaluate it. I will say more about preferential hiring shortly. Likewise, as the occasion warrants, I will discuss some other troublesome terms: "qualifications," "compensation," and "equal opportunity."

FORMAL JUSTICE

It surely is not always wrong to make favorable or unfavorable distinctions among people. What about, however, when these distinctions are based on race? Some believe there is an easy, general answer to this question. They urge that racial discrimination violates the *formal principle of justice*. That principle tells us that likes must be treated alike.[10] It says that it is wrong to treat two persons differently if there is no morally relevant difference between them. It does not proscribe treating people differently, only treating people differently who are not different.

But what is to count as a difference, a morally revelant difference? When are people relevantly alike? The formal principle of justice does not say. How, then, can this principle, unsupplemented by other moral premises, condemn the use of race as a selection criterion?

Not only is the formal principle silent on what is to count as alikeness and unalikeness for purposes of treatment, it is not even clear that the principle applies to all of our dealings with one another. Suppose Jane loves Tom rather than Tim. It seems beside the point to ask if there is some morally relevant difference between the two which justifies Jane in bestowing her affections on Tom and not Tim. Is there any need for Jane to justify herself? Justify herself to whom?

We can avoid the problem about the scope of the formal principle of justice because we are interested primarily in a narrow range of treatment, namely, bestowal of benefits or burdens by government or as a result of government policy. Our focus is on the permissibility of the government's instituting, through legislation, executive order, or judicial decree, a policy of permitting or requiring racial preferences in hiring. Here the formal principle seems indisputably to have purchase. The government, unlike Jane, is required to justify its choices and is not permitted to exercise a preference for white skin (or black), the Christian religion, male sex, etc., unless these properties happen to be morally relevant characteristics for the purpose of conferring benefits and burdens.

Those who believe that the formal principle of justice always forbids racial discrimination or racial preferences of any sort are thus committed to the view that race can never, under any circumstances, be a morally relevant characteristic in regard to state action. This view—that race is always an arbitrary and unacceptable basis for social choice—is widely held. Consider this representative claim:

"All men are created equal" means that all distinctions and discriminations on the basis of race, color, religion, and the like are evil, and these bases should never be criteria for differential treatment.[11]

But why does "all men are created equal" mean that such distinctions are always evil? Why must race be, from a moral point of view, always an arbitrary and illegitimate basis for differential treatment?

The essence of government legislative activity or policy-making is classification. Legislation creates classes of persons who receive special benefits or suffer special burdens. The blind are eligible for special assistance but are disqualified from holding a driver's license. Corporations which pollute the air are subject to fines which do not fall on non-polluting companies. Tax law treats those whose taxable income is over $50,000 differently from those whose taxable income is under $10,000. Penal law treats those who get drunk in private differently from those who get drunk in public.[12] Differentiation, distinction, classification—this is what much of government is all about, as we shall note again in a later chapter. Sometimes underlying a legislative classification will be some prior difference that we intuitively take to be morally relevant. The comparative helplessness of the blind provides a reason for government to provide to blind persons seeing-eye dogs while at the same time not providing dogs to the public at large. But on other occasions, the legislative classification itself creates the basis for differential treatment, as when a law permits persons at age 16 to acquire a driver's license. There is clearly no prior notable distinctions to be drawn between individuals who are 15 years, 11 months old and those who are 16 years, one month old.

Our perception that government acts justly in framing legislative classifications involves two elements: first, the acceptance of the purpose of the legislation as morally legitimate and, second, a belief that the state has adopted classifications reasonably related to the promotion of the legislative purpose. If the state adopts a statute for the purpose of promoting home-ownership but denies blacks the benefits available under the statute to whites, we judge this unjust discrimination because we discern no rational connection between the discrimination and the putative purpose of the statute. We can condemn the discrimination by reference to the demands of formal justice: the state's action seems arbitrary and inconsistent with its avowed purpose.

But if the state takes as its explicit purpose the separation of the races and the subordination of blacks, and thus takes as its aim the denial to blacks of home-ownership, then legislation which assisted only whites would involve a discrimination which was obviously rationally related to state purpose. Here, we cannot condemn the state by showing its actions inconsistent with its aims. We must condemn the state's aims themselves. But this will require, in the end, reference to some substantive principles of justice, not mere recitation of the injunction to treat likes alike.

The belief that formal justice condemns all racial discrimination because race is never a morally relevant characteristic upon which to base differential treatment presupposes, then, the substantive judgment that racial classifications are never materially related to the promotion of any morally legitimate state purpose. This seems a very strong claim. Is it illegitimate for the state to make as its explicit end the improvement of the conditions of a particular race when the particular race in question represents an impoverished group or has been the victim of a history of abuse and exploitation? I do not think we can dismiss out of hand the legitimacy of such an aim; and the materiality of the use of racial preferences to such an aim seems quite apparent. It may be wise or even mandatory never to use race as a basis of preference, but this will need to be established by substantive moral argument.

FOCUS

We want, then, to turn to the substantive arguments. In particular, we want to consider the arguments that bear upon the legitimacy or illegitimacy of favoring blacks in employment because they are black. Now, one background consideration is what we might term a principle of merit: that it is reasonable to select for each job the best qualified for it. If a black is chosen over a white because the black is more qualified, it is difficult to imagine what principled basis for complaint there could be. It might be urged that in such a case, a black is not being chosen on account of his race. But we must not be too quick; we must not rule out the possibility, without argument, that being black can be a job qualification. If it can be, then there can be instances of a black's being hired on account of his race which conform to the merit principle. What raises the great controversy, then, is not so much a black's being favored on account of his race but his being favored on account of his race in circumstances where being black is not a job-related qualification.

This explains why I have adopted the following usage in this book: *a black is preferentially hired over a white when the black, because he is black, is chosen over at least one better qualified white, where being black is not a job-related qualification.* Where race is irrelevant to the performance of the job, if a black is hired over a white but would not have been hired over another black with the same qualifications as the white, then this is an instance of preferential hiring.[13] If a black is hired because he is black but being black is a job-related qualification, then this is not a case of preferential hiring as I have defined it.

My definition leaves open the possibility that blackness can be a genuine job-related qualification.[14] Many might oppose using race as a criterion even when it bears on job performance. Others might dispute whether race ever is a proper qualification. These matters are aired in a later chapter. For now, it is important for the reader to take notice of how I shall be using the phrase "preferential hiring" throughout the rest of this book. Other writers use the phrase in different ways.

2

The Types of Argument

SOCIAL UTILITY ARGUMENTS

The defender of preferential hiring of blacks might point to the many social goals such a policy would likely serve. A well-designed, successfully executed policy of preferential hiring would increase the well-being of many people since it would move many blacks upward on the economic scale. It would provide additional role models for young blacks by placing blacks in greater than token numbers in more visible and desirable positions. It might result in better services being provided to the black community. Overall, the upshot of the policy would be to break down racial stereotypes and to move America closer toward being a racially integrated society. These gains, of course, would be bought at a certain cost, but the defender of preferential hiring can claim that the benefits to society outweigh the costs.

This is a very familiar kind of argument. To give it a name, I will call it the *Social Utility Argument*. It takes the form of showing that the aggregate well-being of society is promoted by some policy. The benefits of the policy are discounted by its costs. If the social "utility" (i.e., aggregate well-being) is raised, and raised at least as high as it would be by any other alternative, then the policy is said to be "in the public interest," or "for the common good."

Although arguments of this type are common, they are infected by notorious problems. First is a practical problem: how do we accurately project all the foreseeable consequences of any complex and far-reaching social policy? The second problem is conceptual: how are we to define and interpret social well-being? What is to be counted as contributing to or detracting from social utility? Finally, there is a theoretical problem: if the utility of society is composed of the well-being of individuals in society, how are these individual utilities to be measured, compared, totaled-up?

Despite these difficulties, social utility arguments are popular and frequently persuasive. Sometimes it is pretty obvious that a certain policy will substantially improve the social lot. But sometimes this is not the case. Often it will be true that, despite the best application of the tools of economic analysis and sociological research, our judgments about the expectable effects of a policy will rest in large part on hunch and guess-work. It will also often be true that, even in the face of agreement about expectable effects, we will lack a common measure for gaining consensus about the proper weights to be assigned to good and bad consequences. Where these things are true, there will be ample room for controversy and disagreement, even among reasonable and well-informed people.

In regard to preferential hiring, opponents of such a policy might claim that its costs are far greater than its proponents concede, or that its benefits are very much smaller, or that in any case its benefit-to-cost ratio is unfavorable compared to other alternatives. Perhaps there are non-preferential ways of breaking down racial stereotypes, improving the economic condition of blacks, and fostering integration which, though not as effective as preferences, are not as costly either.

How do we measure the projected benefits and costs of preferential hiring? How extensive will preferential hiring be? How long will it last? How many will it effect? Will such a policy actually promote racial stereotypes at the same time that it is working to undermine them? I will discuss the Social Utility Argument for preferential hiring in greater detail in a subsequent chapter. It seems reasonable enough to conjecture here, however, that the argument will not foreclose the possibility of considerable differences of informed opinion about the desirability of preferential hiring.

DISTRIBUTIVE JUSTICE ARGUMENTS

A different kind of argument for preferential hiring might urge that government has a positive duty, even at considerable social cost, to channel resources, including jobs, so as to increase the opportunities and improve the condition of those who "are toward the bottom of the socio-economic-political pecking order, and unlikely to rise as things are presently arranged."[1] Preferential hiring can be viewed as one instrument for carrying out this redistribution. Because a very large proportion of blacks are in the lower socio-economic classes, a device which favors blacks in employment will in effect favor a substantial segment of society's poor. By such means as preferential hiring, deficiencies in opportunities for blacks can be ameliorated and the economic status of blacks improved. I will call such an argument the *Distributive Justice Argument* for preferential hiring.

Appeals to justice are nearly as common as appeals to the general welfare. Such appeals respond to deep elements in our common moral sense. We believe that people ought to have what is due to them. Any argument which claims that people are entitled to a certain share of this or that good is an argument that appeals to this sense.

Arguments that make such appeals are frequently difficult to evaluate because there is so much controversy and uncertainty about the appropriate principles of distributive justice. Moreover, arguments often fail to distinguish between grounds of distributive justice and grounds of charity. We believe that it is good to help those in distress. But what does this belief come to, precisely? Does it express anything more than an idea of charity, the idea that we ought to provide some measure of relief to the needy but that no person is entitled to demand such relief as his right? Is there a separate, stronger principle to the effect that the poor and disadvantaged have a moral right to our help, that they can claim resources from us as their due so that we have no right not to give aid?

Those who contend that preferential hiring is required or justified by principles of distributive justice must be explicit. What kind and how much redistribution is due to whom? Under what circumstances? How are resources for redistribution to be appropriated? Unless questions like these are given full and specific answers, appeals to distributive justice degenerate into appeals to our vague and ill-formed intuitions of fairness and fittingness.

Many people oppose preferential hiring on grounds of justice. Although they would agree that the putative aims of preferences—a rise in aggregate social utility or a redistribution of resources to the poor—may be laudable in themselves, they would hold preferential hiring itself to be unjust because it places the costs of achieving these aims not on everybody equally but only on a few, namely those white job applicants disadvantaged by being in competition with preferred blacks. Most people support improving the lot of the poor and making society better off, but many instinctively feel that preferential hiring is not a fair way to accomplish these things. If the advocate of preferences has nothing more to offer than his own competing intuition that giving racial preferences is fair, then there is simply a stalemate in the dispute.

Is there any way beyond mere gut feelings of fairness or

unfairness? The proponent of preferential hiring believes it gives blacks their due. The opponent believes it denies whites theirs. Who is right? Both? Neither? Is there any way to decide? We will explore the complexities of a Distributive Justice Argument for preferential hiring in later chapters.

RIGHTS

One thing due to an individual is recognition of his rights. Do blacks, all of them or some, have rights to be preferred in employment? How were these rights acquired? Do they derive from principles of distributive justice or from other grounds?

Are there any moral rights that are infringed by preferential hiring? Neither the Social Utility Argument nor the Distributive Justice Argument speaks to the possibility of existing rights (moral or legal) of individuals to some or all of the resources to be channeled to raise utility or improve the lot of the poor. These defenses of preferential hiring leave out of account the possibility that preferences violate the rights of some persons. Even if we believe the poor have redistributive rights, we must recognize that others have various rights as well and that redistributive policies must be adjusted to those rights.

But what rights could individuals have that would be violated by giving employment preferences to blacks? Opponents of preferential hiring might claim that each citizen has a constitutional right to "equal protection of the laws," guaranteed by the Fourteenth Amendment, and that this right is violated by racial preferences.[2] Moreover, the opponents might urge that each individual has a right to equal opportunity and that preferential hiring must violate this right. Since I will explore in detail in later chapters the meaning of constitutional "equal protection," let us focus here on the second claim, that there is a right to equal opportunity which stands in the way of preferential hiring.

Many, including both defenders and opposers of preferential hiring, claim that all persons have a right to equal opportunity. But this claim is quite vague. What is equal opportunity? In saying that a person has a right to equality of opportunity, what in particular are we saying he has a right to? Before we can decide whether or not preferential hiring violates the rights of some to equal opportunity, the alleged right must be specified in a more detailed and concrete way. Let us make some preliminary moves here.

The 125 professors mentioned in the newspaper story in Chapter One, who opposed the statement by 90 other professors supporting preferential treatment for minorities, were reported as saying that

just as no one truly dedicated to civil liberties would contemplate a "temporary" suspension of, say, the right to counsel or the right to a fair trial as a means of dealing with a crime wave, so no one truly dedicated to equality of opportunity should contemplate a "temporary" suspension of equal rights of individuals in order to achieve a goal of greater representation.[3]

The 125 professors evidently take equal opportunity to be an individual right (they speak of "suspension of equal rights") and one that is violated by any use of racial preferences. Moreover, it is reasonable to assume that they hold that this right is, or ought to be, a constitutional one, since they compare it with a person's right to a fair trial.

If we restrict our focus to racial preferences in employment, what would the right to equal opportunity amount to? As a first approximation, let us posit for each person a right to *equal consideration for a job*. This does not mean that any person has a right to a job. Rather, it means that if an individual applies for a job for which he is qualified, he must be considered equally with all other candidates. But what does this mean? Suppose we further specify the right in question as one which asserts that *each job applicant has a right that the successful applicant*

be chosen solely on the basis of his job-related qualifications.
Here we have a right which is specific and which is violated by
preferential hiring (as defined). For short, I will call this the
right to equal consideration (RTEC).

Is this a right we wish to endorse? It is certainly one feasible
specific interpretation of equal opportunity in employment. If
there were such a right we would have a ready explanation of
the moral evil of past job discrimination against blacks: their
rights to equal consideration were violated. The existence of
such a right would provide a firm moral foundation for
legislation prohibiting any racial discrimination in hiring practices.

If we assume the existence of RTEC, we can see the force of
the claim by the 125 professors that preferential hiring violates
the equal opportunity rights of individuals. Preferential hiring
appears to be a violation because it is the hiring of people for
reasons not based on job-related qualifications. Even if we
assume RTEC, however, might it not be possible that, despite
initial appearances, preferential hiring does *not* violate any
rights? If preferential hiring could be shown to be justified even
in the face of assuming RTEC, then it ought to be capable of
justification under any weaker assumption. For this reason,
and because so many believe there is a right to equal opportunity, it might prove useful to proceed by assuming RTEC and
seeing what follows from this. That is the strategy I will
adopt. Later I will relax the assumption and see what happens
to the case for preferential hiring.

It might be thought, however, that any justification of
preferential hiring of blacks has been rendered altogether
impossible by the assumption of a right to equal consideration
(RTEC). Preferential hiring as I have defined it will necessarily
involve assigning jobs partly or wholly on the basis of the race
of applicants. Since race is not, where preferential hiring
occurs, a job-related qualification, preferential hiring would
seem necessarily to violate some persons' rights. However, this

conclusion need not follow. Perhaps there are occasions on which a person's rights may without violation be overridden. And even if not, nevertheless there are ways that individuals may *waive* or *forfeit* rights they have.

One kind of argument for preferential hiring that we have not yet noted can readily exploit this last possibility. In brief, the argument which I will term the *Argument from Compensatory Justice* advances on the proposition that those who wrongfully injure or unjustly exploit others acquire an obligation to compensate their victims for their losses. By their behavior the wrong-doers forfeit or qualify their existing rights, since their newly acquired obligations will alter the contours of some of those rights. The assumption of a right to equal consideration (RTEC) may pose no obstacle to justifying preferential hiring if it can be shown that blacks are owed compensation for past wrongs against them and that whites have lost or forfeited their rights to equal consideration for a job. This is what the Argument from Compensatory Justice tries to establish.

FORFEITED RIGHTS AND THE OBLIGATION TO COMPENSATE

In 1969, James Forman presented the Black Manifesto to American churches, demanding that they pay blacks $500 million in reparations. The argument of the Black Manifesto was that for three and a half centuries blacks in America have been "exploited and degraded, brutalized, killed and persecuted" by whites; that this was part of persistent institutional patterns of, first, legal slavery and, then, legal discrimination and forced segregation; and that through slavery and discrimination whites have extracted enormous wealth from black labor with little return to blacks. These facts constitute grounds for reparations on a massive scale. The American churches were but the first institutions to be asked for reparations.[4]

The Black Manifesto did not receive any widespread public support. Rather, it tended to be dismissed if not ridiculed as a crack-pot idea. This is somewhat surprising, for the basic moral ideas underlying Forman's demand are deeply imbedded in our common law and our common morality. The basic ideas are that wrongful injury and unjust enrichment both provide moral grounds for a demand for compensation by the injured or exploited. In fact, such wrongs create rights on the part of the victims and corresponding obligations on the part of the victimizers.

Although the idea of American institutions paying reparations to blacks was not taken seriously in 1969, in recent years one of the most frequent defenses of preferential treatment of blacks characterizes the special treatment as compensation for past injuries suffered under discrimination. Preferential hiring is a way of "making up for past discrimination," of "remedying the effects of past discrimination," of "making up for the wrongs done to blacks." Such language is ubiquitous in arguments about preferential treatment. One recent defense of preferences in employment goes as follows:

Justice requires compensating for past injuries, not just forbidding their reoccurrence. . . . Compensatory justice requires more than an assurance of future "good behavior"; rather, it requires that benefits be provided to those individuals who have been wrongfully injured in order to raise them to the level they would now have if they had not been disadvantaged. . . . Thus preferential policies may be warranted for those members of groups who were previously unable to acquire . . . positions due to discrimination.[5]

This is a statement of the Argument from Compensatory Justice. This may prove to be a forceful and effective defense of preferential hiring. It does not rest upon highly speculative conjectures about the future effects of preferences and it does not appeal to highly controversial principles of distributive justice. Instead, it appeals to a widely accepted moral principle, that those who wrongfully cause injury should compensate their victims and make them whole again if possible. And because the principle includes the idea of forfeiture of rights, the Argument from Compensatory Justice promises to be able to get around the obstacle that the assumption of RTEC creates for the other defenses of preferential hiring. It is worth exploring this argument in some detail to see if it fulfills its potential to be an effective defense of preferences.

Let us begin, then, with a *simple model* of compensation and develop its features. We can then determine if the model can be extended to cover preferential hiring. Suppose I negligently or deliberately back my car through your fence, breaking a hole in it. As a result of my wrongful action, I incur an obligation to pay you the cost of having your fence repaired. Prior to my backing into your fence, I owed you nothing. I was at liberty to spend my money without regard to you. But after I damage your fence, I do not have that liberty. You have a specific right that I use some of my money to pay for the repair of your fence. Your claim against me qualifies and limits my right to spend my money as I please.

There is a variation on this example that is relevant to our purposes. Suppose I am working for the phone company when I break your fence. It may be that it is the phone company instead of me that acquires the obligation to fix your fence. If so, the relationship between you and the phone company would be the same as that between you and me in the initial version of the example. In any event, the heart of the compensation situation is the creation of specific rights holding between particular entities as a consequence of their relationship to a particular episode or episodes. In any claim to compensation, we need to ask: *Who* owes *what* to *whom?*

We should pause here to note an important ambigiuity in the idea of compensation. What I have been calling compensatory justice is about making up for injuries or disadvantages caused by wrongful acts (deliberate or negligent). In its most general sense, however, to compensate simply means to make up for, with no necessary reference to the genesis of the lack or deficiency being compensated for. We might believe that we ought to provide special assistance to the handicapped, the disadvantaged, and so on—to compensate them, in the general sense, for their lesser ability to compete or participate in important social activities. We might even say this is required by a principle of compensation, but such a principle would not be a part of compensatory justice as I am using the phrase but a part of distributive justice. Such a principle would enjoin us to make up for the deficiencies of some without regard to how those deficiences were created.

It is very important to keep the two ideas of compensation distinct. They belong to different parts of morality. Whatever the nature of rights to assistance or redistribution, if there are any, rights arising under compensatory justice are always specific and limited rights against particular persons or entities. Thus, when I speak of compensation I shall be referring to reparations, restitution, indemnification, and the like.

Having noted this, let us return to the simple model of compensation. In the two examples used to illustrate the simple model, there seem to be these possibilities:

I back over your fence and I personally owe you.
I back over your fence while working for the phone company and both I and the phone company owe you.
I back over your fence while working for the phone company and the phone company owes you but I do not.

Depending upon the particular circumstances of my damaging your fence, any one of these might obtain. What does not seem a possibility, however, is this:

I back over your fence while working for the phone company and Sue, who works for the phone company, owes you.

How could Sue owe? It seems ruled out by the simple model unless in some way Sue has agreed to take on my debts or the phone company's.

Can the Argument from Compensatory Justice successfully apply the simple model to preferential hiring?

3

Compensatory Justice

THE SIMPLE MODEL OF COMPENSATION APPLIED

The argument in the Black Manifesto charges wrongs to white America, not to specific white Americans. There is no effort to single out individuals for accusation. It is the nation collectively that is indicted. This is as it should be. The wrongs done to blacks are not simply the sum of individual wrongs done by whites. They are corporate wrongs flowing from the legal practices and legislative policies of the state itself. If the merely personal wrongs of private individuals were at issue, many if not most of the debts of compensation founded on these wrongs would have been extinguished by now. Most of those who constructed and supported the edifice of slavery and subsequent segregation have long since passed from the scene. It is because so many of these were acting in official capacity, on behalf of the nation and not merely as private individuals, that their actions can be the basis of an enduring national debt, inherited by living Americans.

The answer, then, to the question, "Who owes compensation?" is: our government. The whole community, taken corporately, owes. This answer does not rule it out that specific individuals also have personal debts. But neither does it identify any culpable individuals. And this poses an immediate problem for the successful application of the simple model to preferential hiring.

Suppose the government seeks to discharge its debt by mandating a general policy of preferential hiring. That policy will be blind in this sense: it will not ask any job applicant whether he is guilty of wrongs against blacks. It will ask only if he is white. If he is, then he can be discriminated against. Let W be a white applicant and B a black one, both in competition for the same job. What are we to say of the government's discharging its obligation to blacks by favoring B over W for the job?

Recall the assumption we are making that W has a right to equal consideration for the job (RTEC). This means that he has the right that the choice between B and him be decided on the basis of their respective job-related qualifications. If the government adopts a program of preferring blacks in employment, it requires or permits choice by reference to a factor—race—which is not a job-related qualification. This seems to violate W's right. There has been no showing that he has forfeited any right or done anything to make himself liable to the loss of any right. It is the community, not W, which has incurred a compensatory obligation.

Doesn't W's possession of RTEC block the government from legitimately discriminating against him, just as the right to a fair trial blocks the government from engaging in summary executions? The Argument from Compensatory Justice seems to falter at this crucial point. It seems necessary to show that W (and other white job applicants) have forfeited RTEC. If we show only that the community as a whole owes a compensatory debt, we have failed to show that W, for example, is liable for that debt. This is a serious failure.

Although someone may owe compensation to another, he is

not thereby warranted in discharging that debt in any way that is convenient. He must still honor the rights of others. He must pay his debts with what is rightfully his to pay. There is a corollary to this: though one may have a right to be compensated, that right is against a particular actor and embraces no more than what that actor has available to pay as compensation.

These points are vitally important and can be illustrated by an example. Suppose you steal from me a rare musket, the jewel of my gun collection. Before you can be made to return it, the gun is destroyed. There is only one other musket like it in existence and by coincidence it is possessed by your neighbor. Now, I have been wrongfully injured by you and I have a right against you that you make good my loss. But the only thing that can truly make good my loss is the return of my musket—impossible now—or of one just like it. Does it follow that I have a right to your neighbor's gun? Do you have a right to appropriate it to give to me in discharge of your ob'igation? When these questions are put, they answer themselves. You have no right to take your neighbor's gun to give to me and the fact that you owe me compensation doesn't alter that at all.

The simple model of compensation establishes that I do, indeed, have a right to be compensated in this case, but my right is against *you,* and thus it is a right to be compensated by whatever *you* have to compensate me with. If what you have is inadequate, that is unfortunate for me but not grounds for either of us invading your neighbor's rights.

What is true of individuals is also true of governments. Suppose you are a Treasury agent and expropriate and destroy my musket in the mistaken belief that it is contraband. Now my right lies against the government. But the government is no more justified in giving me your neighbor's musket as replacement than you were in the previous example. Thus, establishing that the government is liable to pay something to B does not establish a particular liability in W. If the government decides to discharge its debt to *B* by inaugurating a program that denies *W* his right to equal consideration, this seems as much a case of theft as your paying me with your neighbor's gun.

Because it is usually overlooked in arguments about preferential treatment, this general point deserves to be repeated a third time: one may have a right to compensation for an injury suffered but *that right lies against a specific party and encompasses what that party rightfully has as a means of payment.* If one's claim is against the government—or the community taken corporately—then one's claim is to what the government can rightfully command as means of payment. If taking *W*'s non-forfeited, in-force right is not one of the morally available options, the government is morally foreclosed from that means of payment. If preferential hiring entails taking *W*'s right, then it appears to be illegitimate. It is blocked from consideration.

If we wish successfully to defend preferential hiring by the Argument from Compensatory Justice, we cannot be content merely to show that there is an obligation on the part of the community at large. We must show that in some way *W* has incurred a liability, that in some way his right to equal consideration (RTEC) has become qualified or limited and is *not* violated when the government adopts a scheme of preferential hiring.

FORMS OF VICARIOUS LIABILITY

Sometimes an agent need not commit a particular act in order to be liable for obligations that arise from it. For example, a father may be liable for the debts of his minor children. Many who defend preferential hiring as being an expression of compensatory justice may feel that *W* is liable to a legitimate limitation of his right to equal consideration even if he personally never injured any black. I will consider two arguments to this effect. The first rests on this inference:

> The community owes B
> W is a member of the community
> Therefore, W owes B

Many may, indeed, assume some such inference without actually being aware of it. If the inference were acceptable, it would remove a major impediment to a defense of preferential hiring. If W is personally liable to B, even if only indirectly through his membership in the community, then the community is surely justified in enforcing W's obligation and in doing so it violates no right of W's.

The problem with this inference is that it contains an equivocation. Once this is seen, the inference loses any respectability it might initially appear to have. The problem is this: the phrase "the community" can be taken either distributively or corporately. In the first case, the inference should be restated this way:

> Each member of the community owes B
> W is a member of the community
> Therefore, W owes B

This inference is perfectly valid but the problem with it is that it begs the question. The first premise assumes precisely what is in dispute. The charge in the Black Manifesto was laid at the feet of the community taken corporately, i.e., taken as a complex organization with special governmental bodies and associated roles, functions, and responsibilities.[1] It was also addressed at other organized institutions within the community. The inference suggested by this sort of charge is not the one given immediately above but this one:

> The community's institutions and its government owe B
> W is a member of the community (and its institutions).
> Therefore, W owes B

But this inference is unacceptable. Liability is not something that generally distributes from a corporate entity to each of its members. The phone company example illustrates this fact. It is the same with national obligations. During the Nixon administration, the President imposed by executive order a surcharge on Japanese imports. A federal court ruled that the President's action exceeded his constitutional authority and ordered an award of hundreds of millions of dollars to several Japanese companies. The U.S. Government thereby owed the Japanese companies, but did you or I or even President Nixon owe the companies anything? Not one of us acquired any personal debt to the Japanese although the nation acquired a debt.

This example is sufficient, I think, to remind us of what we already believe in reflective moments: that we should reject the assertion that because an individual is a member of a community he acquires its debts and its liabilities. There may be special cases where debts transfer, but mere group membership does not generally suffice. Because *W* is a member of the community and the community owes *B* is not sufficient ground for saying that *W* owes *B*.

DO INDIVIDUALS OWE NOTHING?

To say that the community owes *B* and that *W* is a part of the community is not to say that *W* owes *B*. But it does not follow from the fact that he does not owe *B* that thereby he owes nothing in regard to the community's compensating *B*. *W* may owe the community. But what could he owe the community simply in virtue of his citizenship?

In general, *W* owes his fair share to support the community's discharging its legitimate obligation. When the United States acquired a debt to Japanese companies, *W* did not acquire a debt to the companies but he did acquire an obligation to provide his fair share of the additional tax revenues from which the government paid its debt. If the community owes *B* and other blacks compensation, *W* owes it to the community to shoulder his fair share of the burden of compensation. What, then, is his fair share?

This raises the question of what is compatible with his rights. The standing obligation to do one's part to support legitimate government ends cannot be a blank check upon which government may draw as it pleases. For example, the government cannot pursue the legitimate goal of efficient prosecution of crime by allowing prosecution witnesses to give testimony anonymously at trial. The right of a defendant to confront and cross examine his accusers is a part of his right to a fair trial. We cannot say to a person tried under such circumstances that deprivation of his right constitutes his fair share of the costs of fighting crime.

Rights as basic and as important as a right to a fair trial cannot legitimately be abrogated by government except in genuine emergency situations. If we take RTEC to be as basic as the right to a fair trial, as the 125 professors apparently do, then we will find it exceedingly difficult to show that *W*'s fair share in supporting legitimate government compensation consists in his being deprived of his right to equal consideration, especially when this deprivation will not fall on all white applicants.

Opponents of preferential hiring of blacks need not oppose the idea that blacks are owed compensation by the nation. They may be concerned, rather, that preferential hiring lies outside the permissible means of compensating blacks. They may be concerned that it violates a basic individual right. A program which violates basic rights is unacceptable; for the signal function of a structure of basic individual rights is to specify the limits to policy beyond which the state cannot proceed no matter how worthy its aims.

So long as opponents of preferential hiring are allowed to assert a right to equal opportunity and to characterize it as specifically and as strongly as RTEC, the argument seems to lie on their side unless defenders of preferences can convincingly show that white job applicants have effectively waived or forfeited the right. The alternative is to deny that anyone has a strong right to equal employment opportunity.

VICARIOUS LIABILITY DUE TO WRONGFUL BENEFITS

W has not been shown to have done any wrongs to blacks. If it could be shown that in spite of this fact he nevertheless has a liability which justifies the government in breaching his right to equal consideration, then the defense of preferential hiring would be greatly facilitated. The problem of violating W's right would not arise. One argument, examined and discarded in the previous section, held that W owes B because the community owes B and W is a member of the community. A second argument is this: Although W has not personally injured any black, he is nevertheless not for that reason "innocent" of the injuries done them. He has *benefited* from past racial injustice.

The Black Manifesto partly rested its demands for reparations on the claim that all whites have benefited from the exploitation of blacks. Since these benefits derived from great wrongs, possession of them constitutes an unjust enrichment and the possessor is under an obligation to restore the benefits to their rightful recipients. Possession of illicit benefits undermines one's claim to "innocence." Such possession makes one an accessory after the fact, so to speak. The wrongful possession serves the same function as personal fault; it makes one liable to pay appropriate compensation. So the argument might go.

The proponent of preferential hiring might adapt this argument to his own purposes. He could claim that all white job applicants have benefited from previous wrongful exclusion of blacks from important segments of the labor market.[2] Thus an applicant such as W is not "innocent." Having benefited from wrongs, he is not in a position to assert his right to equal consideration now that it comes time to pay for the wrongs. A policy of preferential hiring does not, as a consequence, violate W's right.

What about this argument? Will it successfully establish that W's right to equal consideration has been qualified and limited through his receiving "stolen goods"?

White workers unquestionably have been the beneficiaries of the artificial limitation of portions of the labor market to whites only. The relegation of blacks to the least desirable jobs meant less competition among whites for the better positions. Further, whites have tended to have competitive advantages deriving from superior educational preparation, this deriving at least in part from educational discrimination against blacks. Now, it may be arguable whether every single white applicant has received net benefits from past discrimination. Rather than debate the point, let us agree that every white has benefited in some way. Is this sufficient to establish that no white applicant has standing to assert his right to equal consideration (RTEC)? Does it establish that W is "not innocent"?

Many who defend preferential hiring view the losses it imposes on whites as simply their "paying back" benefits that are not legitimately theirs. This view is bound to have some purchase on our sentiments because it rests on a widely held intuition that no one is entitled to benefits gained through wrong. But the issue here is more difficult than it seems. We need a clearer appreciation of how benefiting from wrongs makes us liable and we need to see in what way benefits we are not entitled to can be taken away from us.

The complications here can best be exhibited by an example. My neighbor contracts to have his driveway repaved while he is out of town. Having paid the contractor in advance, he leaves a set of directions in his mailbox, indicating which driveway to pave. An enemy of my neighbor takes the directions from the mailbox and replaces them with others which describe my driveway to the contractor. The contractor arrives while I am out of town as well and, following the directions he finds, resurfaces my driveway. When my neighbor returns, the mistake is discovered. My neighbor has suffered an injury, he has been done a wrong. Somebody owes him compensation. Is it I? Is it the contractor? Or is it the enemy? The obvious answer is: the enemy. But his identity is unknown. My neighbor is faced with an uncompensated loss. Since I benefited by the wrong done to him, am I obligated to compensate my neighbor if the enemy cannot be found?

First, consider the question of whether I am entitled to the benefit that has befallen me. Clearly, I am not. If the surface of my driveway could be stripped off without changing the previous condition of the driveway, then I would have no claim against its being removed. But here is the rub. The benefit that I am not entitled to cannot be removed without disturbing my other rights. Compensating my neighbor means I must pay the cost of the contractor. Taking away the surface of the driveway would leave me no better off and no worse off than before the harm was done, but if I must pay the cost of the contractor, I am left worse off than I was. Presumably I valued other things more dearly than having my own driveway repaved; otherwise I would have had it done myself.

Given, then, that the undeserved benefit cannot be taken from me and my neighbor cannot be compensated by me without my incurring a loss, am I under an obligation to pay compensation? I do not see that I am. It would indeed be generous of me, and if the cost to me were not very great, common decency would suggest I reimburse my neighbor. But if I have little money and have other pressing needs, I am not bound to relieve my neighbor of his loss. By contrast, if the enemy could be found, he would be bound to pay whether he could easily afford it or not. The difference between the enemy and me is that I cannot return the unjustified benefit without suffering a harm that I have a right not to suffer, whereas the enemy, for his wrongful deed, forfeits any right not to suffer whatever harm is necessary to make my neighbor whole again.

To hold that I am bound to pay would be to collapse any moral distinction between myself and the enemy.

I conclude, then, that the fact that I benefited from a wrong is not by itself sufficient to place me under a compensatory obligation and I conclude that this principle is false:

> *P:* He who benefits from a wrong must help pay for the wrong.

If this principle were true, then mere receipt of the benefit would make me liable to bear my neighbor's costs. But the principle fails to take into account a special feature of the situation, one which relieves me of obligation. This feature is the fact that I had no choice in the matter, no means of avoiding the benefit. A principle which incorporates this feature would be preferable to *P*. Such a principle might be:

> *P':* He who knowingly and willingly benefits from a wrong must help pay for the wrong.

How does this example of the driveway apply to preferential hiring? It is argued that *W* has benefited from wrongs done to blacks. These benefits produce competitive advantages to which *W* is not entitled. These advantages can be and ought to be corrected for, and preferential hiring does this. The problem with this argument is that preferential hiring takes away *W*'s undeserved advantage by taking away his right to equal consideration (RTEC); and although he is not entitled to the advantage, he *is* entitled to RTEC. The situation seems to be analogous to the driveway example.

We must ask not whether *W* benefited from wrongs done to blacks but whether he deliberately took advantage of the benefits or refused to avoid them when he easily could have. Now, some white applicants may meet this condition. But it is not obvious that every white will. When employment discrimination against blacks was pervasive, white workers obviously reaped competitive advantages. But in order for many of them to have avoided the taint of advantage it would have been necessary for them to have foregone employment entirely. Employment advantages that accrued to whites due to segregation in the labor market may not have been truly avoidable by them or may have been avoidable only at great cost.

Unavoidability of benefits is even more pronounced for those very general, intangible benefits of racism described by Judith Thomson:

Many [white males] have been direct beneficiaries of policies which have down-graded blacks and women . . . and even those who did not directly benefit . . . had, at any rate, the advantage in the competition which comes of the confidence in one's full membership [in the community], and of one's rights being recognized as a matter of course.[3]

Whites, or white males anyway, may have a general competitive advantage over blacks because of their more secure sense of self-respect and self-confidence, an advantage deriving from a racist system which denied self-respect and self-confidence to blacks. Now, even if this is true, this sort of benefit or advantage is one which is unavoidable because it derives from an individual's early socialization and from other factors beyond his control. Young children have no power to determine the kind of socialization they receive, and by the time they are old enough to understand society and evaluate its practices, the basic features of personality, including self-confidence and self-respect, are already in place. Even in adult years, when one's sense of self-respect is reinforced and enhanced by "confidence in one's full membership in the community," one cannot avoid that reinforcement. One cannot stop others from treating him in ways that augment his self-respect and self-confidence.

Much the same is true about basic educational advantages. Basic reading, mathematical, and other educational skills are already in place before an individual has reached the age of choice. If advantage in these skills derives from injustice done to blacks, there is little conceivable way the advantage could have been avoided by the individual white.

I am not trying to absolve all whites from complicity in the evils of our racist system. Many of us have lived without protest under a social system which has been unjust to blacks. Many of us in large and small ways may be personally culpable for wrongs done to blacks. The point is that it is this personal culpability which is crucial to the creation of personal obligations. Mere possession of benefits produced by someone else's wrong-doing is not enough to obligate. Not all whites will meet the conditions of personal obligation specified by principle P'. Consequently, they will have no personal obligation which obliges them to forego their right to equal consideration. If the government adopts a program which abrogates their right, then it violates the right.

This discussion illuminates the role played in our argument by RTEC. A proponent of preferential hiring might urge that taking away an unjust advantage from an individual is not denying him "equal consideration." In some sense of "equal consideration" this may be true. But remember that I have defined "equal consideration for a job" as the right that jobs be determined on the basis of job-related qualifications. It is precisely because we assume RTEC that it is impossible to use preferential hiring to deny W an undeserved competitive advantage without denying him something that he is entitled to. This reveals once more what a strong assumption RTEC is and may prompt us to reconsider whether we wish to endorse this right or not. We will have occasion to return to this question in the latter chapters of this book.

WARNINGS ABOUT VICARIOUS LIABILITY

There are grounds for imputing vicarious liability. Principle P', for example, is a principle for holding a person liable for a wrong he did not commit. There are other principles of this sort, such as the principle that holds a parent liable for the debts incurred by his minor children and such as those principles of criminal law which make a participant in a felony liable for the culpable acts of his co-participants. Now, it may be that there are acceptable principles that I have not considered which can successfully impute vicarious liability to *every* white applicant for the wrongs done to blacks. (Principle *P'* will not do so, in my judgment.) The advocate of preferential hiring who favors the Argument from Compensatory Justice may wish to offer and defend possible principles that he feels I have overlooked.

We must exercise great caution, however, in accepting principles of vicarious liability. Although there seems a proper place in morality and law for some limited principles of this sort, it is nevertheless a basic part of our common morality that it is wrong to make people liable for what they could not avoid or could not help. The principles mentioned above all rest on the fact that the person made liable possesses some control that would allow him to avoid liability. A parent by exercising proper control over his children can see to it that they do not incur unwanted debts. A person can avoid commiting felonies and thus avoid the risk of liability for the felonious acts of his co-felons. And, clearly, a person can refrain from knowingly and voluntarily receiving stolen goods and thus avoid becoming an accessory.

Broad and uncritical principles of "collective responsibility" or "guilt by association" are to be rejected. Unfortunately, some of our worst traits as humans involve imputing vicarious liability to "enemies." When a Hatfield kills a McCoy, a McCoy will take any Hatfield as a suitable object of retaliation. And Hatfields will look at McCoys in the same way. Blood feuds, primitive and not so primitive, thrive on attributing to all in a group the guilt for the crime of one of its kinsmen. It is only in relatively recent times that Christian denominations have officially abandoned the doctrine that all Jews are guilty of the murder of Christ, a doctrine used throughout the centuries in Europe to justify the worst abominations. And this is only one egregious example of the vicious effect of primitive notions of vicarious liability.

However emotionally satisfying it may be for blacks to believe that all whites owe some sacrifice simply because they are whites, it would be a terrible irony if we were to endorse this view as respectable. It involves the same kind of typecasting and "tainting" which lies at the very core of racism itself.

4

Rights

OVERRIDING RIGHTS

Judith Thomson presents a different argument for imposing the costs of compensating *B* directly upon *W*. Rather than challenge *W*'s faultlessness or claim that he has forfeited his right to equal consideration, she argues that the community may justly *override* *W*'s right. Sometimes a right may be overridden without this being a violation. Thomson says:

> Now it is, I think, widely believed that we may, without injustice, refuse to grant a man what he has a right to do only if *either* someone else has a conflicting and more stringent right, *or* there is some very great benefit to be obtained by doing so—perhaps that a disaster of some kind is thereby averted.[1]

If these were the only grounds for overriding rights, acknowledges Thomson, then preferential hiring would violate *W*'s right to equal consideration rather than justly override it. However, she says, "there are other ways in which a right may be overridden" (378). The other ways amount to overriding a right in order to pay a debt. Thomson offers two examples, both of which are supposed to be examples of justly overriding a right in order to pay a debt of gratitude and both of which are supposed to be analogous to the community's overriding *W*'s right to equal consideration (RTEC) in order to pay a debt of compensation to *B*. The first example involves an eating club which, by majority vote, gives Smith preferential seating privileges out of gratitude for Smith's services to the club. The example is supposed to appeal to our moral intuitions and I suppose that no one would be very inclined to think that another member, for example Jones, was unjustly deprived of any rights if he were made to wait while Smith was seated first though Jones arrived before him. There may be several reasons for this feeling that nothing is terribly amiss here, but one reason, surely, is our perception of the trivial nature of the "burden" Jones is required to bear. He is deprived of nothing important in regard to the benefits of the club. He will be served dinner, being inconvenienced for a few minutes until another table is available. Moreover, the favoring of Smith over Jones in this way does not reflect adversely upon Jones' standing in the club.

The triviality of the deprivation caused Jones and the nebulousness of the very right supposedly overridden (was it Jones' right to be seated before Smith, his right to an impartial seating procedure, or his right to be treated fairly by the club?) unfit this example to be instructive for the preferential hiring case. The right to equal consideration (RTEC), which is at stake in the preferential hiring situation, must be counted a basic right. Even if we are prepared to deny the existence of RTEC, we must still concede that the deprivation imposed on *W* by preferential hiring is not a mere inconvenience, a trivial burden.

Thomson's second example of a just overriding is very much more apt:

. . . suppose two candidates for a civil service job have equally good test scores, but there is only one job available. We could decide between them by coin-tossing. But in fact we do allow for declaring for *A* straightway, where *A* is a veteran, and *B* is not. It may be that *B* is a non-veteran through no fault of his own. . . . Yet the fact is that *B* is not a veteran and *A* is. On the assumption that the veteran has served his country, the country owes him something. And it is plain that giving him preference is not an unjust way in which part of that debt of gratitude can be paid. (379–380.)

This is an important example because giving preferences to veterans in employment is structurally the same as giving blacks preference in employment. In both cases, a factor not related to job performance is employed as a selection criterion. Veteran's preference is established by law; proponents of preferential hiring of blacks claim it is or ought to be mandated by law. Veteran's preference is justified as a way of paying a debt (of gratitude); preferential hiring is argued to be a way of paying a debt (of compensation). In both cases assumedly innocent parties bear the burden of the community's debt. If veteran's preference is acceptable, why is preference of blacks unacceptable? It is hard to see how a person can defend the former without defending the latter.

Veteran's preference has been a pervasive feature of public employment in America for more than half a century. Since 1944, the Federal government has added five points to the civil service examination scores of veterans with prescribed periods of military service (disabled veterans receive more points). Similar preferences are also commonly given by the states.

Although Thomson thinks "it is plain" that veteran's preference is not unjust, this evidently has not been plain to scores of individuals who over the decades have mounted legal challenges to its validity. And it is especially not plain if we assume that each job applicant has the right to equal consideration (RTEC). Thomson doubtlessly relies on the ready legal acceptance of veteran's preference as evidence that its justifiability is plain. However, this legal acceptance is predicated on the assumption that there *is no right like RTEC*. The clearest expression of this position occurs in a recent case, *Feinerman v. Jones,* in which the court sustained the constitutionality of veteran's preference against a challenge based on the Fourteenth Amendment's equal protection clause. The court specifically denied the appellant's claim that she had a right to be considered fairly for public employment.

In the absence of such a right, the state has little difficulty in justifying, at least legally, the use of preferential hiring to "reward those veterans who . . . have served their country in time of war" (*Feinerman* at 259). If we do not assume RTEC, it is easier for our moral intuitions to approve of veteran's preference. If we do assume RTEC, then the ready acceptance by the courts of veteran's preference will not be decisive in our moral evaluation of the practice. Once we assume a right to equal consideration, the preferring of *A* over *B* because *A* is a veteran looks very much like a *violation* of *B*'s right.[2] (Because of the way veteran's preferences parallel racial preferences, we will examine them in more detail in a later chapter.)

Thomson's two examples, then, provide no persuasive support to the idea that important rights may be overridden without injustice in order for the community to pay a debt. The first example is unpersuasive because the alleged right is too trivial. The second is not persuasive, either, because the standard legal acceptance of veteran's preference rests on denying there is any right which is being overridden. Once we assume RTEC, our intuitions about veteran's preference surely become as unhelpful as our intuitions about racial preferences.

CONFLICT OF RIGHTS

Thomson claimed that rights can be overridden if they are in conflict with more stringent rights. Suppose the following argument is made: *W* has a right to equal consideration but *B* has a right to compensation. In the present instance the two rights conflict—to adopt preferential hiring is to override W's right, to refuse to adopt it is to deny B's right. The preceding arguments against preferential hiring rest on the fact that such a policy overrides (and thus violates) someone's rights. But, in fact, someone's rights will be overridden *both* by the adoption of a policy of preference and by the non-adoption of such a policy. So the argument against preferential hiring of blacks rests on the covert and undefended assumption that W's right is more important than B's right.

Let us accept the assertion that a right may be justifiably overridden when it is in conflict with a stronger right. Does this require us to examine W's right to equal consideration and B's right to compensation to determine which is the stronger? Are the two rights in conflict? The answer is no.

If B's having a right to compensation were his having a right to anything from anyone which would make good his loss, then perhaps a conflict of rights would arise between B and W. If a job were the only thing that would compensate B then he would have a right to be preferred for the job; and if W were better qualified he would have a right to be chosen for the job. Each would have a claim to the same resource but only one claim could be accommodated. This would be a genuine conflict of rights.

However, as we have already noted, B's right to compensation has particular contours. It is a right against the community to be compensated by whatever resources the community may legitimately offer. If preference for employment means violating W's right to equal consideration (RTEC), then giving such preference is not in the first place among the eligible items the community may offer, and thus not within the scope of the resources B may claim from the community as a matter of right. Consequently, there is no conflict of rights between B and W, and in holding against preferential hiring one need not be making a covert judgment that W's right is stronger than B's. Since there is no conflict of rights between W and B, we cannot argue that W's right might be justifiably overridden on account of a conflict of rights.

There is a kind of situation that is easily confused with a conflict of rights. It is a situation where I have a right to do something but I cannot do what I have a right to do so long as we honor others' rights. For example, each man has a right to marry. Suppose all females of age marry other men, there being more men than women. Then, I cannot marry even though I have the right to. This is unfortunate for me but it is not the case that my right to marry has been denied me or overridden; nor is there any conflict between my right to marry and anyone else's right. There is indeed a conflict of *interest* between me and other males but not a conflict of rights. My right is not a right that a particular person will marry me or a right that marriageable women be made available to me. It is a right (a liberty) to marry if I can find someone who will marry me.

Consider a more apposite example. In the case of the stolen musket discussed earlier, honoring your neighbor's right to his gun meant that you could not fully compensate me. But there is no conflict of rights between me and your neighbor. I do not have a right to be compensated with your neighbor's gun; I have only the right to be compensated by whatever is yours to compensate me with.[3]

RIGHTS

Thomson also claimed that a right could be overridden to avoid a catastrophe or to secure some very great good. Suppose a proponent of preferential hiring claims that it yields a very great good and this justifies overriding the rights of others.

There are situations where it does seem that overriding a right in order to secure some public good is justified. Motorists may have a right to travel north on Elm Street but if a traffic policeman waves me to an alternative street in order to relieve traffic congestion at an intersection, this seems proper and legitimate. Now, we may be inclined to view this situation in different ways. Some may say that the right I have is not to travel north on Elm Street but to travel north *conditions permitting*. In blocking me from going further north on Elm, the policeman is not overriding my right. Others may hold that my right is the right to travel north on Elm Street *simpliciter*, and that the policeman overrides my right. If we view the matter in the second way, then we appear to have an example where a right can be overridden in order to secure a good, and not at very great good at that.

Undoubtedly there are many examples of this sort. However, I do not believe they will serve to show that the right to equal consideration (RTEC) may be overridden so that blacks may be preferred in employment. They will fail because the right to equal consideration is of the greatest weight. It is assumed to be as basic and as inviolable as the right to a fair trial. Now, whatever the traffic policeman may do on Elm Street, I think it is apparent that the state cannot override an individual's right to a fair trial in order to secure some good, even some very great good. Suspension of a right to a fair trial is warranted, if ever, only in times of extreme emergency. If RTEC is analogously basic, it cannot be justifiably overridden either.

Once again, our conclusion exhibits the strength of the assumption that there is a right to equal consideration (RTEC). By assuming it, we appear to have thoroughly blocked any defense of preferential hiring. We must wonder whether the assumption is justified.

Is there such a right as RTEC? This remains to be seen. I shall not at this point try to persuade you that there is. It should be noted that if there is no RTEC, then neither whites nor blacks possess such a right. If white applicants do have such a right but it is weak, easily overridden by the social goods produced by preferential hiring of blacks, then the right of black applicants to equal consideration for employment is not strong either, and may stand in jeopardy of being overridden in other circumstances in order to achieve some important social aim. Whatever general opportunity rights there are, whites and blacks have the same rights.

Consider the provisional conclusion that we are brought to. If there is a right to equal consideration (RTEC), it is a fundamental right. If it is a fundamental right, it cannot be overridden to achieve some substantial social good. White applicants have not, in general, forfeited this right. If it is in force and cannot be overridden, then it seems to block absolutely any justification of preferential hiring.

This conclusion may be too hasty, however. We need to reconsider the proposition that rights cannot be overridden to achieve some desirable purpose. There is an important qualification to be noted. Consider the following example. The state needs to build a new highway to replace a dangerous and inadequate road. Not only will the new highway save lives, it will spur economic development, make social services more accessible, and so on. But in order to build the highway the state takes my land. Isn't this overriding my property rights? And isn't this plainly acceptable?

However, the state may not merely take my land for the public good. It may take what is mine only on condition that it compensate me. Otherwise, its taking is simply theft. This suggests that sometimes a right may be overridden if we are willing to compensate the right-bearer.

Suppose we apply this idea to preferential hiring. Perhaps the state has good reason to favor blacks in employment—for example, in order to pay a debt of compensation to blacks— but it can give preferences to blacks only by denying to white applicants something that is theirs: the right to equal consideration for a job (RTEC). We have been assuming that this right poses an absolute barrier to the state's imposing preferential hiring. But perhaps the state can be justified in denying white applicants what is theirs *if it compensates them for their losses.*[4] How it would do so I leave aside. At least, in theory, compensating whites for their losses under preferential hiring presents a way over the obstacle that they have equal opportunity rights which are incompatible with giving blacks preferences in employment.[5]

No actual proposal for preferential hiring includes this idea, however, and if the state proposes to inaugurate preferential hiring of blacks on the model of veteran's preference, then the problem of white applicants' rights looms as a serious obstacle to justifying such a policy. In fact, if each individual possesses RTEC and it is fundamental, neither preferring blacks nor preferring veterans can be justified where compensation to those who are harmed by the preferences is not offered.

DOES PREFERENTIAL HIRING COMPENSATE?

Up to this point we have been concentrating on the "who" in the question "Who owes what to whom?" This preoccupation is certainly reasonable since we ought to be very careful about imposing substantial involuntary costs upon anyone without adequate reason. We must be especially careful if there are rights involved. However, we must not neglect the other parts of the question. Who is owed compensation and what is he owed? To put the issue another way, does preferential hiring actually compensate?

We have already seen a general answer to the question of "what": a person is owed, of the things the wrong-doer has available to pay, that which will best make up for the injury or loss. The general answer to "who is owed" is: the one who was injured or harmed.

Whom would preferential hiring benefit? Would it benefit those who are owed compensation? Consider the example with which the book began. The Boston School Committee will hire one black for each white in filling a number of positions. It will seek out blacks (and whites) with appropriate educational qualifications and then select from a pool of qualified applicants on a ratio basis. Assuming there are less black applicants than white applicants, the hiring scheme will have to extend preferences to blacks (unless all the blacks rank at the top of the qualifications list). The School Committee will inquire into each applicant's qualifications, but *not* into his past injuries or unjust losses. The preferential scheme will benefit some blacks, but how are we to be assured that it compensates anyone?

It might be urged that it is unnecessary to inquire into the past history of each black applicant since all blacks have been harmed by discrimination and thus all blacks are owed compensation. Thus, if the Boston School Committee's preferential scheme is benefiting blacks it is compensating them. Is it true that every black is owed compensation? Has every black suffered compensable injury under discrimination?

This is certainly a reasonable question to ask. The claim that every black job applicant has suffered injury as a result of discrimination needs to be argued for, not just assumed. Nevertheless, suppose for purposes of argument we accept that every black has suffered in some way under discrimination. Even so, it does not follow that every black is owed the same compensation. For not every black was injured in the same way or to the same degree.

Implicit in our commonsense views of compensation is a *proportionality requirement*. A wrong-doer owes for the injury he caused. Thus, the greater the injury he caused, the more he owes; the lesser the injury caused, the less he owes. The victim of injury has a right to be made whole. The greater the injury he suffers, the more he is owed; the lesser the injury, the less he is owed.[6]

Preferential hiring is going to impose the greatest burden on younger white job-seekers, those most active in the labor market, without fixed and stable positions. These whites are generally the least responsible for injuries caused blacks. So, independently of the question of rights, preferential hiring will violate one side of the proportionality requirement. Will it violate the other side as well? Does it distribute the greatest benefits to those least injured? Preferential hiring may be subject to this accusation as well.

No feasible program of preferential hiring will require the hiring of thoroughly unqualified workers. Any workable program will give preferences to blacks who meet minimal qualifications. In the case of skilled labor positions and white collar jobs, these minimal qualifications will be pretty substantial, requiring a fairly high level of skill, educational achievement, and experience. Except in the case of unskilled jobs, preferential hiring will favor the most qualified blacks, those with the best skills and education.[7]

Does this establish that preferential hiring most benefits those least deserving of compensation? Is it implausible to generalize that those blacks who have the best education and the greatest job skills are those least harmed by racial discrimination? If we can accept this generalization as a fair one, then we may conclude that preferential hiring of blacks will tend to benefit most those blacks to whom least compensation is owed.

On the other hand, preferential hiring will provide little or no benefit to those most harmed by racial discrimination. Surely the most harmed by past employment discrimination are those black men and women over fifty years of age who were denied an adequate education, kept out of the unions, legally excluded from many jobs, who have lived in poverty or close to it, and whose income-producing days are nearly at an end. Preferential hiring programs will have virtually no effect on these people at all. Thus, preferential hiring will tend not to benefit those most deserving of compensation.

SUMMARY

For several chapters we have been considering the claim that preferential hiring is justified as a method of compensating blacks for the wrongs done them. We have seen that it is quite possible that preferential hiring violates an important right. Even if it does not, it violates the requirement that those who did greatest injury should pay greatest compensation, those who did least should pay least. Moreover, if not every black is owed compensation, then preferential hiring programs may be overinclusive, benefiting some who are owed no benefit. Even if every black is owed compensation, a preferential hiring program is likely to be underinclusive, failing to benefit some who are owed benefit. And, finally, preferential hiring very likely inverts the proper proportionality, benefiting most those owed the least and benefiting the least those owed the most.

The proponent of preferential hiring might concede that by itself preferential hiring is not very compensatory but argue that it is justified as one element of a total mix of compensatory programs, the overall effect of which is roughly proportional to the desert of all blacks. The opponent of preferential hiring may not find this a persuasive defense. Since preferential hiring seems so weakly compensatory in its effect, its contribution to any mixed program of adequate compensation must be quite limited. Consequently its omission from an effective mixed program should do little to diminish that program's overall effects.

The Argument from Compensatory Justice, which appeared promising as a defense of preferential hiring, turns out to be less appealing than it seemed. There are several infirmities in the defense of preferential hiring as a requirement of compensatory justice. Most serious is the possibility that it violates a fundamental right of many individuals. Whether this violation is actual depends upon our deciding just what equal opportunity rights people have. I will turn to this question later in the book. But even apart from possible violation of rights, we have reason to believe that preferential hiring is not truly what it is touted to be: compensatory.

5

Group Rights?

Many persons believe that the defense of preferential hiring of blacks lies in the demands of compensatory justice. In the previous chapters I have examined the way in which individual rights and obligations arise under the principle of compensation. This examination has raised critical problems for a defense of preferential hiring.

It might be objected that the entire preceding investigation has been misconceived and that I have failed to understand the meaning of the compensatory justification given by the proponents of preferential hiring. I have made the mistake of construing the issue as one of individual rights and individual compensation, whereas it is really one of group rights and group compensation. When the matter is conceived as one of individual rights, great difficulties arise about establishing individual liability, individual desert, proportionality, and so on. These difficulties threaten to undermine a successful defense of preferential hiring. When the matter is conceived in terms of group rights these problems disappear and the

57

Argument from Compensatory Justice is effective. Blacks-as-a-group have a right to compensation and the problem of identifying individual blacks who have been injured by discrimination is beside the point; "as compensation is owed the group, it is group claims that must be weighed, not individual ones."[1]

How can a group have a claim? If we mean, in saying that blacks-as-a-group have a claim, that many or most or all black persons have a claim, then talking about the "group claim" is innocent enough. It is just an elliptical way of talking about the claims of individuals.[2] Invoking group rights in this way does not avoid any of the problems faced in earlier chapters in making preferential hiring compatible with individual rights and individual deserts.

In order to side-step these problems, we would need to attribute to the group a right which was distinct from and independent of the rights of its members. How could there be such a right? What would we be talking about if we were not talking about the rights of individuals? Is a group a kind of individual itself? There are certainly many instances in which we would be mistaken in thinking so.

When our talk about groups is no more than a summary or shorthand way of talking about individuals, no sticky philosophical questions arise. The talk is straightforwardly about entities whose existence we fully grasp. It is often economical or convenient to talk this way. Nevertheless, talk about groups can also lead us into serious equivocations if we are not careful. There are numerous instances of this in discussions about reverse discrimination and preferential treatment. One example is provided in this claim by Alfred Blumrosen about discrimination and compensation:

. . . discrimination is a phenomenon addressed against a class, and . . . it can be redressed in part by providing improved situations for the class or group as a whole. Some individual victims of discrimination might never be compensated, for they might be unidentifiable, but other members of the class of victims would become the vehicle of improving the condition of the entire class. In short, the consequences test [of discrimination] involves recognition that discrimination laws are aimed at vindicating the group interest of the victims of discrimination.[3]

What is the "group interest" of a victim of discrimination? How can a victim's injury be made good by making someone else better off? Blumrosen evidently is led to believe this is possible by failing to notice that he is talking about two distinct classes of people. The origin of the confusion lies in the claim that "discrimination is a phenomenon addressed against a class." Discrimination is addressed against a class only in the trivial sense that discrimination against any individual is always based on some property or characteristic which the individual can have in common with others.

I discriminate against a person because he is smelly, or because he is my enemy, or because he is a philosopher, or because he is a lover of Wagner's music, or whatever. There is *something* about the person that leads me to treat him adversely. Now, on the basis of such a property, we can always define a logical class.

All smelly persons
All persons who are my enemy
All philosophers
All lovers of Wagner's music
All etc.

If I discriminate against you because you are smelly, for example, my discrimination is addressed to a class only in the sense that I discriminate against you on the basis of a property common to others and all those who have that property constitute a class. But to suppose that in injuring you because you are smelly I injure all smelly persons would be to confuse my discriminating against you on the basis of a group-characteristic with my discriminating against other individuals with the same group-characteristic. This is exactly the mistake made by Blumrosen. The "class against which discrimination is addressed," in the first sentence of the passage, is transformed in the second sentence into the class of victims of discrimination. But these two classes are not the same at all. If I discriminate against you because you are smelly, then the "class against which my discrimination is addressed," in the trivial sense, is the class of all smelly persons, but the class of victims of my discrimination is the class that contains only you.[4]

If I discriminate against you, I injure your interests. If I do it in a public way that causes Smith, who is also smelly, to take insult, then perhaps I injure his interests as well. However many individuals I injure, these are still just so many individual injuries. What could there be besides these individuals to be injured?

Could there be more here than a failure to be careful in talking about groups? Can we avoid muddles and equivocations and still talk about some *thing*—the group itself—which has an interest that is harmed when individual members of the group are discriminated against? Kenneth Karst and Harold Horowitz write:

It is group interests . . . which underlie the constitutional claim [to racial equality]. . . . Thus, while the claim to racial equality . . . is one in which individuals may join, from the judicial standpoint it is a group claim.[5]

Here there is no obvious equivocation. Instead there seems to be the thesis that the group claim is something quite distinct from any individual claims. This is both philosophically interesting and puzzling. What is this group interest in racial equality, an interest upon which can be founded a claim or right? We can easily enough comprehend that individual blacks have interests in being treated equally with individuals of other races. But the group interest we are trying to fathom cannot be the sum of these individual interests. It is supposed to be a distinct interest.

Now, a group can be the *object* of a person's interest. A black could not only desire equal treatment for himself but for all blacks and in this sense desire equal treatment for the group. Moreover, he could further desire such things as that average black income be equal to average white income. If many or most blacks felt this way, then policies which raised the average income of blacks would not only satisfy the interests of those whose incomes actually improved but the interests of other blacks as well. We could say that raising average income for blacks would satisfy "group interests." But these would be simply the group-oriented interests of individual blacks, and the sum of them could not be the group interest we are looking for.

It is puzzling to know where to look. How can a right be founded upon an interest that is not somebody's interest? Is the group itself a "somebody"? In fact, attributing rights to blacks-as-a-group, where this is not a shorthand way of talking about individuals, seems to require that we treat a group as if it were itself an individual. There must be something which possesses the right.

CORPORATE RIGHTS

There is at least one condition under which it is not an error to treat a group of individuals as itself an individual. This is when the group is a *corporation*. A corporate group is not a mere collection, assemblage, class, assortment, or crowd, but a union of persons organized for common action. The United States is a corporate group, as is General Motors, the Roman Catholic Church, and the NAACP. Because of the way corporate groups are organized, they are capable of acting in ways that make it feasible to treat them as individuals.

Crowds can act, too, but only in an anemic sense. A crowd, for example, can trample the grass into dust. No individual in the crowd performs this particular act. Nevertheless, the act of the crowd is no more than the causal consequence of all the individual acts of trampling. In the case of corporations, they can perform acts generically different than the acts performed by the individuals in them. Consider the United States declaring war. That act is not simply the causal consequence of numerous smaller acts by American individuals. Rather, because of the rules defining the internal organization of the nation, the acts of certain individuals *count as* an act of the United States. Members of Congress vote for war. The acts of those who form a majority *count as* an act of Congress. In turn, on the matter of declaring war, the act of Congress *counts as* the act of the United States. Even though this act of declaring war is constituted by the acts of various persons, it is a different act from any of those which constitute it and it is not merely the causal consequence of those acts.[6]

Thus, in a full-blooded way we can attribute acts, goals, intentions, aims, and interests to the corporation itself in the same way we do to individual persons. Corporations can have legal and moral relations to other external individuals (persons and other corporations). Through its internal structure, the individuals who comprise the corporation will have various rights and duties with respect to it. This is how it can be that the United States Government can owe Japanese companies yet none of us owe any Japanese. Although we owe nothing to Japanese companies, we owe something to our government. This follows from the particular internal structure of our society: a general contribution rule requires each of us to bear his fair share in contributing toward the legitimate expenses of government. Different corporations can have different ways of covering their expenses. The phone company pays its expenses by charging its customers rather than by taxing its workers.

Now, the argument that blacks-as-a-group have a right to compensation might be taken as a claim that blacks constitute a corporate group in the United States and have *corporate rights* to reparations. This, for example, apparently is the claim of Cornelius Golightly:

> . . . the 14th Amendment vests rights in individuals while the affirmative action requirement vests rights in the group or nation of women, the group or nation of Blacks, the group or nation of American Indians, and the group or nation of Orientals.[7]

Golightly is mistaken in claiming that anti-discrimination statutes and regulations vest any "group rights" in blacks.[8] He is correct in saying that there are no such constitutional rights.[9] There are no legal rights vested in the "black nation" in the United States. If we take the argument about group rights to be a claim that there are such rights, the argument is false.

However, the argument can be recast as one which claims that blacks are morally a "people" or "nation" and this *ought* to be legally recognized. The United States should alter its legal and political structure so as to become a federation of corporate bodies defined along racial or ethnic lines. In 1967, the Newark Black Power Conference considered a resolution calling for the possible partitioning of the United States into two separate nations, one a homeland for whites, the other a homeland for blacks.[10] Less extreme is the proposal by Gidon Gottlieb that constitutional relations be revised so as to recognize and give legal standing to "peoples."

> New legal arrangements are . . . needed where the poor, the blacks, and other ethnic minorities are concerned.

> The emancipation of the blacks as one people may demand that our legal structure grant recognition of the rights of "peoples" under our system of government.

> Such judicial developments would parallel the legal recognition of labor unions in the last century.[11]

Such proposals call for sweeping changes in the American political-legal system. Whether a development in this direction would ultimately be desirable or not is a question that lies outside the scope of this book.[12] For our purposes, it is enough to observe that a proposal to reorganize America into "peoples" or "nations" is just that—a proposal. It is not itself a ground for asserting any existing political or constitutional right.

Moreover, the basis for calling blacks a "nation" is itself fuzzy. What constitutes a "nation"? How are distinct "nations" to be identified? We are not here talking about nations as states; those are relatively easy to identify. In the sense that concerns us, a state may contain many nations and a nation may be spread over many states. A nation is a population the members of which are presumably bound together by one or more common characteristics. What characteristics define a population's nationhood? Common language, race, culture, history, values, antipathy to other groups? Is it enough that a population calls itself a nation? Does this create a moral claim upon others also to call it a nation?[13]

Because of the fuzziness of the concept of "nationhood," it is hard to evaluate the claim that blacks are a nation. Are American blacks a distinct nation or are they a part of one nation of blacks spread across the earth? Is common race itself sufficient to constitute nationhood despite all other differences? If American blacks are a distinct nation, is this due to their unique history as slaves? What about the common history American blacks share with American whites?

If the nation is no more than a population with a common language, or a common culture, or whatever, how can it qualify as a corporate group? It would lack any internal structure which authorized the deeds of some to count as the acts of all. It would lack a common decision-making mechanism. It would not be a true union of persons. Can we attribute "national rights" to it in such a case? If the nation must have an internal organization, do American blacks possess an organizational structure of the requisite sort? Until these questions and others are given satisfactory answers, we are on very uncertain footing in talking about the "group rights" of blacks even when we purport to be talking about corporations and nations.

CONCLUSIONS ABOUT COMPENSATION

We began in Chapter Two to explore our basic intuitions about compensation for wrongs in order to see if by elaborating them we could find an adequate defense of preferential hiring. We saw that in the paradigm compensatory situations special rights and obligations are created. These rights and obligations lodge against particular agents. Their specific content will partly be determined by the existence of other rights and obligations. In cases of compensation, rights and obligations are proportional to responsibility for doing injury and to degree of injury suffered. Complicity in wrongs requires some knowing and voluntary acceptance of the fruits of the wrongs. Because we do not have at hand a fully worked-out moral theory of compensation, applying the complexities just noted to the preferential hiring case is problematical. I have relied, therefore, on simple and clear examples to lead us to some conclusions about preferential hiring.

1. If we assume that every individual has a basic right to equal consideration (RTEC), then preferential hiring, without side compensation to those who are discriminated against, violates this right. White applicants have not, by and large, forfeited their right to equal consideration and while it is in force this right stands in the way of preferring applicants on grounds—for example, race—not related to job performance. Since RTEC is an interpretation of a "right to equal opportunity," a defense of preferential hiring must deny that there is any right to equal opportunity or must offer an alternative account

of this right which is not violated by some uses of racial preferences.

The assumption of RTEC works as much against the Argument from Compensatory Justice as it does against the Social Utility Argument and the Distributive Justice Argument. Let us now drop the assumption. Our investigations in the past few chapters have shown that even if we drop the assumption of RTEC, thus removing one decisive objection to preferential hiring, there are still other serious objections to the Compensatory Justice Defense.

2. For example, a general policy of preferential hiring will inevitably impose its costs on only a few whites and they are likely to be those least responsible for the injuries caused blacks. This inequality of burden and lack of proportionality must be a matter of concern even if it violates no rights.

3. On the other side, preferential hiring's direct effects are only weakly compensatory. It will not significantly, if at all, benefit those blacks most deserving compensation. It will favor the young instead of the old, the trained over the untrained. We must wonder, thus, why it is so imperative to employ such an inefficient compensatory device in the face of the inequitable costs it imposes. Perhaps more than real compensation, preferential hiring delivers symbolic compensation. Favoring blacks in hiring is a symbolic substitute for an actual program of compensation and restitution aimed at redressing the actual injuries of individual blacks.

To reject preferential hiring as a form of compensation for blacks is not necessarily to reject either preferential hiring or the idea of compensation for blacks. There may be an alternative defense of preferential hiring that is persuasive. And there is every reason, at least from a moral point of view, to take seriously the idea promulgated in the Black Manifesto. The idea of substantial monetary compensation to blacks may be politically unpopular, and would face important practical difficulties of administration, but is not morally fanciful.

Moreover, there may be other forms of special treatment for blacks which are more nearly compensatory than preferential hiring.

I conclude that there are reasons for a person to reject preferential hiring as a justified form of compensation to blacks. The reasons may not be decisive, especially in light of the complexities of the issues and the consequent room for uncertainty, but they are of considerable weight. They seem to me strong enough to prompt the defender of preferential hiring to look elsewhere for support. Now that we have dropped the assumption of RTEC, that support might be found in an argument drawn from social utility.

6

Social Utility

The pursuit of highest social utility—the public interest, the common good—must be limited by basic moral and constitutional rights. Where rights pose no barriers, social policy is free to be determined on the basis of simple cost-benefit analysis. Once we drop the assumption of a fundamental right to equal consideration (RTEC), a defense of this sort becomes available for preferential hiring. Favoring blacks in employment will generate both positive and negative effects. The proponent of favoritism may urge, with considerable plausibility, that an effective preferential policy would result in net positive social effects of significant magnitude.

First, there will be important economic benefits. Any policy which will significantly increase the representation of black workers in the better paying jobs in industry, business, government, and education will raise the average income of black families and this, in turn, will have important benefits for the whole society. A great economic burden on society derives from the poverty in which large numbers of blacks find themselves and which seems to perpetuate itself. Breaking the cycle of poverty for blacks will economically benefit society as a whole.

A look at the position of black workers in Philadelphia provides a microcosm of the problem to be overcome. In the Philadelphia area, 30 percent of the construction work force was, in 1971, black (and other minorities). Yet, in the skilled construction trades, only 1 percent of the workers was non-white. The overwhelming bulk of non-white workers was relegated to the lowest paying jobs. Construction jobs represent one significant avenue to better pay and higher income for blacks, but this avenue is significantly diminished if the best paying construction jobs are not open to them. A program of preferential treatment, involving preferential admissions to unions and preferential hiring, which could bring blacks into the lucrative trades in numbers proportionate to their population in the construction labor force, would dramatically improve the condition of blacks in Philadelphia.[1]

What is true in Philadelphia is true in other major cities. And what is true in the construction industry is true of the economy in general. Blacks are effectively excluded, whether by discrimination or for other reasons, from significant movement into better-paying positions. Change this and we begin to break the cycle of poverty creating poverty.

It might be objected that the economic consequences of preferential hiring of blacks will, in fact, be zero, since every black gain must be matched by a corresponding white loss, the losses and gains cancelling each other out. Nothing is added to social utility by preferential hiring. The distribution of the economic total is merely shifted around among subgroups in society.

It is precisely this shifting around, however, which can increase the size of the total. The positive economic effects of the extra blacks employed in higher paying jobs would likely be greater than the negative effects of white losses. This is because black poverty is concentrated. Consequently, a significant rise in the incomes of a substantial number of blacks will have a concentrated positive effect. We might truly say that black job gain will represent community gain, while white job loss will represent individual loss.

There are other, non-economic, benefits that might expectably derive from an effective preferential hiring program. One important benefit may be the reduction of racism. Whatever the causes of racism, it involves stereotyping and this stereotyping feeds on a perceived association between race and poverty. Anything that lifts the economic position of blacks will have the effect of diminishing this perceived association and thus weakening one of the psychological supports of racism. Moreover, as there come to be more and more black managers, administrators, executives, supervisors, foremen, and so on, white workers will find their stereotypes of blacks breaking down and they will become accustomed to seeing and thinking of blacks not just as inferiors. Finally, as more and more blacks occupy decision-making roles, the decisions made in those roles are less likely to reflect prejudice against blacks.

Preferential hiring can be expected to have negative social effects, too. Among the most important of these is the possibility that it will create resentment and hostility in groups adversely affected by preferences extended to blacks and this resentment could fuel new racism.[2] And there is the cost imposed on individual whites who are discriminated against. This cost cannot be ignored.

Nevertheless, it might be argued that, everything considered, preferential hiring is a beneficial policy. The effect of preferential hiring in breaking down racist stereotypes will be greater than the new racism it generates. The net effect of preferential hiring will be to promote community and fraternity in the whole population. The development of a substantial black middle class, the influx of greater incomes into the black community, the creation of a tradition of skilled labor and professionalism among blacks, all of these will not only benefit blacks but the entire community as well.

These very great benefits will derive from a program that imposes its costs unevenly on some whites. This is regretable but justified, so long as there are no basic rights violated. Nearly all desirable social policy imposes sacrifices or losses of benefits on some persons, and so long as we are willing to let social policy be set by the calculus of collective benefit, these individual losses are acceptable. So might the proponent of preferential hiring argue.

Of course, a crucial question concerns the existence of rights which might be violated by preferential hiring. This concerned us in previous chapters. We will return to take up directly this issue later. Here, we assume that there is no right such as RTEC which precludes a defense of preferential hiring by appeal to its social benefits.

The proponent of preferential hiring has the makings, here, of a persuasive argument. Much more would be needed, of course, to make it compelling. A complete argument would require an exhaustive listing and assessment of all the directly foreseeable and measurable costs and benefits. But how does one successfully do this for the multiple and complex ramifications of a social policy like preferential hiring? Even if fairly plausible projections of economic impact could be made, how could we say with certainty how much brotherhood or fraternity will be fostered, how much hostility created? Moreover, how are we to weigh the various elements involved? Is a small increase in racism offset by a small increase in economic welfare or only by a big one?

The defense we are considering argues that the benefits of preferential hiring outweigh its costs. Even if we accept this as true, a question still remains. What about alternative means for increasing black incomes, getting more blacks into better jobs, diminishing racism, and so on? Might not some alternative policy work as well or better than preferential hiring but without the costs incurred by using race as a criterion of hiring? To be fully defensible, preferential hiring must not only be a good policy, it must be better than its alternatives. It must be necessary to produce the goods it aims at; otherwise, any scheme for producing those goods which did not need to take race into account would be far preferable.

We need to know, then, what alternatives there might be. We need to know how fast blacks would enter the construction trades without preferences being used. How fast would blacks enter managerial ranks? What would the black employment profile be in 30 years in various job categories in the absence of discrimination but without the assistance of preferential policies?

The Social Utility Argument for preferential hiring, even when complete and made with the greatest cogency, will unavoidably be highly conjectural, imprecise, debatable. There will be ample room for reasonable people of good will to disagree on the wisdom of preferential hiring. Some would point to the inevitable incompleteness of a social utility defense of preferential hiring as a decisive reason for not adopting such a policy. This is a mistake. Social utility arguments against preferential hiring are also incomplete, imprecise, conjectural, and so on. The Social Utility Argument for preferential hiring need only show preferential hiring sufficiently promising as a superior alternative to justify a social experiment using it. The only real test of social programs is how they work when they are put into effect.

QUALIFICATIONS AND EFFICIENCY

It might be objected that in my cursory listing of the costs and benefits of preferential hiring, I overlooked a very substantial cost: the cost of reduced efficiency in industry, business, education, and government caused by the *lowering of qualification standards*. One of commonest criticisms of preferential hiring is that it will lead to the hiring of unqualified or under-qualified workers. The clear implication is that we will all end up receiving inferior goods and services.[3]

As I have defined it, preferential hiring does result in less-than-the-best-qualified being selected. If a black candidate were best qualified for a job, there would be no occasion to select him because of his race. His job-related qualifications alone would be sufficient for his selection. Preferential hiring, as I have defined it, involves appealing to criteria of choice which are not job-related.

Although preferential hiring means hiring the less-than-best-qualified, this does not mean there is any substance to the critic's fear that the upshot of favoring blacks in employment will be unqualified workers and inefficient work. Part of the problem in deciding whether the critic is right stems from the confusions that surround the idea of *qualifications*. What are qualifications?

When we speak about a person being qualified or not for a job, we typically have in mind a range of performances required by the job and we judge whether the applicant can operate effectively over that range. Can he do, and do well, the things he will be called on to do.

If an employer needs a bookkeeper, then surely one qualification is being able to add and subtract. The bookkeeper will be called on at least to do these. More than adding and subtracting may be desirable. Traits like punctuality, honesty, reliability, and so on, will help a person do well the things the employer wants his bookkeeper to do. Whatever conduces to a better bookkeeping performance could be counted as a qualification for that job.

Taken generally, this idea leads to some important implications. Virtually every trait of personality can have a bearing on job performance. Traits like curiosity, industriousness, loyalty, amiability, ambition, patience, etc., can contribute as vitally to a successful job performance as skills like adding and subtracting. Theoretically, there may be no objection to counting *any* facet of a person as a job qualification. It all depends on the job. In practice, however, there are limits to what may be or ought to be counted as a qualification.

Before we consider those limitations, we should note that there is another way of looking at qualifications. An employer may advertise a job, stating a number of requirements. One "qualifies for" the job by meeting the requirements. Thus, an employer may advertise for a bookkeeper with five years' previous experience and a college degree. Jones, without five years' experience and without a college degree, is not qualified for the job, in the sense that he does not meet the employer's requirements, even though he might do a better job than any other applicant and thus is qualified in the more general sense.

An employer might require anything from an applicant, including traits or characteristics that are plainly irrelevant to doing the job well. As a matter of social policy, we may forbid an employer from requiring some traits that are irrelevant to job performance, especially when these requirements have to do with race, sex, religious belief, and similar properties. However, I think it needs to be emphasized that we are also prepared to limit what an employer may require even when what he would require is relevant to performance. This is because of another feature of qualifications.

Qualifications must be spotted, determined, discovered. An employer will need to have methods or techniques for testing or measuring job-related qualifications. The process of testing or measuring might itself have such important negative effects on people that we decide to forbid an employer to test for or measure a qualification in a particular way or to use the results of a particular test or method of determining qualifications. Consider some cases.

An airline seeks pilots. Among the factors involved in job performance is safety, avoidance of crashes. A person with a propensity to have a heart attack could possibly have that attack in flight, jeopardizing the safety of the passengers. How does the airline pick out persons with a propensity to have a heart attack and eliminate them from consideration? It must rely upon reliable generalizations. The airline might, accordingly, refuse to hire any overweight person as a pilot on the grounds that there is a statistically greater chance such a person will have a heart attack while piloting a plane than will a non-overweight person. On the basis of a statistical generalization about heart-attack rates for different weights, the airline inquires into the weight of its pilot applicants and makes being under a certain weight a "qualification" for the job. I imagine most of us would accept the airline's procedure as legitimate.

Suppose, however, the case involved an automobile manufacturer with reliable statistics showing a higher rate of absenteeism among black workers in the industry than among white workers. If the company employs thousands of workers, it stands to save millions of dollars a year if it can cut its absenteeism by even a bit. Will we accept the company inquiring into the race of its applicants and adopting a policy of hiring whites only? In fact, as a matter of law and social policy, the automobile company may not follow this course.

It isn't that the automobile company uses a dubious generalization and the airline company a sound one. It isn't that blackness, on average, plays no role in total production whereas fatness, on average, does play a role in total performance safety. It is, rather, for reasons that lie altogether outside job performance that society has *decided* that whiteness shall not be a qualification and blackness a disqualification, even where these properties are connected by accurate generalizations to job performance. Of the things an employer might like to count as a job qualification, society may forbid his counting some factors that are relevant to job performance taken in the aggregate. It may forbid his reliance on certain generalizations.[4]

Consider, now, a slightly different sort of case. Suppose it were established that people who have good sex lives are more productive on the job and are less prone to on-the-job accidents. Will we let a company, then, inquire into the sexual experiences of its applicants. Surely we would not. The inquiry would be sufficiently invasive of applicants' privacy that it ought to be forbidden, even if sexual experience is related to job performance. Again, of the things an employer might desire to count as a job-qualification, and which may be relevant to job performance, some may be forbidden him for reasons that lie beyond productivity or efficiency.[5]

Some inquiries about qualifications may be forbidden an employer, as well as the use of generalizations based on race. Aside from these limitations, there may be yet other kinds of generalizations involved in the effort to identify qualified applicants that will be looked on with suspicion. For example, suppose a company has only one entry level. All other jobs are filled by promotions and transfers of the occupants of the entry level positions. In such a case, the employer will be most interested in an applicant's general aptitude for acquiring the skills that characterize the range of jobs to be learned and performed. The most important attribute of an applicant will be his trainability.

But trainability is not a concept about which we can be precise. Measuring it is a matter of some controversy. Employers commonly use standardized aptitude tests. These tests provide numerical scores indicating success at certain verbal, mathematical, and conceptual tasks. Success at these tasks is presumably related to success in learning the jobs into which the applicant will eventually be placed.

As a matter of fact, these tests seem to disqualify a disproportionately greater percentage of black (and minority) applicants than white applicants. There are several reasons given for this fact. One claim is that the tests are guilty of "cultural bias," that is, they test for culture-specific knowledge as much as for real aptitude. Even if this is not the full answer to why these aptitude tests yield such differential results, we may be concerned about the widespread use of such tests to determine an applicant's qualifications for employment. This is because it is very difficult to establish the connection between what the tests test for and the actual success of individuals at various kinds of work.

Extreme pressure has been put on employers to demonstrate by stringent scientific tests that the written tests they use are truly related to the specific performances required by the employer's jobs. Employer tests which produce a disproportionate disqualification of blacks and minorities are viewed by law as racially discriminatory unless the tests can be validated in regard to the genuine job-relatedness of the factors tested for.[6]

We have drifted from our initial concern with the critic's claim that preferential hiring will lead to the hiring of the unqualified. We first digressed to consider what qualifications are. We can view qualifications from two perspectives. First, there is the job to be done, the actions, deeds, performances, skills, etc., it requires. Second, there is the perspective of the employer and what he proposes to require by way of qualifications and what he proposes to do in the way of testing for qualifications. Our general conclusions were these: (1) theoretically, any personal trait or property might be a job-related qualification, regardless of the perspective we adopt; (2) we are prepared to forbid employers the use of certain tests or generalizations, even in instances where they bear directly upon the productiveness or efficiency of the employer's operation.

Having digressed, let us return to the claim that preferential hiring will result in the hiring of the unqualified. Why must this be so? Although by definition it involves hiring the *lesser* qualified, why must preferential hiring in practice involve the hiring of the unqualified? Certainly, any feasible program will extend preferences only to those that are at least minimally qualified. Moreover, the differences in qualifications between the best qualified and those actually preferred may not be very great, especially if minimal qualifications are set high enough. Finally, the differences in qualifications may not be reflected in markedly reduced efficiency of the employer's operation. Perhaps preferential hiring would result in some degree of diminished efficiency in American business, education, government, and so on, but this depends on what efficiency amounts too, a matter I will discuss in a few pages, and it depends upon what actually happens when some scheme of preferential hiring is tested.

RACE AS A QUALIFICATION

One way to reply to the critic who claims preferential hiring leads to hiring the unqualified is to assert that race itself may be a legitimate qualification for a job. This way of attacking the critic denies, in fact, that preferential hiring is even taking place even though race is being used as a selection criterion: the critic mistakenly thinks the lesser qualified are being hired over the more qualified because he fails to note that in these cases being black is itself a qualification. Many have taken this position, both in regard to hiring and in regard to admissions to professional schools. Consider the following position of the American Association of University Professors regarding the use of race in connection with academic employment:

The point [namely, taking the age of an applicant into account so as to produce a balance between younger and older faculty] may be generalized: meeting a felt shortage of tenured professors by preferring a more experienced and senior person; broadening the professional profile within the department, most of whose faculty secured their degrees from the same institution, by preferring in the next several appointments well-qualified persons of a differing academic graduate exposure or professional background; leavening a faculty predominantly oriented toward research and publications with others more interested in exploring new teaching methods, and vice-versa. It is useless to deny that we believe such considerations are relevant, as indeed we familiarly and unselfconsciously take them into account all the time, and rightly so; never in lieu of seeking the "best qualified person," but as contributing to a reasonable decision of what constitutes the *best qualified person in terms of existing needs and circumstances.*

As we do not think this Association would disapprove conscientious efforts by academic faculties to register an affirmative interest, as they often have, in the positive improvement of their departments in the several ways just illustrated, but rather that this Association would (and does) regard those efforts as wholly conducive to fairness and equality, we do not see any sufficient reason to be less approving of the affirmative consideration of race or sex. We would go further to say that special efforts to attract persons {to} improve the overall diversity of a faculty, and to broaden it specifically from its unisex or unirace sameness, seem to us to state a variety of affirmative action which deserves encouragement. A preference in these terms, asserted affirmatively to enrich a faculty in its own experience as well as in what it projects in its example of mutually able men and women, and mutually able blacks and whites, seems to us to state a *neutral, principled,* and altogether precedented policy of preference.

The argument to the special relevance of race and sex as *qualifying* characteristics draws its strength from a recognition of the richness which a variety of intellectual perspectives and life experiences can bring to the educational program. It is more than simply providing jobs for persons from groups which have in the past been unfairly excluded from an opportunity to compete for them; it is a matter of reorganizing the academic institution to fulfill its basic commitment to those who are seriously concerned to maintain the academic enterprise as a vital social force. The law now requires the elimination of discriminatory practices and equality of access for all persons regardless of race or sex. . . .[7]

The AAUP position rests on the idea that *institutional needs* are a legitimate factor in establishing job qualifications and that one important institutional need may be for a greater racial or sexual balance, thus making race or sex a legitimate job qualification. As we have already seen, we cannot rule out *a priori* any factor as one which might possibly contribute to the performance of a job. This means that we cannot, *a priori*, rule out race or sex as a possible job qualification. The AAUP's position is not without its plausibility.

A similar use of the idea of institutional needs was made by the Federal District Court of New Jersey in a 1969 case, *Porcelli* v. *Titus*. The case involved a suspension by the Newark School Board of its examination system and promotion list for principals and the appointment of several black principals who would not have qualified under the examination system. The court sustained the School Board, holding that although the Board had taken race into account in its appointment of principals, its actions were intended "not simply to appoint Negroes to promotional positions but to obtain for those positions qualified persons, white or black, whose qualifications were based on an awareness of, and sensitivity to, the problems of educating the Newark school population" (*Porcelli* at 732-733). The court relied heavily on testimony "that the education of Newark's largely black student body was suffering from the absence in the administration of the schools of black authority figures with whom the pupils could identify."[8] Thus, the court appeared to sanction the use of color as itself a job qualification.

As we shall see in the next section on efficiency, there are other circumstances in which being black can be alleged to be a job qualification. We have already noted that Congress explicitly refused to countenance the use of color as a possible job-related qualification in the 1964 Civil Rights Act.[9] Nevertheless, we may think that it should have allowed race to count.

There are arguments for allowing race to count as a qualification and there are arguments against it. What we must keep in mind is that we cannot have our cake and eat it too.

Whatever position we take on race as a qualification, we must be consistent in our position. Whether a position like the AAUP's is "principled" and "neutral" depends upon the willingness of the advocate of such a position to accept all of its implications. Some of those implications may not be easy to accept. Consider the following testimony by Dr. Mary Gray, representing the AAUP before the O'Hara Hearings, on the matter of sex as a qualification. After she read the AAUP report, previously quoted, into the record, we find the following exchange:

> Dr. Gray: That is correct. What I said was: I thought you can consider what was *serving the needs of the institution* and, in this case, that might require that you give special consideration to hiring more women.
> Rep. Dellenback: And it would also be possible and proper in the reverse situation, if the decision-makers felt that the institution was better served by having a male president, to insist that it be a male even though there be an equally well qualified, or even academically superior, female?
> Dr. Gray: What we are talking about is remedying effects of past discrimination and we are not talking about general policies as to what people think is best and what people think is not best, because for years people have thought it was best for the institutions not to hire women and what we are trying to do is write some sort, or enforce some sort of guidelines which are going to overcome the effect of this past policy, which we believe to be incorrect. (O'Hara Hearings, 589. Emphasis added.)

Here we have a complete flip-flop in what is represented as the AAUP's position. The AAUP Council, as we quoted it above, said that race or sex could legitimately be taken into account because of institutional need. The AAUP spokeswoman, Dr. Gray, offers this position in the first sentence of the quoted exchange between herself and Representative Dellenback. But when the Representative suggests that her (and the AAUP) position might commit her, in certain circumstances, to favoring a male over a female because of institutional needs, Dr. Gray reverses her position and claims that the justification for favoring women is not institutional needs ("what people think is best and what people think is not best") but "remedying [the] effects of past discrimination."

Dr. Gray's unwillingness to stick by her original position is understandable, since the position commits its holder to precisely the kind of possibilities Representative Dellenback suggests. If factors like "institutional need" can legitimize the use of race or sex as job qualifications, then we must notice that there is no guarantee that institutional need will *always favor the hiring of blacks or women.* Dr. Gray's testimony may not be representative of a willingness or unwillingness of AAUP members in general to stick by their Council position, but the association's position on race as a qualification is "principled" and "neutral" only if the association is willing to concede that institutional needs may not only make blackness a job qualification and whiteness a disqualification but may also make whiteness a qualification and blackness a disqualification. If, in fact, the AAUP's position is that blacks may be favored because of institutional needs but may never be disfavored, then its position is neither "principled" nor "neutral."

If the preferences of black students can make blackness a qualification for being a school principal, then cannot the hostility of white students make blackness a disqualification in an all-white school? If a company's workers resist working for a black or female foreman, is the company justified in taking race or sex into account in hiring a foreman? If church members resist the idea of female priests, is this a good reason for excluding females from the priesthood? If providing an appropriate distribution of role models is an institutional need, is massive discrimination against female elementary school teachers warranted?[10]

These are hard questions that must be answered by one who urges that race can be a legitimate job qualification. Once race is permitted to count as a job qualification, there is no way of preventing the racial sword from cutting both ways. There is nothing about the concept of qualifications itself which excludes or rules out race as a relevant job qualification. One may decide that, on balance, letting race be counted as a qualification is best; but this means being prepared, at least on some occasions, to view blackness not as an added qualification but as an added disqualification. It cannot be the case that job performance needs or institutional needs make blackness a qualification but never a disqualification. It is all a matter of the needs!

On the other hand, one may decide that, even though on occasion race may be a relevant factor in doing a job or in an institution's fulfilling its mission, race ought not to be allowed to count as a qualification. This position might be taken for a number of reasons. One might fear the abuses from letting employers make racially-based choices. One might prefer more strongly that blacks not be disfavored on account of their color than that they be favored, and since allowing race to count as a qualification may lead to both, prefer that race not be considered at all. For whatever reasons, Congress in 1964 allowed sex and religion to count on some occasions as "bona fide occupational qualifications," but not race.

OBJECTIVE VERSUS SUBJECTIVE DECISION PROCEDURES

Focusing on the procedures permitted employers brings out an important division over what may properly be considered by hiring officers. On the one hand, there is pressure to make the selection procedure more *objective,* so that the biases of hiring officers have less room for effect. The more cut-and-dried the hiring criteria, the more public and objective the standards of choice, the more difficult it is to discriminate on the basis of irrelevant features. Many federal regulations require that job requirements be as public as possible, that tests be scientifically validated, that all criteria be shown to be as job-related as possible.

On the other side, there is also pressure towards making the choice procedure more *subjective*. The complaint is that the use of objective tests and procedures leaves out or ignores too many relevant factors about an applicant. A procedure that allowed the hiring officer greater latitude of subjective judgment would permit him to take into account a greater range of relevant but intangible, difficult-to-measure, personal qualities of applicants. The *Porcelli* court, for example, gave support to the idea that more than test scores should be taken into account in choosing principals, that such factors as life-experience, sympathetic understanding of black students, and so on, should also be considered. And Justice Powell, in his *Bakke* decision, commended a school admissions procedure which took into account various personal features of candidates apart from such objective indices as their grades and test scores.

In general, the more objective the selection process, the more narrow the criteria for selection. The broader the criteria and the more room for interpretation and judgment, the more subjective the process. An objective process may leave out much that is relevant but also protects against employer bias. The more subjective the choice procedure and the more that relevant but unmeasurable factors can be taken into account, the more that personal prejudice can obtrude upon the selection outcomes.

In this connection, it is interesting to read the testimony of Representative Patricia Schroeder and former Representative Andrew Young before the O'Hara Subcommittee in 1974. Both complain of having personally encountered discrimination in their careers; but they draw different lessons from the experience. Here is one exchange:

Rep. Schroeder: I think if they can make a good case—this is why I feel so strongly about setting up the job qualifications—if they can make a good case that someone has more teaching experience or a higher grade point or has written more scholarly articles or something, I could accept that. *But I don't like this fuzzy stuff.*

Rep. O'Hara: I agree completely with that. I see no reason why they can't set up job descriptions and objective criteria so that they can be checked on what they do. (O'Hara Hearings, 212-213. Emphasis added.)

Contrast this with Representative Young's testimony:

Rep. Young: My feeling is that society working toward affirmative action and towards inclusiveness is going to be a stronger and relevant society than the one that accepts the limited concepts of objectivity which we now consider permanent.

Rep. Dellenback: I am not sure I would agree with you, Andy, when you said that there can be no objective measurements . . . .

Rep. Young: . . .I do feel that there is [sic] no purely objective criteria. (O'Hara Hearings, 220, 223.)

Representative Schroeder wants to eliminate the "fuzzy stuff" from job selection. She means the vague and imprecise job requirements and the subjective judgments. She will be satisfied that hiring is fair if we can point to a successful applicant's superiority in terms of numbers of articles published, higher grade point average, more years of teaching and other such objective items. Representative Young, on the other hand, wants more of the "fuzzy stuff." He complains that objective criteria leave out too many of the individual's special qualities and distinctive experiences and perspectives which he could bring to a job.

Shall hiring decisions be made as objective as possible? Or, shall hiring decisions be based upon the broadest consideration of all an individual's personal qualities? Shall employers be permitted to use race as a qualification where relevant? Or shall they be forbidden from ever counting race as a criterion, even where race bears on job performance or institutional needs? It is important to see that these issues are matters of *social choice*. They are not matters that can be decided merely by asking what a qualification is.

EFFICIENCY

The critic has said that preferential hiring will result in the hiring of the unqualified and that this will result in reduced efficiency. We have questioned whether preferential hiring must necessarily result in the hiring of the unqualified. We have also seen that the concept of a qualification is broad and that there is no *a priori* reason why race itself might not be a job-related qualification. But what we will allow an employer to *count* as a qualification is another matter. Even if race is relevant on occasion, we may want social policy always to forbid its use in hiring.

By definition, preferential hiring involves lesser qualified persons being chosen over better qualified persons, the selection being predicated on a factor (race) that is not job-related. (Thus, when race is job-related and is used in hiring, the hiring is not necessarily preferential.) If the issue is one of some lesser qualified workers being chosen over better qualified ones, it remains to be seen whether efficiency of production and quality of services in industry, business, education, and government will suffer, and to what extent. In thinking about efficiency, we must carefully distinguish two different issues: (1) race and efficiency and (2) preferential hiring and efficiency.

1. *Efficiency and selection by race.* We have already argued that there is no reason to suppose that race is never a job-related

qualification, i.e., never a factor that affects job performance. Thus, there is no reason to suppose that choosing a candidate on the basis of his race always diminishes the efficiency of an activity or enterprise. On the contrary, race-consciousness may enhance efficiency. To see this more sharply, we need to look at how the efficiency of an operation may be determined.

Sometimes efficiency is additive, so to speak. The efficiency of an operation will be a simple function of the efficiency of each worker taken separately. For example, the efficiency of a glass factory might be simply a function of the individual skills of each of its glass blowers. The employer makes his business more efficient by hiring workers with the best glass blowing skills. It is as simple as that.

In other situations, however, efficiency may be compositive, to coin a term. How well the enterprise succeeds depends not only upon the individual skills of the workers but also upon how well they interact with one another and how well others interact with them.

[T]he performance of a group of workers . . . is affected not only by their individual capacities and qualifications but also by the composition of the work force of which they are a part. Productivity may be enhanced by having a socially homogenous work force. . . . Some jobs may be done best by a work force which is 'representative' of the population within which it works; others by a work force which has no connection with the population it serves.[11]

Consequently, an organization that ranks applicants according to their independent and objectively measurable skills and then chooses its work force by picking from the list top down, taking the highest ranked applicant first, may not end up with the most productive or effective operation. For example:

a police force which serves a varied population may be better able to deal with various community problems if the force itself mirrors that variety . . . and [an] efficiency argument can be made for a recruitment policy which—roughly—mirrors the heterogeneity of the population served. Similar arguments can be made for a representative labor force in other "service" jobs. Teachers, health workers of all sorts, social workers, prison wardens, lawyers and government officials may all be more effective when they are selected in a way which produces a representative labor force, even when this means not selecting from the top of the list.[12]

Arguments from efficiency or productivity do not necessarily disfavor selection by race. An all-white police force which serves a racially mixed population may be less effective than a police force as racially mixed as the population it serves. If selecting in rank order from a list of applicants yields an entirely or predominantly white police force, the police department might do better to depart from the list and explicitly include racial minority members in its ranks.

We have already seen that "institutional needs" can make race a legitimate job-related qualification. It is only a small step to see that race-conscious hiring might enhance efficiency or productiveness. These are just two sides of the same coin.

2. *Preferential hiring and efficiency.* Preferential hiring, which involves selecting the lesser qualified, can be expected to have at least some minimal effect on efficiency. But what can we expect about the size and significance of this effect? As we have already argued, preferential hiring need not entail hiring the *un*qualified. Whether hiring the lesser qualified will diminish a business's efficiency or degrade an enterprise's quality of service is an empirical matter and surely difficult to generalize about. Effects on efficiency would need to be analyzed on a case by case basis.

Divide work into three types: high skill (e.g., airline pilot, chemical engineer), medium skill (e.g., plumber, secretary), and low skill (delivery truck driver, toll booth attendant). The effects of preferential hiring on efficiency will surely vary according to the job categories. In high skill jobs, there will be a premium in selecting the very best qualified and the adverse consequences of selecting less than the best qualified will be probably the greatest. Even here, though, one must be careful in saying this. If the spread between the best qualified and the minimally qualified is narrow, that is, if all the applicants are very qualified, then there may be little noticeable effect if those further down the qualification list are chosen over those further up.

Moreover, in talking about a qualification list and the best qualified, we are talking about qualifications-as-they-have-been-detected-and-assessed. Now, whether we eliminate the "fuzzy stuff" in employment choices or allow it, our predictions of job success based on qualifications-as-we-can-detect-and-assess them are far from perfect. So many circumstances enter into the success of an individual's job performance (happy family life, happiness with the job, expectations about the future, financial pressures, style of life, etc.) that where paper qualifications of applicants are not greatly different, we may do just as well to choose at random than to choose from the top of the list down. Selecting "less qualified" over "more qualified" may produce little discernible effects regarding efficiency.

In the case of low skilled jobs, effects on efficiency from hiring the less than best qualified may not be noticeable at all. Choosing a lesser qualified person to drive a bread truck is not likely to result in a significant deterioration of bread delivery, so long as the successful applicant can drive a truck at all.

I would conclude with the following observations:

1. Choosing a worker on the basis of his race need not be inefficient.
2. Preferential hiring may or may not produce significant inefficiencies. It depends upon the kind of work involved and how qualified the lesser qualified are. The actual effects of preferential hiring await a test.

We should note a further point, as well. Small declines in efficiency may be perfectly acceptable in order to achieve other important social aims. There is nothing so sacred about efficiency that says it can never be sacrificed to justice or social peace or diminished racism. In fact, to be willing to adopt a rule that all hiring must be colorblind is itself to be willing to compromise efficiency on occasion. The defender of preferential hiring is not the only one who must justify the less efficient procedure.

In short: some color-conscious decisions may promote efficiency; some color-conscious decisions may detract from efficiency; some colorblind decisions may detract from efficiency. Moreover, efficiency is not always our prime concern in deciding the desirability of colorblind versus color-conscious choices.

CONCLUSIONS ABOUT THE SOCIAL UTILITY ARGUMENT

If we adopt a cost-benefit approach, plausible arguments can be made for trying out, experimentally at least, preferential hiring of blacks. This is not to deny that plausible arguments can be made against the desirability of preferential hiring. Given the complex nature of the costs and benefits involved, plausible arguments can be made on both sides. There is no decisive way to demonstrate the desirable consequences of a proposed program except to put it into effect. The Social Utility Argument may bring enough plausibility to the case for preferential hiring so as to warrant a legislative experiment. The risks inherent in giving preferences to blacks may be worth taking.

In many ways, the Social Utility Argument seems a more persuasive defense of preferential hiring than the Compensatory Justice Argument. There is certainly a closer fit between instrument and aim on the Social Utility Argument. The instrument is preferential hiring and the aim, according to the

Argument from Compensatory Justice, is to compensate. But preferential hiring is weakly compensatory. The instrument is not well-fitted to the aim. On the Social Utility Argument, on the other hand, the aim of preferential hiring of blacks is to quickly increase the number of blacks in certain jobs. The instrument is well suited to the aim which allegedly justifies its use. Moreover, the fact that preferential hiring will tend to benefit the better qualified blacks is perfectly consistent with the reasons for extending preferences, since there will be greater overall social utility in preferring the best qualified blacks.

If the proper defense of preferential hiring of blacks lies in its maximization of social welfare, then an important implication should be noted. If the legitimacy of preferential hiring derives from the fact that it is in the public interest, then no black can claim *as a right* the preference accorded him. It is merely fortuitous that *he* receives an employment preference since his receiving it is due entirely to the adventitious circumstance that benefiting him is an effective way of benefiting society. The Social Utility Argument does not entail individual rights, as does the Compensatory Justice Argument.

If social utility considerations now favor specially benefiting some blacks, conditions may not always make this so. In fact, conditions may become such that it is socially useful to deny some blacks employment opportunities. Persons receiving benefits justified solely by the social utility of their receiving them cannot complain when these benefits are taken away because new utility maximizing policies are adopted. Nor can they complain when they are called upon to make sacrifices for the public interest if their previous immunity from sacrifice derived only from the public interest. The public interest can change.

It is this fact which gives rise to social theories which imply moral limits to the scope of public interest arguments. Acknowledging certain fundamental rights is a way of acknowledging that an individual has standing to complain about some sacrifices, some losses of benefits. Whether there are any fundamental rights that limit social policies in the area of employment is the crucial question that has yet to be answered.

7

Distributive Justice

DISTRIBUTIVE JUSTICE AND PREFERENTIAL HIRING

There is a third general ground upon which one might attempt a defense of preferential hiring of blacks. One might argue that the poverty and lack of opportunities of the mass of blacks must, as a matter of *distributive justice,* be addressed by the most effective means, including preferential hiring. Distributive justice would favor aid to blacks regardless of the reason why they need it and regardless of whether this is a way of maximizing social utility.

Is there a persuasive defense of preferential hiring to be found in such a line of argument? The answer to this depends upon the clarity and power of the principles of distributive justice. Since arguments about distributive justice turn out to be highly controversial, arguments for preferential hiring that rely on principles of distributive justice will turn out to be controversial as well.

The basic idea of compensating a person for wrongful injury is not very controversial, and there are many intuitions about such compensation that we all share in common. Similarly, the justificatory power of social utility arguments, within limits, is uncontested. The same is not true when we turn to what is called distributive justice. There is agreement neither about what it is nor even that it is morally legitimate. Hayek, for example, believes that the idea of distributive justice is a dangerous illusion and a totalitarian snare.[1] Others are sympathetic to the idea of distributive justice but disagree about its content. Does a just society assure that the rewards people receive are commensurate to their need? Or their effort? Or their contribution? Or their moral desert? All of these? None of these? Or, does a just society distribute and redistribute resources so as to make each person's income, wealth, or social position approximately equal to everyone else's? All of these and others have been offered as requirements of distributive justice.[2]

It is not uncommon for people to appeal to the precept of need in certain situations, to the precept of contribution in others, and to the precept of effort in still other circumstances. Can any one or combination of these precepts be thought of as the most general principle of justice? If so, what would it say? What would it tell us to do? Would it express a social ideal or something stronger: a requirement? Is the principle supposed to imply a structure of individual rights? To what? Against whom do the rights obtain? These questions will have to be answered by any theory of distributive justice.

Perhaps a Distributive Justice Argument for preferential hiring of blacks might go like this. Because of their poverty, inferior education and training, and so on, blacks labor under unfair disadvantages in competing for decent jobs and positions. Giving blacks employment preferences compensates for (in the general sense of "makes up for") the unfair competitive advantages had by whites. The idea here is expressed in an analogy used by President Johnson in 1965:

Imagine a hundred yard dash in which one of the two runners has his legs shackled together. He has progressed 10 yards, while the unshackled runner has gone 50 yards. How do they rectify the situation? Do they merely remove the shackles and allow the race to proceed? Then they could say that "equal opportunity" now prevailed. But one of the runners would still be forty yards ahead of the other. Would it not be the better part of justice to allow the previously shackled runner to make-up the forty yard gap; or to start the race all over again? That would be affirmative action towards equality.[3]

In the competition for the good things of life everyone ought to be free of certain "shackles" and it is only fair to give special help to those who have been "shackled." From the point of view of distributive justice, it is irrelevant what caused the shackles. Even if they derived from natural causes rather than unjust oppression, the "better part of justice" would still have us allow the recently unshackled runner "to make-up the forty yard gap."

I will term this argument the Unjust Advantage Argument.[4] It rests on a widespread feeling that it is good to assist the underprivileged, to help the handicapped, to assist the needy, etc. It remains to be seen, however, whether this feeling can provide the basis for a compelling and specific theory of distributive justice. The argument assumes that it is unfair that some have to labor under certain disadvantages no matter how these came about. But this assumption is too vague to serve as a critical standard. There are innumerable disadvantages under which individuals labor. Is it a serious requirement of justice that every disadvantage be removed? At what cost? If not every disadvantage is the concern of justice, which are? What sorts of claims do the relevant disadvantages give rise to? Rights against the government or other people for specific kinds of help? Or weaker claims than this? What are the limitations on the means that government may employ to eliminate or make up for disadvantages? Of the various aims government may have, what priority are we to assign to the elimination or amelioration of disadvantage?

Perhaps we can take a clue from President Johnson's speech and agree that "equal opportunity" provides one of the touchstones of distributive justice. It is unjust that people suffer under disadvantages which deny them equality of opportunity. This does not advance us very far, however. Which disadvantages deny us equal opportunity? What *is* equality of opportunity?

We have already touched briefly on this last question in previous chapters. In trying to give some precision and specificity to the idea of a right to equality of opportunity in employment, I defined a right which I called a right to equal consideration in employment (RTEC). As defined, it was the right of a job applicant that the choice of a successful applicant be made solely on the basis of his job-related qualifications. Is this what equal employment opportunity means? This is the appropriate place to take up that question.

EQUALITY OF OPPORTUNITY

Here we come face to face with an issue as muddled and controversial as it is important. Reference to equality of opportunity is ubiquitous in political arguments of all stripes. Like "freedom" and "democracy," it is a notion every party wants to enlist on his side. Equality of opportunity has been raised to the level of a national goal by equal employment and educational opportunity legislation. The assumption of a "right" to equality of opportunity seems to underlie President Johnson's remarks, which were made in conjunction with the issuance of Executive Order 11246, requiring every federal contractor to affirm its status as an "equal opportunity employer."

Some contend that preferential hiring is wrong precisely because it violates equality of opportunity, since it is a kind of favoritism. Others contend that, in fact, preferential hiring is necessary to realize equality of opportunity. Are they talking about the same thing? Who is right? In the next few pages, I will try to indicate what an opportunity is, define the *concept* of equal opportunity, and then proceed to describe some of the different *conceptions* of equality of opportunity that can be constructed on the concept.[5]

Opportunity is a species of freedom or liberty; and since freedoms involve absences of restrictions or obstacles, the idea of absence of some obstacle is implicated in the notion of opportunity. Opportunities arise when obstacles that normally block achievement of a goal are not present. However, it is not enough to focus merely upon the obstacles that have been removed; otherwise there would be no distinguishing between opportunities and plain freedoms. By calling something an opportunity, our focus is as much on what remains to be done as on what no longer stands in the way.

Although an opportunity arises when some obstacles to achievement are removed, *other obstacles, needing effort to overcome them, will still remain.* Opportunities can be grasped or let pass, seized or squandered. The agent must decide. It is an essential part of something's being called an opportunity that both an agent's choices and efforts are called for. Thus, an opportunity for something is not, strictly speaking, to be equated with a chance for that thing; "a chance occurs when a person is in a situation where he might, or is likely to, obtain a desirable goal or possession but where whether or not he does so does not depend on his efforts."[6]

Opportunities, thus, involve three components: first, an agent who has the opportunity; second, the goal or aim of the agent; third, the absence of some obstacles to achievement of the goal or aim such that effortful action by the agent can overcome the remaining obstacles. Using this analysis, we can now say when *opportunities are equal:*

The opportunities of persons X and Y are equal with respect to some goal A if they face the same obstacles in attaining A.

This gives us the *concept* of equal opportunity.

Equal opportunities for something are not the same thing as equal chances for it. An equal chance principle will say that the appropriate equality holds between X and Y with respect to A when the likelihood of X's receiving A is the same as the likelihood of Y's receiving it, no matter what. Equal opportunity principles will not imply that chances of X and Y with respect to A must be the same regardless of their personal choices and efforts.[7]

Having an analysis of the concept of equal opportunity leaves us far short of having a substantive principle which will imply conclusions about preferential hiring or other social policies. The terms of the concept must be fleshed out in various ways to yield a concrete conception of equal opportunity. A substantive view will have to answer a number of questions. Among them are: (1) Society must equalize opportunities to do what? (2) Society must equalize with respect to which obstacles?

Can distributive justice require society to equalize opportunities for every goal a citizen may have? Consider the goal of becoming Miss America. Is society required as a matter of justice to offer free nose bobs to those whose looks disqualify them from competing successfully for the title? Or consider the goal of becoming a mafia chieftan. Must society remove special barriers which stand in the way of some succeeding in this goal?

We can expect that any substantive view of equal opportunity will require society to equalize obstacles to the attainment of *some* goals and not others. Every view of equal opportunity, accordingly, includes implicit if not explicit affirmation of some goals over others. Thus, a view of equality of opportunity will have this form:

> Justice requires that X and Y have equal opportunities for achieving or having $G_1, G_2, G_3, \ldots, G_n$.

(G_1, etc., stand for specific goals or goods.) Which goals are judged basic and subject to equal opportunity of attainment can be a matter of dispute between different views of equal opportunity. Different conceptions are obtained by adding to or subtracting from the list $G_1 \ldots G_n$.

Room for variation and disagreement is even more apparent in regard to question (2), the question of which obstacles to equalize. Even if we agree on the goals for which there must be equal opportunity of attainment, must society equalize with respect to every barrier or obstacle which stands in the way of attainment? Suppose we agree that the goal of holding elective office is one for which there should be equality of opportunity. Suppose Mary and Sue, equally capable, run for office. Mary has friends and family who are very supportive, who always provide encouragement, and so on. Sue's family and friends are indifferent or hostile to her political ambitions and are non-supportive. Obviously, their non-support is a motivational burden borne by Sue, and no similar burden is borne by Mary. Must an equal opportunity society see to it that Sue's family and friends are as supportive as Mary's? How a principle of equal opportunity answers this question will depend upon how *extensive* or how *limited* it is. On the matter of obstacles to be equalized, a view of equal opportunity will have this form:

> X and Y have equal opportunity with respect to A if, of the possible obstacles to A, obstacles O_1, O_2, $\ldots O_n$ are equalized for X and Y.

Some views of equal opportunity may be modest in the obstacles they select for equalization; others may be ambitious in seeking to equalize most obstacles to their chosen goals.

Finally, there is another question to be faced. In speaking of the concept of equal opportunity, we spoke of X and Y facing the same or equal obstacles. How is "same obstacle" or "equal obstacle" to be interpreted? Suppose we say that X and Y face equal obstacles to achieving A if it requires as much effort from X as from Y to achieve A. We are still faced with an interpretation problem, since effort can be understood in two ways: objectively and subjectively. Consider an example. Suppose X and Y are engaged in the high jump and the bar is set at seven feet. In the objective sense of effort, the same effort is required of X and Y to pass over the bar, namely, the effort to jump seven feet. This represents a *task* notion of effort and the equal effort condition is satisfied when equal tasks are set. In the subjective sense of effort, it may take X more effort (expenditure of energy, concentration, etc.) to jump the bar because he may be shorter, out of shape, winded from previous contests, or whatever. This is the *energy* notion of effort and the equal effort condition is satisfied on this interpretation when equal amounts of energy expenditure are required of X and Y.

There are yet other complications involving equality of opportunity, but the ones already noted should give sufficient evidence that there is a vast number of possible principles of equal opportunity. Consider, for example, these schematic principles:

P1: Justice requires that X and Y have equal opportunities for achieving or having G_1 and G_2; and this is accomplished if, of the possible obstacles to G_1 and G_2, obstacles O_1, O_2, and O_3 are equalized (in the objective sense of effort) for X and Y.

P2: Justice requires that X and Y have equal opportunities for achieving or having G_1, G_2, G_3, and G_4; and this is accomplished if, of the possible obstacles to these goals, obstacles O_1 through O_{10} are equalized (in the subjective sense of effort) for X and Y.

P3: Justice requires that X and Y have equal opportunities for achieving or having G_1, G_2, G_3, and G_4; and this is accomplished if, of the possible obstacles to these goals, obstacles O_1, O_2, and O_3 present the same tasks to X and Y while O_4, O_5, and O_6 require the same energy of X and Y.

And so on. Principles can differ with respect to the goals they posit, the obstacles they attack, and the notion of effort they presuppose.

Because of the endless variations possible, it should be obvious that there is no one answer to the question: Does equal opportunity forbid, permit, or require preferential hiring of blacks under current conditions? Some views may permit or even require use of legal handicaps such as racial favoritism. Legal obstacles to employment are to be made unequal in order that other obstacles are equalized. Yet other views of equal opportunity will be incompatible with the use of racial preferences. Unless we have a decisive way of determining the correct or preferred conception of distributive justice and of equal opportunity, we are not going to be in a position to decisively evaluate arguments for or against preferential hiring that rest on those grounds. In what follows, I propose to describe two major views of equal opportunity which *do not* support preferential hiring. These views have the advantage of being standard, popular, fairly precise and comprehensible, and limited.[8] This, of course, does not guarantee their superiority.

FORMAL EQUAL OPPORTUNITY

On the view that I will call Formal Equal Opportunity (FEO), X and Y have equal opportunity in regard to A so long as neither faces a legal or quasi-legal barrier to achieving A the other does not face.[9] Applied to employment, FEO reads: X and Y have equal opportunity in regard to jobs so long as neither faces a legal or quasi-legal barrier to employment the other does not face.

Suppose there were a program of preferential hiring giving employment preferences to whites. If X were white, and Y black, then Y would labor under a legal burden not borne by X. Their employment opportunities would not be equal.

Suppose there were a program of preferential hiring giving preferences to blacks. Then X would labor under a legal barrier not faced by Y. Again, X's and Y's employment opportunities would not be equal, according to FEO. Suppose we recognize a right to equal employment opportunity and we understand equal employment opportunity in terms of FEO. Are we not then compelled to reject any use of race in hiring, any use of preferential hiring?

This conclusion may not be compelled. It depends upon how we construe the phrase "opportunity in regard to jobs" in the FEO formula and how race or racial preferences might be used in hiring. Does "jobs" refer to each specific job opportunity an individual might have or does it refer to the totality of his job opportunities over a working life? Suppose "jobs" is taken to mean each individual job opportunity. Then it is evident that any use of racial preferences violates FEO. If a specific job is determined by a racial criterion, pursuant to some official policy, then applicants of the disfavored race will face a legal barrier to attaining that job not faced by all other applicants.

Suppose, however, we take "jobs" to refer to the totality of a person's employment opportunities. It is not clear, in this case, that FEO rules out every possible use of racial preferences in hiring. Consider some scheme of proportional hiring by race, so that industries, businesses, governments, educational institutions, etc., were required to hire in proportion to the racial composition of their labor pools. It is conceivable that such a scheme might be devised and operated so that over any person's career of employment he faced no greater total of legal barriers than any other person, though in regard to specific occasions he might have faced greater or lesser legal barriers to jobs.

It is possible, then, that there might be a form of explicitly taking race into account so that the total of each individual's employment opportunities is equal to every other individual's.[10] Such a use of race, however, could not uniformly favor one race over another. If blacks exceeded their quota in an industry, whites would thereafter be favored until balance was achieved. If whites exceeded their allotted number, blacks would be favored. If our conceivable proportional hiring scheme were sufficiently fine-tuned, it would leave no individual facing greater legal barriers, in total over his whole employment career, than any other individual. Such a scheme would be consistent with one interpretation of FEO.

Although such a scheme may be conceivable, it is difficult to see how it could be practically possible. It would require, among other things, a mammoth accounting mechanism to keep score of total legally enforced move-aheads or move-behinds experienced by each worker over the whole of his employment career. In the absence of such monitoring there could be no possibility of government intervening to even things out, and in the absence of government intervention there could be no assurance that some individuals won't come out net losers.

In contrast to the insuperable difficulties of bringing off the proportional hiring scheme, if we want to assure equal legal barriers to employment there is one very easy way to take a step in that direction: forbid any use of race in employment that is not genuinely job-related. If race is never used as a legal impediment to a job, then, at least in regard to race, everyone will face equal legal barriers to employment, namely no racial barriers at all.

This is why it is, perhaps, natural to understand FEO as requiring "careers open to talents." We can guarantee equal opportunity in the sense of FEO simply be extruding from the law the use of race, sex, religion, social position, royal or common birth, and any other irrelevant factors, in the selection of persons for jobs.

Equal opportunity understood as "careers open to talents" has a distinguished heritage.

This formal interpretation of equal opportunity is part and parcel of the classical liberal tradition of political thought, in that it is mainly an extension of the idea of securing the equal liberties of all persons. Just as the removal of class, income, race and sex obstacles could make all persons able to vote, hold property, serve on juries, hold office, and so on, so a removal of legal obstacles could open up places of . . . employment to persons from all social groups. Where access to . . . a type of employment had to be restricted, selection procedures which took account not of social status, but of relevant qualifications, were devised. The career open to talents is a career entered by competitive examination.[11]

Only the applicant's ability to do the job should count, only his job-related qualifications should have a bearing.

If we see equality of opportunity as an essential element of distributive justice, if we interpret equality of opportunity (in regard to employment) as FEO, and if we interpret FEO as "careers open to talents," then we must conclude, I believe, that distributive justice, rather than providing a justification for preferential hiring, condemns it.

Indeed, if we wish to assert a right to equal employment opportunity, on the interpretation of equal opportunity as "careers open to talents," it would be natural to define that right as the right to equal consideration for a job (RTEC). This is the right of job applicants that the choice of a successful applicant be made solely on the basis of job-related qualifications. In earlier chapters, we have already seen that preferential hiring of blacks is incompatible with the recognition of RTEC.

LIBERAL EQUAL OPPORTUNITY

Formal Equal Opportunity, interpreted as "careers open to talents," forbids the use of racial criteria in job selection unless race is a genuine job-related qualification. Such a conception of equal opportunity might seem too weak, however. There are many significant barriers to employment besides legal ones, and FEO addresses none of them. "Careers are open to talents" but talents must be developed and cultivated. Barriers to such development can effectively bar large numbers of people from any meaningful competition for the better jobs in society. Individuals who are equally talented and equally willing to work might nevertheless have greatly different employment prospects because of their command or lack of command of educational and training resources.

These concerns may prompt us to turn to an alternative view of equality of opportunity, one which I will call Liberal Equal Opportunity (LEO). LEO is concerned not only with legal obstacles to employment (and other goods) but with important non-legal barriers to the development and display of talent.

Verbal, conceptual, and logical skills of a fairly high order are necessary to perform most of the non-menial jobs in our society. Failure to possess these minimum skills effectively excludes an individual from the competition for the better jobs. More than this, educational certification of various sorts is generally a prerequisite for most good jobs.

The state is deeply implicated in this certification process. First of all, it controls the means of certification through its power to accredit courses of study, recognize degrees and diplomas, etc. The state is further deeply involved in controlling access to various occupations through its monopoly control of licensing to practice particular trades. Often, a condition of acquiring a license is prior educational certification of some sort. Finally, the state controls access to and provides the means to free education. For these reasons alone, it may be urged, the state has a responsibility to equalize with respect to at least the basic educational and preparatory conditions of employment.

It is not enough, however, that a person have the resources to develop his talents and then succeed in actually developing them. In order to compete for jobs, he must be able to *show* he is talented and trained. But sometimes there are serious obstacles to showing an employer one's abilities. Some of these obstacles derive from the operations of the labor market.

Our social system leaves firms free to choose workers who will, in the firms' judgments, most benefit them. Firms must adopt procedures for making these judgments. They need ways of determining the qualifications of the job candidates. The costs of information frequently make it efficient for firms to use disqualifying generalizations, a matter we have already talked about in Chapter Six. Recall the example of the airline that disqualifies all overweight applicants from being considered as pilots. The airline uses a generalization to disqualify an entire class of people. This practice is one which we generally justify in the name of safety, efficiency, convenience, or whatever.

There are occasions, however, when such generalizations and their consequent group disqualifications are so seriously harmful to the opportunities of many persons that they should not be used even when they have a business justification. Recall the case of the automobile manufacturer which wanted to rely on the finding that there is statistically less absenteeism among white workers than among black workers. Even a small statistical difference might be sufficient to prompt the manufacturer to seek labor costs savings by preferring whites. The upshot would be diminished opportunities for blacks.

The costs to a company of determining the qualifications of each individual separately may be so high that it is cheaper to rely on generalizations, even those that are only marginally sound. If to even a minor degree black workers on average were felt to be less disciplined, less motivated, and more prone to absenteeism than white workers, and if employers sought to use such generalizations to disqualify blacks in general, *all* black workers would be disadvantaged regardless of their individual qualities as workers. Reliable, able, highly motivated black applicants would be unable to show they could do the job because it would not be worth the companies' while to examine them separately, it being cheaper to disqualify them as a group. Under such circumstances, each black would labor under a persistent obstacle to showing how capable he is, an obstacle not shared by white applicants. For reasons of this sort, legislation does not allow employers to use such racial generalizations in hiring. It is perfectly reasonable to view this legislation as designed to enhance equality of employment opportunity.

The same problems can be generated by the employer's use of such devices as aptitude tests. Such tests, for various reasons, may disproportionately down-score and thus disqualify certain groups. The employment opportunities of members of such groups are diminished. We may surely demand more than a showing of business convenience before allowing such tests into ubiquitous use. [12]

One criticism of FEO was that people with equal native ability may nevertheless have very unequal employment prospects unless some equalization of basic educational and training resources is provided along with "careers open to talents." A second criticism was that FEO ignores certain unequal obstacles to showing one's talents. Liberal Equal Opportunity (LEO) seeks to address both of these matters, to assure that lack of means does not stand in the way of getting at least a basic education and to assure that an individual does not face pervasive and enduring barriers to showing he is able to do the job.

This general characterization of LEO leaves it unclear whether it would favor or oppose preferential hiring. It will be necessary further to flesh out our account of LEO. There are two directions the development can take. One direction is to build the account of LEO on FEO. [13] This will have the effect, of course, of making LEO incompatible with preferential hiring, since FEO (interpreted as "careers open to talents") is incompatible.

LEO #1: X and Y have equal employment opportunities when (i) each has equal basic education, (ii) neither faces a legal or economic barrier to further education or training based on race, sex, or other factor not related to ability to benefit from such further education or training, (iii) neither faces a legal or quasi-legal barrier to employment based on race, sex, or other factor irrelevant to job competence, and (iv) neither faces pervasive special labor market barriers to demonstrating job competency not faced by the other.

LEO #1 defines a concrete, specific conception of equality of opportunity in employment. It seeks to assure that no one suffers from a lack of basic training, irrelevant legal barriers to jobs, pervasive group-disqualifying generalizations, or lack of means to higher education. LEO #1 is a conception of equal opportunity that probably commands wide acceptance. It is feasible to implement as social policy; it "treats individuals as individuals" so far as this is possible, and it honors personal liberty and choice. And it is incompatible with preferential hiring by race.

Clause (iii) guarantees this incompatibility, expressing the substance of FEO. LEO #1 supplements FEO with further requirements. If any version of equality of opportunity is to be compatible with preferential hiring, it must break free from FEO. Consider, then, this version of LEO:

LEO #2: X and Y have equal employment opportunities when neither faces a total package of educational, legal, and market barriers which is distinctly greater than the package faced by the other.

LEO #2 concerns itself with the same obstacles as LEO #1 but it differs in not making it necessary that each obstacle, taken individually, be equal for X and Y. Instead, it requires that the mix of these obstacles for each, X and Y, result in approximately equal totals.

Consequently, LEO #2 leaves it open that some may face differential legal barriers to employment even though equality of employment opportunity is satisfied. X may face lesser educational barriers but greater legal barriers; Y may face greater educational barriers but lesser legal ones. This might be arranged through perferential hiring.

LEO #2 is very much vaguer than LEO #1. It leaves a great deal to intuition in deciding what variations of opportunities create the appropriate balanced totals of opportunity. Moreover, it would appear to require very much more intervention and manipulation and monitoring to assure that variations in opportunities balance out. It may be subject, then, to some of the same criticisms posed against the proportional hiring scheme discussed earlier.

8

Equal Opportunity and Rights

BROADER CONCEPTIONS OF DISTRIBUTIVE JUSTICE

The concept of equal opportunity speaks of equalizing obstacles to agents' goals. If we restrict our consideration to employment goals alone, there are vast numbers of impediments and obstacles which can diminish an individual's prospects for good employment: quality of family life, cultural background, health, geographical location, luck, religious values, and so on. A vision of equal opportunity less modest than FEO, LEO #1, or even LEO #2, might seek to control for as many of these factors as possible, resorting to handicaps, quotas, special assistance, and other devices to assure that total employment prospects are equal for all. One impulse that might lead us in this direction is unhappiness with the unequal results allowable under FEO or LEO. The desire to see the outcomes of effort and choice reflect ability may prompt us to want to control as many factors as possible which bear on employment prospects. We may even be prompted to control for lack of effort and incentive themselves. We may be led, in fact, to abandon equal opportunity as an aim, substituting instead the goal of *equal condition.*

An egalitarian may think that the essence of distributive justice is not equality of opportunity but equality of material condition. Liberties and opportunities may be viewed as less important than the elimination of economic class differences. If quota hiring, racial preferences, and other such devices are effective in bringing about a greater equality of income, health, self-esteem, and so on, then they are justified.

In connection with egalitarian views, we might discuss one additional alleged view of equal opportunity, a view called Actuarial Equal Opportunity (AEO). On this view, X and Y are said to have equal opportunity with respect to A if X and Y belong to social groups whose rates of success at obtaining A are equal.[1] A black applicant has equal opportunity with a white applicant if the rate of employment success of blacks is equal to the rate of employment success of whites.

This view will be satisfied where there is proportional representation of racial groups in employment. Suppose that 100 whites and 25 blacks apply for 50 jobs. The rates of success for the two groups—blacks and whites—are equal if approximately 40 of the jobs go to whites and the rest go to blacks.[2] If our aim is to assure equal rates of employment success to the major racial groups, then racially preferential hiring may be called for when other employment procedures fail to generate the appropriate racial profile.

Although proportional representation of races may be a desirable aim, it is difficult to understand why this should be called "equal opportunity." Certainly, AEO is not a conception of *individual* equal opportunity. Suppose that X and Y belong to the *same* group. Each's group, then, has equal employment success rates! Nevertheless, opportunities of X and Y may be very different.

It is highly misleading to call X's and Y's opportunities equal when they belong to groups with equal success rates. X's and Y's opportunities are equal only in the sense that X's average opportunity as a member of his group is the same as Y's average opportunity as a member of his group. This tells us nothing about the actual opportunities of X and Y. The average opportunity of X is the average of opportunities possessed by all in X's group. This average is as uninformative about X's actual opportunities as average family size is about the actual size of his family.[3]

AEO is concerned about equal success rates of social groups—equal results—and not about equal opportunity for individuals. AEO is satisfied if success rates (outcomes) among basic social groups is the same regardless of the disparities of opportunities within the groups. It reflects a group-oriented egalitarianism.

EQUAL OPPORTUNITY RIGHTS

As we have already seen, questions about rights arise when we discuss preferential hiring—rights to compensation, rights which might be violated by preferential hiring, and so on. Asking about rights is especially important in regard to equal opportunity rights.

We have been examining some principles and views of equal opportunity. How are we to understand the force of these principles? Are they meant to imply any specific individual rights? It is commonplace for people to talk about a right to equal opportunity. Is this talk to be understood literally? Might not talk about a right to equal opportunity simply be a loose way of indicating that equality of opportunity—of some vague sort, perhaps—ought to be a social ideal?[4] This need not imply that any individual has any specific rights at all. And on some of the broader views of equal opportunity, it is difficult to see what individual rights could be entailed.

But let us take seriously the language of equal opportunity

rights and suppose that some, at least, are prepared to assert quite literally that individuals have a right to equal employment opportunity. What could this right amount to? Against whom would it obtain? What would be the corresponding obligations? Once we try to provide some cash value to our talk about equal opportunity rights, we face increasingly greater difficulties as our conceptions of equal opportunity become broader and vaguer. Both FEO and LEO #1 are relatively specific and we can imagine fairly specific rights which could be founded on these conceptions. The essential idea in FEO, "careers open to talents," is promoted by recognizing a right that employers not use race or other irrelevant criteria in hiring but select from applicants solely on the basis of job-related qualifications. This is the right previously defined and called the right to equal consideration for a job (RTEC). Since LEO #1 incorporates FEO, RTEC will promote the former's values as well.

We may imagine that this right is a right possessed by each participant in the labor market and that it applies, in the first instance, against employers and, in the second instance, against government to enforce a prohibition against the use of irrelevant hiring criteria. The Civil Rights Act of 1964 (Title VII of which deals with employment discrimination) appears in the guise of legislation to protect individuals' *rights*.

LEO #1 would support additional individual rights. It would give individuals a positive claim against society for a basic education, for easy access to other educational resources, and for government intervention to prevent the labor market from imposing certain persistent barriers to showing one's ability to do a job. This repertoire of rights has a fairly definite structure and content and can be implemented without serious conflict with other social values such as efficiency and maximum personal liberty.

Ambitious conceptions of equal opportunity which break away from FEO lend themselves less easily to analysis regard-

ing the rights they might be taken to imply. If these conceptions ground rights, the rights must surely involve yet greater
positive claims on social resources and on governmental
performance. At the same time, the conceptions seem to imply
less protection against (at least temporary) legal discrimination
and are more likely to justify interferences with personal
liberties.

Because people can subscribe to different conceptions of
equality of opportunity, they can mean different things by
saying that a person has a right to equality of opportunity.
Until we have a way of determining the preferred conception
of equality of opportunity, we have no effective way of
deciding between different interpretations of the right to equal
opportunity. Before we can say more about equal opportunity
and about employment policies in general, more groundwork
must be established. I shall later return to the question of an
equal employment opportunity right in connection with the
discussion of constitutional equality.

MAKING UP FOR LACK OF EQUAL OPPORTUNITY

Suppose we agree on a certain conception of equal opportunity. What are we to say about a situation where this equality of
opportunity *has not in fact obtained?* This seems to be one of
the questions raised in President Johnson's analogy. Equal
opportunity in the 100 yard dash consists (at least) in running
the race without shackles. Yet the race is half run with one
runner shackled. The shackles are now removed; but the other
runner is 40 yards ahead. What is to be done?

Many who urge that equality of opportunity requires for the
time being preferential hiring of blacks have in mind, I believe,
this situation. Blacks have been the victims of discrimination
and are now far behind in the competition for jobs. In the case
of the 100 yard dash, perhaps the race can be started anew, with
both runners unshackled from the start. But the "race of life,"

which includes the competition for jobs, cannot be started over. If we decide that some competitors have been shackled and release their shackles, they must compete with those who have been unshackled all along.

Equality of opportunity has not obtained. In order for it now to obtain for the never-shackled and the newly-unshackled alike, it is argued, there must be some way of pushing the latter forward in relation to the former, since the race cannot be started again. Thus, legal policies involving temporary preferences to blacks in hiring will serve to restore equality of employment opportunity in a situation where it has long been absent.

This argument is powerfully persuasive to many, but let us consider what kind of view of equal opportunity it presupposes. For, as we have seen, there are many competing views of equal opportunity and this argument may succeed on some of these views and not on others. On FEO and LEO #1, equal employment opportunity is to be understood as at least requiring implementation of RTEC; people are chosen on the basis of their qualifications. If a person has been denied equal employment opportunity in the past, we can give him equal opportunity by seeing to it that when he applies for a job, he will be considered solely on the basis of his job-related qualifications. Being so considered is what, or partly what, equal employment opportunity means.

It might be protested that this still leaves the victim of past discrimination laboring under the accumulated effects of that discrimination. So it is specious to say that we have now given him equal opportunity by no longer discriminating. We remove the shackles from the runner but now he is forty yards behind and no amount of effort will allow him to catch up unless he is moved forward. How can simply removing the shackles be termed "equal opportunity"? Even President Johnson deprecated this view.

But, what does equal opportunity mean in the context of the

race? Suppose it is claimed that equal opportunity means: "not being shackled and not having to suffer any disadvantages from having previously been shackled." We need to consider, now, whether this claim derives from a principle of equal opportunity or from a principle of compensation. If the shackled runner has been wrongfully shackled, then he has suffered an unjust injury and a principle of compensation will have us attempt to make good his loss. Is it this fact which would have us move him forward, or is it the requirements of equal opportunity itself? To complicate matters further, on some occasions opportunity may be the medium in which compensation is paid. A call for "equal opportunity," in the sense of a restored balance of competition, might then derive not from a principle of equal opportunity (a part of distributive justice) but from the particular requirements in a particular situation of the principle of compensation.

Let us consider how the 100 yard dash analogy can mislead us, making us think of the elimination of discrimination as specious equal opportunity. Our tendency to deprecate unshackling the runner as "restoring" equal opportunity (competitive equality) stems partly from our appreciation of the emptiness of the gesture. There is only one prize in the race and that comes from winning. The second runner is by now out of contention unless he is moved forward. If he is not to be moved forward, it seems to matter little whether we trouble to unshackle him or not.

In the same vein, one may see it an empty gesture to simply stop discriminating against a person when he seeks employment. He, like, the racer, is far behind in the competition. But it is mistaken to see the matter this way. The "race of life" is not like the 100 yard dash in crucial respects. In fact, it is not a race at all. There is no one prize at the end but innumerable benefits along the path of a person's life which can be gained or lost. By judging a victim of past discrimination now on the basis of his qualifications alone, he may not be able to get a job he might have gotten had he not been previously discriminated against. This is true. But judging him on his qualifications now may mean that he can get a better paying job than the one he has. And that constitutes a real improvement in his life. It is not a trivial or empty gesture to make that improvement possible.

As to the genuine loss or injury he has suffered under past discrimination, this is a matter that the victim should be compensated for in some fashion. But as we have seen from our examination of compensatory justice in the earlier chapters, this may not mean giving employment preferences.

None of this is meant as a defense of the superiority of FEO or LEO #1. These conceptions of equal opportunity may be too weak or unacceptable for other reasons. I have tried, however, to show that implementing and abiding by RTEC is not a necessarily "empty" or "unreasonable" expression of equal employment opportunity. The 100 yard dash analogy can mislead us.

If equal opportunity includes RTEC, then racial preferences violate equal opportunity. If equal opportunity does not include RTEC—if, in other words, we subscribe to one of the broader views of equal opportunity—then equal opportunity may well require or permit racial preferences where equality of opportunity has not previously obtained for all. If equal opportunity is looked at as some kind of equilibrium, then we can see nothing amiss about tampering with a situation that has got into disequilibrium. We add and subtract weights here and there until equilibrium is restored. The persuasiveness of the argument we have been considering rests upon holding particular views about equal opportunity.

RAWLS' THEORY OF JUSTICE

By now, a person genuinely interested in examining the rights and wrongs of preferential hiring and willing to follow out the arguments on all sides may be despairing of the possibility of coming to any hard and fast conclusions. In the early chapters, the weight of argument seemed to go against the Compensatory Justice Defense, but nothing like a decisive case was made. Too much rested upon assumptions about rights, when they could be overridden and when not, and so on. Moreover, the method of argument relied almost entirely upon appeal to intuition and consensus about examples.

When, in subsequent chapters, we turned to arguments based on social utility, we again found indeterminancy. The consequences of preferential hiring are to a large extent speculative. A person optimistic about our ability to design effective social policies might reasonably believe, on the evidence, that preferential hiring will be justified by the good it will bring about. But, the contrary belief is not unreasonable, either.

Now, when we turn to considerations of basic social justice and equal opportunity, we find ourselves dealing with principles which are vague, imprecise, lacking a comprehensive framework, and which are, as a consequence, subject to widely differing interpretations. There is no agreement on how we are to order the relations between principles of liberty, principles of opportunity, and principles of assistance, nor even on what these principles say. In our disagreement, we might proceed to exchange examples about fair contests and the like, but we need not be pessimists to doubt the ultimate efficacy of this approach.

It might be suggested that there is advantage in turning to the most rigorously developed and comprehensive theory of social justice that we currently have available, the theory of John Rawls. This monumental treatment of distributive justice, perhaps, can provide some backbone to our examination of equal opportunity.

In *A Theory of Justice*[5] Rawls seeks to state and justify the most general principles of distributive justice, to defend particular interpretations of them, to establish priority relations in their enforcement, and to indicate how they might be applied to actual societies. According to Rawls, the basic principles are these:

1. Each person is to have an equal right to the most extensive total system of equal basic liberties compatible with a similar system of liberty for all (Equal Liberties Principle).
2. Social and economic inequalities are to be arranged so that they are both:
   (a) to the greatest benefit of the least advantaged . . . (Difference Principle), and
   (b) attached to offices and positions open to all under conditions of fair equality of opportunity (Equal Opportunity Principle).[6]

The principles are related to one another hierarchically, in descending order: Equal Liberties Principle; Equal Opportunity Principle; Difference Principle. This means that a just society must fully satisfy the Equal Liberties Principle before it may implement the Equal Opportunity Principle; and it must fully satisfy the Equal Liberties Principle and the Equal Opportunity Principle before it may implement the Difference Principle. Basic liberties cannot be sacrificed for increased opportunities; fair opportunity cannot be sacrificed to material gain.

When Rawls discusses the Equal Liberties Principle, it is in terms primarily of rights to political participation, free speech, and liberty of conscience. However, he would apparently count as basic liberties the right to travel freely and the right of individual choice of occupation (*TJ*, 310). Thus, an employment scheme which assigned occupations to individuals would apparently violate the Equal Liberties Principle and would be unjust even if it did benefit the least advantaged.

Rawls' discussion of the Equal Opportunity Principle is brief and vague. One interpretation of equality of opportunity, he notes, is "formal equality of opportunity" where "all have at least the same legal rights to access to all advantaged social positions" (*TJ*, 72). It would not be unnatural to view this interpretation as forbidding the use of legal policies which use race or other irrelevant criteria for filling jobs. However, for reasons which become plain in the next few paragraphs, one must be circumspect in imputing certain consequences to Rawls' three principles.

Rawls' preferred interpretation of equality of opportunity is what he calls "fair equality of opportunity." Here is what he says about this:

> The thought here is that positions are to be not only open in a formal sense, but that all should have a fair chance to obtain them. Offhand it is not clear what is meant, but we might say that those with similar abilities and skills should have similar life chances. More specifically . . . those who are at the same level of talent and ability, and have the same willingness to use them, should have the same prospects of success regardless of the income class into which they are born. In all sectors of society there should be roughly equal prospects of culture and achievement for everyone similarly motivated and endowed. The expectations of those with the same abilities and aspirations should not be affected by their social class. (*TJ*, 73.)

Not only is the idea of fair equality of opportunity general, it is not possible, according to Rawls, to completely realize it in any social setting; it can be only imperfectly carried out (*TJ*, 74). This characterization of fair equality of opportunity does not give us many clues about how we are to judge specific social policies.

This lack of specific direction is not so much due to Rawls' failure to attend more carefully to the issues as it is a reflection of one of the basic features of the theory itself. According to Rawls, the most basic principles of distributive justice are not about individual holdings and entitlements, specific shares and opportunities. The principles have as their subject the basic social structure and not the micro-level of specific social

policy. Rawls believes that there are no general criteria for
directly judging the justice or injustice of the multifarious
individual transactions and exchanges that take place in society, or for judging the variety of concrete social policies. The
principles of justice tell us instead how to create the conditions
of "background justice." They tell us how to judge and design
fair basic economic, legal, and political structures. The justice
of individual dealings, individual shares, individual entitlements, individual opportunities, etc., becomes a matter of
"pure procedural justice." This means that the justice of
individual situations is determined by the actual operations of
the fair structures themselves (*TJ*, 83-90).

That is why we must be circumspect in attributing any
implications about preferential hiring or other particular social
policies to Rawls' principles. The principles are not meant for
judging those kinds of cases. Instead, the principles are to be
applied through a four-stage sequence. First, there is the stage,
elaborately described by Rawls, in which imaginary rational,
self-interested individuals, by means of a social contract, adopt
the basic principles themselves (i.e., adopt the three principles). This stage, the stage of the "original position," is an
intellectual device which allows us to discover the very general,
basic principles of justice. Next, we are to imagine a constitutional stage, in which the institutional arrangements for society
are actually settled upon, selected from among those that are
compatible with the three principles. Next comes the legislative stage, where specific social policies are decided upon in
accordance with procedures provided by the constitution.
Finally, there is the judicial stage, in which legislative rules are
applied to specific cases and individuals.

The decisions made at the constitutional and legislative
stages give meaning to the three principles of justice. There can
be alternative constitutional arrangements compatible with the
principles. And under a specific constitution, there can be
alternative legislative policies which support constitutional

values and promote the public welfare. At the lower stages, but especially at the legislative stage, political judgment is called for. This political judgment, made in the context of fair political procedures, fills the space left by the generality of the principles of justice.

Two just societies could, accordingly, differ in regard to at least some of the constitutional and statutory rights afforded citizens, and differ in their institutions. This means that a *general* theory of justice (with its general principles) is indeterminate in regard to specific social policies like preferential hiring. The Equal Opportunity Principle expresses a fairly vague and quite general ideal which must be implemented in its detail by the political judgments of fair institutions. We cannot conclude from the bare statement of the principle that it will not countenance racial preferences in hiring. We cannot even conclude that equality of opportunity can never be sacrificed. Under the full statement of his Second Priority Rule (*TJ*, 302–303), Rawls contemplates the possibility that inequality of opportunity might be justified if that inequality enhances the opportunities of those with the least opportunities. The possibility exists that under appropriate social conditions, sound political judgment may dictate policies that deliberately limit the opportunities of some in the name of fair equality of opportunity.

CONCLUSIONS

Can we judge the justice or injustice of preferential hiring by talking about justice in the abstract? Can we bandy about precepts ("From each according to his ability, to each according to his need"), exchange examples (shackled runners), and arrive at answers with which we will all agree? Can we state our general principles as carefully as we are able and then cautiously and elaborately trace out their implications for a specific policy in a specific society at a specific time?

Examples call on our intuitions, and our intuitions may differ, may fade and blur at crucial junctures, may abandon us altogether in certain hard cases. General principles leave room for varying interpretations of key phrases and words. This is a feature of language that affects all principles, and all kinds of arguments, not just moral arguments. Finally, if Rawls is right, the general principles of justice are not supposed to be applied to specific policy, anyway. How, then, are we to resolve our doubts and questions about preferential hiring of blacks? We surely desire a reasonable basis for our opinions. It is dismaying, in an area of so much emotional controversy, to think that there is no other recourse than to rely upon our gut reactions to racial preferences.

Moral argument becomes frustratingly indecisive. Perhaps we can short cut it altogether. Perhaps we would do better to turn to the law, and simply ask whether preferential hiring is legal or not. This is a tempting idea. First, whereas moral argument is indeterminate, the law on the matter should be fixed and clear. Second, if an institutional theory of justice like Rawls' is correct, we have no recourse anyway except to turn to the actual constitutional principles and political framework of society for further guidance.

We will find, unfortunately, that the fixity and clarity of the law are illusions. And we will find, when we turn to constitutional interpretation, that we are soon driven back to moral principles of high generality. But these findings are at the end, not the beginning, of the story. So let us now turn to the law.

9

Discrimination and the Law

The Civil Rights Act of 1964[1] dealt with racial discrimination in voting, public accommodations, public education, and employment. Title VII, Section 703(a) of that Act, as amended by the Equal Employment Opportunity Act of 1972,[2] reads:

It shall be an unlawful practice for an employer—(1) to fail or refuse to hire or to discharge any individual or otherwise to discriminate against any individual with respect to his compensation, terms, conditions, or privileges of employment, because of such individual's race, color, sex, or national origin; or
(2) to limit, segregate, or classify his employees or applicants for employment in any way which would deprive or tend to deprive any individual of employment opportunities or otherwise adversely affect his status as an employee because of such individual's race, color, religion, sex, or national origin. [42 U.S.C. 2000e—2(a).][3]

It is clear enough that this section prohibits racial discrimination in employment, and it is certainly natural enough to read the words of this section as forbidding preferential hiring on

124

the basis of race. Preferential hiring entails the use of a racially non-neutral selection criterion and will usually necessitate an employer's segregating or classifying his applicants according to race, to the detriment of some of them.

The conclusion that Section 703 thus forbids preferential hiring seems further reinforced by reading Section 703 (j):

Nothing contained in this title shall be interpreted to require any employer . . . to grant preferential treatment to any individual or to any group . . . on account of an imbalance which may exist with respect to the total number or percentage of persons of any race . . . employed by any employer . . . in comparison with the total or percentage of persons of such race . . . in any community, State, section, or other area, or in the available work force in any community, State, section, or other area. [42 U.S.C. 2000e—2(j).]

On the basis of Sections 703(a) and (j) taken together, one might conclude that Title VII categorically disallows racially preferential hiring or other racially preferential treatment in employment. I shall call this the Categorical View of Title VII. According to it, a company that uses an explicit racial ratio in selecting employees is engaged in unlawful discrimination.

But suppose the company is ordered to use a ratio by a federal court. Wouldn't preferential hiring be permissible under this circumstance? After all, Title VII also contains Section 706(g):

If the court finds that the respondent [i.e., the accused employer] has intentionally engaged in or is intentionally engaging in an unlawful employment practice charged in the complaint, the court may enjoin the respondent from engaging in such unlawful employment prac-tice, and order such affirmative action as may be appropriate, which may include, but is not limited to, reinstatement or hiring of employees, with or without backpay . . . , or any other equitable relief as the court deems appropriate. [42 U.S.C. 2000e—5(g).]

Doesn't this give the courts the power to order preferential hiring when this is a suitable remedy? Doesn't this confute the Categorical View?

But why should this section be thought to countenance preferential hiring, even when ordered by a court? Why should not the prohibitions in Section 703 be viewed as limitations which qualify the powers given in 706(g)? This way of looking at Title VII sees it as a rule of this sort:

R1: No employer shall preferentially hire an individual on account of his race [703(a)]; and if an employer is found guilty of discriminating, the court may order any fitting remedy so long as the remedy does not require what is prohibited in the first part of this rule [706(g)].

Now, this is a perfectly consistent way of reading Title VII. However, it is not the only possible reading. In place of the view that Section 703 limits the powers in 706(g), one can take the view that the powers in 706(g) mark out areas of possible exception to the prohibitions in 703.[4] On this view, Title VII expresses a rule of this sort:

R2: No employer shall preferentially hire an individual on account of his race [703(a)]; except insofar as this is ordered by a court as a remedy to the employer's violations of the prohibition in the first part of this rule [706(g)].

Since courts in fact agree that Section 706(g) gives them great latitude in fashioning remedies to unlawful discrimination, *R2* is closer to judicial practices than R1. And R2 allows preferential hiring. Apparently.

The Categorical View, however, can accept *R2* and still hold that preferential hiring always violates Title VII. It can do thus by holding that preferential hiring is never necessary to promote the remedial goals of Title VII. The Title enables courts "to make persons whole for injuries suffered on account of unlawful discrimination,"[5] and doing this does not require or involve preferences.

Is the Categorical View correct in believing that preferential hiring is never necessary to make whole a person who has been discriminated against? This depends, of course, on what we are prepared to call preferential hiring. If we go by the usage established in earlier chapters in this book, then we may have reason to concur in the Categorical View. To see this, consider an example.

Suppose Jones, a black, has been denied a job because of his race and the offending employer has been found guilty by the court. What does it take to make Jones whole? First, suppose the court orders the employer to hire Jones. Is this an instance of preferential hiring? I think we can hold, consistently with the account provided in Chapter One, that it is not.[6] The order to hire Jones rests not on his race but on the fact that he was injured by the employer. Of course, the employer's original injury was related to the fact that Jones is black. But Jones' race is not the operative factor in the order to hire him, nor is it operative in any decision to "make him whole."

If qualifications had determined the employer's selection at the time Jones originally applied for work, he would have been hired then on the basis of his qualifications. Instead, the employer refused Jones employment on grounds that were illegal and extraneous to his qualifications. The court now proposes to set matters right by requiring the employer to give Jones the next job. Suppose you are a present applicant for a job with the employer and suppose you have better qualifications than Jones. Doesn't this show that the order now to hire Jones is racially preferential? The reason we can say it is not is because the employer must take Jones over you whether you are white or black. Your color is irrelevant to whether Jones gets hired and, thus, his color is irrelevant too.

By contrast, if the court ordered the offending employer to

hire not Jones but simply any minimally qualified black applicant, that order would require preferential hiring, since it requires an explicitly racial selection. Your race, now, would affect whether you were hired by the employer. If you are black, then you will be hired if your qualifications are better than those of other black applicants; if you are white you will not be hired at all (for this job).

In this latter case, it is difficult to see how the court could claim that its order was designed to "make whole" a victim of discrimination since it does not inquire whether the beneficiary of its order was a victim or not. Thus, argues the Categorical View, the first court order serves the restitutional purposes of Title VII and does not involve or require preferential hiring while the second court order, which does require preferential hiring, cannot be said to "make whole" the party injured by the employer's unlawful action.

In order to make Jones whole, it further may be necessary to require the employer to give him backpay. It also may be necessary in order to put Jones in his "rightful place" that he be awarded seniority not from the time he is eventually hired but from the time he was initially (and wrongfully) denied employment.[7] Only in this way is Jones put in the position he would have had but for the employer's discrimination against him. Giving Jones this retroactive seniority need not be called preferential treatment on the basis of his race, for like his court-ordered hiring it is given on the basis of his specific identity as a victim of the employer's discrimination. Giving Jones retroactive seniority is not like giving "fictional" seniority to a newly hired black who had never previously applied for a job and had never been discriminated against by the employer.[8] The latter is preferential treatment based on race.

In summary, the Categorical View of Title VII is this. There are two purposes of the Title. First, it outlaws racial discrimination and aims at eliminating discriminatory barriers that have worked against blacks (and other groups). This purpose is effected through the general proscriptions contained in Section 703. The second purpose is remedial. It is effected by Section 706(g). On the basis of the language of that Section, a remedy must (i) be predicated on an employer's violation, and (ii) aim to make whole the victim of that violation. The adjustments involved in moving a victim to his "rightful place," since they are geared to his identity as victim and not to his race, do not involve racial discrimination or preferences and thus do not fall under the proscriptions of Section 703. Racial preferences do not further the functions of 706(g) or promote the ends of 703. Consequently, preferential hiring is categorically against the law.

COURT-ORDERED PREFERENTIAL HIRING

In the case of *Boston Chapter, NAACP* v. *Beecher* (to be referred to as *Boston Chapter* II), the Court of Appeals for the First Circuit upheld a district court order (to be referred to as *Boston Chapter* I) which had imposed preferential hiring. The district court had enjoined the Massachusetts Civil Service Division from using its standard firefighter's examination and the eligibility list based on it. This injunction rested on the court's finding that the examination discriminated against blacks and Spanish-surnamed individuals.[9] The district court had further ordered the Civil Service Division to develop a valid, nondiscriminatory test, and had created four eligibility groups:

Group A: All black and Spanish-surnamed applicants who took and failed any previous test, but who pass any new and valid test.
Group B: All persons on the current eligibility list.
Group C: All blacks and Spanish-surnamed who are not in Group A but who pass the new test.

Group D: All other persons who pass the new exam.

The court had then ordered that new firefighters were to be certified by the Division of Civil Service to the various Massachusetts communities

> by means of a matching procedure designed to assure that each Group receives proportional representation in accordance with their qualifications. Groups A and B are to be given initial preference on a one-to-one basis, and the other Groups are to be drawn upon as A and B are exhausted . . . . In all cases new eligibility lists from successive entrance tests shall be used to replenish Groups C and D. The decree [of the district court] remains in force, for each local fire department, until that department attains sufficient minority firefighters to have a percentage on the force approximately equal to the percentage of minorities in the locality. *(Boston Chapter* II at 1026-1027.)

This order, affirmed by the circuit court, imposes preferential hiring. Even if we put aside any questions about the segregation of applicants into Groups *A* and *B* and the hiring of them on a one-to-one basis, we cannot get around the court's order with respect to Groups *C* and *D*. Everyone in these Groups will have passed the new, valid test and no one in either Group will have been victimized by the old exam. Since the new test will be nondiscriminatory (if there is to be a new test at all), nondiscriminatory hiring is achievable simply by using a *single* eligibility list based on all those who passed the new test. Thus, the first purpose of Title VII is not furthered by the court's order.

Likewise, since the members of Group *C* will have not been discriminated against by the Civil Service exam, the requirement that applicants in this Group be hired on a one-to-one ratio with applicants in Group *D* cannot be construed as putting members of Group *C* into their "rightful places." The one-to-one requirement, at least with respect to these two

Groups, constitutes a requirement that racial preferences be used. After Groups *A* and *B* have been exhausted, a community whose fire department does not have a racial balance proportionate to its population must, under the court order, keep hiring one minority for each white until racial balance is achieved.

How did the two courts justify this order? Section 703(a) apparently forbids an employer to classify or segregate his applicants on the basis of race, yet the courts ordered the Division of Civil Service to do just that. Section 703(j) says that Title VII does not require preferential hiring in order to alter a racial imbalance. Yet the order of the district court was clearly directed, with respect to Groups C and D, to achieving proportional representation by race. From the decisions of the district court and the circuit court, the following defense can be constructed:

1. Section 706(g) gives the federal courts powers to order suitable remedies in discrimination cases.
2. Section 703(j) "deals only with those cases in which racial imbalance has come about completely without regard to the actions of the employers" *(Boston Chapter* II at 1028).
3. Section 703(a) is no bar to preferential hiring orders if an employer has discriminated and such orders are necessary to achieve the purposes of Title VII (R2).
4. One purpose of Title VII is to "eradicate the effects of past discrimination" *(Boston Chapter* I at 520).
5. One effect of an employer's past discrimination is a racial imbalance in his work force.
6. Preferential hiring is necessary to "cure" the employer's racial imbalance.

The key provisions here are 4 and 5. It is because the courts in *Boston Chapter* construe the remedial purposes of Title VII in a broad fashion that their decisions can generate results at odds with the Categorical View.

Generally in Title VII decisions the idea of "eradicating the effects of past discrimination" occurs in the context of the court looking for a way to "make whole" an identified victim of an employer's past discrimination. Thus, the "effects of past discrimination" are the effects upon the victim; and eliminating the effects means eliminating them with respect to this victim. For example, not infrequently courts have ordered companies to alter their job transfer policies on the grounds that initially the companies segregated all of their black employees into undesirable departments and now their facially neutral transfer policies which make interdepartmental transfers difficult continue to penalize the black employees for having been victims of the companies' discrimination in the first place. Courts have ordered such policies liberalized in order to "eradicate the effects of past discrimination" on those blacks.

In cases like these, a narrow conception of remedies is retained. But in *Boston Chapter,* "eliminating the effects of past discrimination" has become detached from the identifiable victims of Massachusetts' discriminatory test. When the court upheld the one-to-one hiring in regard to Groups *C* and *D* by reference to the remedial goals of Title VII, it cannot have been talking about "making whole" the victims of Massachusetts' discrimination or of putting them in their "rightful places." None of the members of Group C had been discriminated against by the Civil Service firefighter's exam. The "effects" to be eradicated could not have been merely the effects on members of Group *A*, since the court order extended far beyond them. The "effects of past discrimination" are identified by the two courts with a general state of affairs: the condition of racial imbalance among firefighters in the different municipalities. The *Boston Chapter* II decision sustained a "remedy" addressed to that broader "effect." The remedy mandated the achievement of proportional representation.

EXCEPTIVE VIEWS

The *Boston Chapter* decisions express what I will call a Moderate Exceptive View of Title VII. It is "exceptive" because it allows a certain amount of preferential hiring under the Title. It is "moderate" because there are other exceptive views which greatly expand the occasions on which preferential hiring is to be counted as legal. It might be thought that the language of 706(g) plainly hews out no further exceptions to Section 703 than those offered by *Boston Chapter*. But there is no consensus on this. In 1977 a court in Kansas City sustained the legality of preferential employment practices adopted voluntarily by an employer. The case is *Germann* v. *Kipp*, involving the Fire Department of that city. The plaintiffs in the case accused the city of practicing discrimination when it promoted minority firefighters over white firefighters who were higher on the eligibility list in order to achieve the goals of the city's affirmative action plan.

The *Germann* court held that the city's actions did not violate Title VII. It noted that there is considerable authority for the courts to use racial quotas. Of course, in the case before the court, the issue was not the imposition of remedies on an employer found guilty of past discrimination but the employer's "voluntary attempt to remedy the 'imbalances (which) may have developed in the utilization of minorities and women'."[10] Even so, the court argued that "[t]he requirement of a finding of past discrimination before a court in the exercise of its broad equitable powers may *compel* implementation of an affirmative action plan, including quota relief, does not necessarily mandate the conclusion that an employer may not *voluntarily* implement a reasonable, short-term affirmative action plan to remedy the effects of historical discrimination." (*Germann* at 1334-1335.)

The *Germann* court did not explain how this could be so if

court-ordered quotas are the only exception to the prohibitions in Section 703. Moreover, although the court couched its decision in the language of remedies, it was no longer talking about the use by a court of its equitable powers to effect restitution; nor, in talking about the "effects of historical discrimination," did it tie remedies to the employer's own discrimination. There is obviously a theory of Title VII at work here which is different from the theory advanced in the *Boston Chapter* decision.

While the *Germann* court was deciding in favor of voluntary quotas, the Court of Appeals for the Fifth Circuit was rendering the opposite decision in *Weber* v. *Kaiser Aluminum & Chemical Corporation* (to be referred to as *Weber* I). Kaiser had implemented a union-management agreement for transfer of workers to on-the-job training programs in the craft jobs at its plants. The agreement called for admission to the program of one minority worker for each white worker until the percentage of minority workers approximated the minority population surrounding each plant.

Eligibility for training still rested on plant seniority, but to implement their affirmative action goal it was necessary to establish dual seniority lists: for each two training vacancies, one black and one white employee would be selected on the basis of seniority within their respective racial groups. (*Weber* I at 220.)

Brian Weber, a white worker at Kaiser's Grammercy, Louisiana, plant brought suit under Title VII. The section applicable to his complaint is 703(d):

It shall be an unlawful employment practice for any employer, labor organization, or joint labor-management committee controlling apprenticeship or other training or retraining, including on-the-job training programs, to discriminate against any individual because of his race, color, religion, sex, or national origin in admissions to, or employment in, any program established to provide apprenticeship or other training. [42 U.S.C. 2000e –2(d).]

This companion to Section 703(a) parallels it in language. An interpretation of 703(d) ought to imply a parallel interpretation of 703(a) and vice versa. If 703(d) permits preferential admissions to on-the-job training, then 703(a) ought to permit preferential hiring. If 703(d) forbids preferential admissions, then 703(a) must forbid preferential hiring.

The *Weber* I court held that Kaiser's program violated 703(d). The argument of the court is important to reconstruct, for reasons that will become apparent. The court observed, first, that Kaiser had not been found guilty of any past discrimination against blacks at the Grammercy plant. No charge was made in court, and no evidence introduced. Thus, *as a matter of legal record,* none of the blacks admitted through the special training program at Grammercy had been discriminated against by Kaiser. This spoke against the legitimacy of the program. "In the absence of prior discrimination," the court argued, "a racial quota loses its character as an equitable *remedy* and must be banned as unlawful racial *preference* prohibited by Title VII, 703(a) and (d)." (*Weber* I at 224.)[11]

In analyzing the remedial powers under Section 706(g), the *Weber* court adopted the "rightful place" theory,[12] rejecting an extremely broad theory of remedies proposed by the defendants. They had argued that the court ought to "approve the on-the-job training ratio not to correct past employment discrimination by Kaiser at this plant but to correct a lack of training blamed on past societal discrimination." (*Weber* I at 225.) The defendants urged a view of Title VII in which the justification for making exceptions to the prohibitions in Section 703 is not the employer's own discrimination but past discrimination in general, and in which the exceptions to the prohibitions in 703 can be made without the authorization of any court.

In a written dissent in *Weber* I, Judge John Minor Wisdom wanted to concede merit to the argument that societal discrimination justifies Kaiser in adopting on its own volition racial quotas. He stopped short, however, of fully endorsing it. In remarks in the *Bakke* decision, Justice Brennan appeared to favor a similar argument in regard to both Title VI and Title VII, speaking on several occasions of institutions justifiably acting to counter "the lingering effects of past societal discrimination." (*Bakke* at 2780; also at 2787, 2789.) These remarks foreshadowed the decision he would render when *Weber* I reached the Supreme Court.

The position argued by Kaiser is obviously difficult to accommodate to the actual terms of Section 706(g). Its position entails that a court order is not a necessary condition of legal preferences; that the employer's own discrimination is not a necessary condition of legal preferences; and that putting identifiable victims in their rightful place is not a necessary condition of legal discrimination. In Kaiser's argument, when it speaks of eliminating the effects of past discrimination, "past discrimination" can stand for anybody's discrimination at any time, and the "lingering effects" of that discrimination can be virtually any difficulty experienced by blacks in competing for jobs.

THE REAL ISSUE IN WEBER

The argument made by Kaiser raises acute questions about the proper interpretation of Title VII, and we will return shortly to this question. But before we do, we should note that the argument considered and addressed by the majority decision does not appear to be the real issue. The court entertained and rejected the argument that Kaiser could employ quotas to "remedy societal discrimination," but the real issue was whether Kaiser may voluntarily adopt quotas to remedy *its own past discrimination*. The real issue was not brought to the center in the trial because there is a catch-22 situation in the law. As Judge Wisdom commented in dissent:

The employer and the union [a co-defendant] are made to walk a high tightrope without a net beneath them. On the one side lies the possibility of liability to minorities in private actions, federal pattern and practice suits, and sanctions under Executive Order 11246. On the other side is the threat of private suits by white employees and, potentially, federal action. (*Weber* I at 230.)

What Wisdom is talking about is this.

Even if a company's employment practices now comply with the requirements of Title VII (and other antidiscrimination regulations), it is likely that its practices in the past, even the recent past, did not.[13] Suppose a company which reasonably believes that its earlier practices were to some extent discriminatory against blacks voluntarily seeks to identify those of its employees which might have been adversely affected and move them to "their rightful place." This might involve moving some black employees ahead of white employees with greater seniority, as the Kaiser program did. What if a white employee then sues the company for reverse discrimination? In order to defend itself against this charge, the company will need to show that its actions are not "preferential" but truly "remedial." In order to do that, it will have to admit officially that it has discriminated in the past. Yet by doing this, the company immediately makes itself liable to lawsuits by other individuals and by the government. On the other side, if the company elects not to admit any past discrimination, its action of moving some blacks ahead does not seem to qualify as remedial and thus finds no justification in Title VII. The company faces a genuine dilemma: it admits it discriminated and falls off one side of the tight-rope, or it refuses to admit this and falls off the other side.

This is the dilemma that Kaiser faced. The company and the unions were under pressure from federal agencies and feared private suits under Title VII. (*Weber* I at 228.) It and the unions sought to forestall litigation by voluntarily adopting a program that would remedy its past discrimination. (Close scrutiny of its past employment practices would undoubtedly have given the company a reasonable basis for believing it had used some discriminatory practices previously.) When Brian Weber sued the company, it elected to embrace one horn of the dilemma: it decided to foreswear any admission of past discrimination.

Thus, the issue argued before the courts was not the real issue but a quite different one: whether Kaiser could right the wrongs of *society* by adopting a racial quota. This was the only way Kaiser could lend an aura of "remedies" to its program without admitting that it was making up for its own wrongs. The majority of the court rejected this defense. The majority held the Kaiser program illegal because the program appeared to have no relation to any past discrimination by the company. No evidence of its own discrimination was offered because neither the plaintiff (Weber) nor the defendants (Kaiser and the unions) wanted to claim that Kaiser had discriminated against blacks.

Consider, then, the question of whether the Kaiser program is legal if it constitutes an effort to remedy the effects of its own discrimination. If the program quotas are aimed at moving to their "rightful places" those of its employees previously victimized by its own violations of law, then the program should be viewed as acceptable on any theory of Title VII. Even on the narrowest conception of remedies, the program qualifies as remedial. If those who are moved forward through the program are victims of Kaiser's past discrimination, then they are not being preferred because of their race.

The question is whether Kaiser can voluntarily institute a remedial program of this sort. There seems no apparent reason why such voluntary efforts are ruled out by the language of Title VII. The Title need not be read as conditioning remedies on a court order. Indeed, this would be at odds with the Title's own provisions. Section 706(b), which deals with the enforcement of the Title, established the Equal Employment Opportunity Commission (EEOC) as the first hearer of discrimination complaints. If the Commission finds merit in a complaint, it is required to "endeavor to eliminate any such unlawful employment practices by informal methods of conference, conciliation, and persuasion" [42 U.S.C. 2000e–5(b)]. Only when such efforts to secure voluntary compliance with the law fail may the Commission or the individual complainant bring suit in court.

Given that Title VII encourages voluntary compliance through conciliation, it should be plain that it does not forbid the same acts of compliance when initiated wholly by the employer himself, before charges are ever filed against him. It is true that the language of 706(b) speaks only of conciliation to end violations; remedies to make up for violations are not spoken of until 706(g) and there only in connection with what a court may order. But Title VII consistently has been read to allow EEOC to achieve in conciliation what a court might achieve in litigation. There should be nothing objectionable about an employer instituting his own remedial measures.

The problem is not with Kaiser's actions themselves, assuming that they are narrowly remedial. The catch-22 pertains to the possible public, legal defense Kaiser can make if those actions are challenged. Because a company does not want to open itself to additional litigation, it does not want to openly admit that it has discriminated in its employment practices. But without such an admission, the defense that the company is acting to remedy its past discrimination is unavailable.

It is only when we drop the assumption that Kaiser's actions are narrowly remedial, i.e., aimed at putting in their rightful places employees it had previously discriminated against, that controversy arises about the actions themselves. If the Kaiser training program extends preferences to blacks who were not victims of Kaiser's own discrimination, then it requires one of the broader views of remedies to bring the program into conformity with Title VII.

SURVEY OF VIEWS

Various interpretations of Title VII's remedial aims are achievable by combining the different views on remedies and their relations to the employer's own acts of discrimination. The combinable elements are these:

remedy	(i)	effects on victim
	(ii)	condition of imbalance
employer's	(i)	necessary
discrimination	(ii)	not necessary

From these elements we can derive these views:

   I. Remedies address the effects on the victims of the employer's own discrimination. (Categorical View)

  II. Remedies address the condition of imbalance caused by the employer's own discrimination. (Moderate Exceptive View)

 III. Remedies address the condition of imbalance caused by societal discrimination. (Kaiser's Argument)

On View I, an employer's voluntary use of quotas would be remedial only if the quotas were a mechanism for making whole the victims of his discrimination. On View II, an employer's quotas would be remedial even though they benefited others than victims if they were directed toward altering a racial imbalance among his workers caused by his own discrimination. On View III, an employer's quotas would be remedial if they were directed toward altering a racial imbalance among his workers due not to his but to society's discrimination.

We must observe that if View III is the correct interpretation

Discrimination and the Law

of Title VII, then we cannot use as a standard for measuring what an employer may do voluntarily any supposition about what a court would have ordered the employer to do had there been litigation. No court can under Title VII order a company to give preferences to blacks in order to alter an imbalance caused by society's discrimination. Section 703(j) should make that plain.[14] Before a court can enter the scene, there must be some chargeable offense under Title VII. If a company has not been and is not discriminating, there is no basis for a charge.[15]

View I, the Categorical View, is well secured in the language of Section 706(g). That language does appear to limit remedies to the victims of an employer's discrimination, since it speaks of remedies ordered by a court in response to a charge of unlawful practices against an employer and designed to afford relief to those damaged by those practices. This has also been the way many courts have read the Title. One typical court speaks thus: "Application of the Act [Title VII] normally involves two steps. First, identification of the employees who are victims of discrimination, and second, prescription of a remedy to correct the violation disclosed in the first step. The Act does not require the application of remedy to employees who are not subject to discrimination."[16]

Finally, strong support for this reading derives from the 1972 Congressional debate on the Equal Employment Opportunity Act which amended Title VII. The House-Senate Conference Report's section-by-section analysis had this to say about Section 706(g):

The provisions of this subsection are intended to give the courts wide discretion exercising their equitable powers to fashion the most complete relief possible. In dealing with the present section 706(g) the courts have stressed that the scope of relief under that section of the Act is intended to make the victims of unlawful discrimination whole, and that the attainment of this objective rests not only upon the elimination of the particular unlawful employment practice complained of, but also requires that persons aggrieved by the consequences and effects of the unlawful employment practice be, so far as possible, restored to a position where they would have been were it not for the unlawful discrimination.[17]

The remedies of Title VII are here tied to putting victims of discrimination in rightful places.

It may be suggested that although Title VII does not require that remedies extend beyond victims, it nevertheless permits it. The order of the *Boston Chapter* courts certainly made non-victims beneficiaries of their preferential orders. The EEOC, in its most recent guidelines encouraging "voluntary affirmative action," urges that an affirmative action plan

> may include the adoption of practices which will eliminate the . . . effects of past discrimination by providing opportunities to groups which have been excluded, regardless of whether the persons benefited were themselves the victims of prior . . . discrimination.[18]

One matter of controversy, then, is whether preferences extended to those who are not victims of an employer's discrimination are truly remedial *under the law*. For as the *Weber* I court argued, racial preferences not remedial within the scope of Title VII are in violation of it. The second and related question is whether preferences given by an employer which are not predicated upon his own past wrongful discrimination can be counted as remedial *under the law*.

10

Remedies and Discrimination

ERADICATING THE EFFECTS OF DISCRIMINATION

The *Boston Chapter* I court justified its preferential order as being designed to "eradicate the effects of past discrimination." It cited a number of cases[1] which, in turn, rely upon *Louisiana* v. *United States,* a case in which the Supreme Court said that in cases of discrimination, "the {district} court has not merely the power but the duty to render a decree which will so far as possible eliminate the discriminatory effects of the past as well as bar like discrimination in the future" (*Louisiana* at 154).

This language—"eradicating the effects of past discrimination," "eliminating the effects of previous practices," and so on—is ubiquitous in court decisions involving Title VII claims. It can be narrowly construed to refer just to the effects on the victims of an employer's discrimination, or broadly construed to refer to *any state of affairs* resulting from either an employer's own discrimination *(Boston Chapter)* or societal discrimination (Kaiser's argument). What warrants taking the language in the broader way, especially in light of the 1972 Congressional view discussed at the end of the previous chapter? We obviously need some theory that explains and justifies the extension of the idea of remedy beyond the "make whole" and "rightful place" conceptions. It is difficult to find a clear defense of this extension anywhere in the case law. Instead, one finds, as in *Boston Chapter,* the recitation of precedents which apply the *Louisiana* proposition, without attention to the fact that the meaning and scope of that injunction is very much in question.

Louisiana was a voting rights case which struck down as discriminatory a Louisiana "interpretations test" for registering to vote. The test had been used to keep black registration exceedingly low. Louisiana proposed to supplant the challenged test with an objective "citizenship" test, but the Supreme Court barred its use until Louisiana registered all eligible voters under an open registration scheme. The Court's ground was that since few blacks had been registered under the old, illegal test, the new test would cut hardest against new black registration and simply maintain the existence of a condition achieved by previous illegal means. It was in that context that the Court pronounced that lower courts have a duty to "eliminate the discriminatory effects of the past."

Now there are important differences to be noted between the order sustained by the Supreme Court and the one sustained in *Boston Chapter* II. The effect of past discrimination to which the Supreme Court addressed itself—the limited black registration—could be eliminated by an order which in no way hindered the rights of anyone to register and vote. Open registration, while registering more blacks, would not de-register or impede the registration of any white. On the other hand, the very source of controversy about preferential hiring is that it benefits some at the expense of others. In preferring some on account of their race, it denies to others jobs that might have been theirs but for their race. The proportional hiring scheme sanctioned by the *Boston Chapter* II court is not benign to all involved.

Secondly, there are implicit limits to the Supreme Court's own rule. The Court itself did not require or countenance attacks on every effect of Louisiana's past voting discrimination. Although it announced a general-sounding rule ("the courts will render decrees that will so far as possible eliminate the effects of past discrimination"), the Court in fact sustained a remedy addressed to one effect: underregistration of blacks. But there were many other effects, important ones. For example, as a result of a long history of virtual disfranchisement, Louisiana blacks in 1965 had no office holders of their race, no vigorous and effective black caucuses, no widespread habits of political participation, and so on. But the Supreme Court would not have sustained a lower court order which mandated open registration for blacks but not for whites, or which struck a proportion of whites from the roles, or which forbade further white registration for a fixed period, or which blocked whites from voting in some elections, or which gave blacks weighted votes, and so on. It is obvious that the Court presupposed limitations on its own rule even if it did not state them.

In fact, the same is true about the lower courts. When they seek to "eliminate the effects of past discrimination," they too recognize implicit limits on the application of the rule. For example, the *Boston Chapter* II court would not have sustained a district court order requiring white firefighters already on the job to be fired and replaced by minority applicants, even though this order would have more quickly "eliminated the effects of past discrimination" than the order it did sustain.[2] So, even for a court which takes the broad view of remedies, the rule of "elimination" is limited to some effects and not others, and some "remedies" may be ordered but not others.

It is precisely because the *Louisiana* rule is implicitly limited that it is necessary to articulate clearly and persuasively what those limits are and why. The *Boston Chapter* II court needs to explain why it draws the line at displacing workers but permits preferential hiring while another court would draw the line at preferential hiring. It is no argument for the broader view of remedies simply to cite the *Louisiana* rule since it must itself be interpreted. The need to advance a clear justificatory theory for construing the remedial aims of Title VII in a broad fashion is even more pressing in the case of the Kaiser view which, on its surface at least, appears to deviate considerably from the language of Section 706(g).

WEBER AND THE SUPREME COURT

The United States Supreme Court accepted appeal from the decision of the Court of Appeals in *Weber* I and in the summer of 1979 rendered an opinion overturning the lower court. The majority opinion in *Kaiser Aluminum & Chemical Corporation* v. *Weber* (to be referred to as *Weber* II) was written by Justice Brennan. He framed the issue thus: "whether Title VII forbids private employers and unions from voluntarily agreeing upon bona fide affirmative action plans that accord racial preferences" (*Weber* II at 4853). His conclusion was that it did not.

Brennan reached this conclusion by rejecting a literal interpretation of Sections 703(a) and (d) of Title VII.

It is [he wrote] a "familiar rule, that a thing may be within the letter of a statute and yet not within the statute, because not within its spirit, nor within the intention of its makers". . . . The prohibition against racial discrimination in ## 703(a) and (d) of Title VII must therefore be read against the background of the legislative history of Title VII and the historical context from which the [Civil Rights] Act arose. . . . (*Weber* II at 4853.)

As Brennan read that history, it was within the "spirit" of Title VII to allow preferential programs like Kaiser's. His position rested upon two arguments. First, it was the purpose of Congress in creating Title VII to "open employment oppor-

tunities for Negroes in occupations which have been traditionally closed to them" (*Weber* II at 4854, quoting Senator Hubert
Humphrey). Thus, concluded Brennan, it would "be ironic
indeed" if Title VII were to be read as forbidding voluntary
actions to open such opportunities.

Brennan's second argument rested upon the language of
Section 703(j). That Section, it will be recalled, says that
nothing in the previous sections "shall be interpreted to *require*
any employer . . . to grant preferential treatment . . . on
account of an imbalance . . ." (emphasis added). Brennan
reasoned that if Congress had meant to forbid voluntary
preferential hiring, it would have said in Section 703(j) that the
Title should not be interpreted to require or *permit* any
employer to grant preferential treatment on account of an
imbalance. Since it did not say this, the "natural inference,"
according to Brennan, is that Congress meant to approve
voluntary "race-conscious affirmative action" (*Weber* II at
4854).

Brennan's arguments are desultory and insubstantial. They
could persuade only a person who had already made up his
mind that Title VII allows preferential hiring. It was indeed
one of the purposes of Congress in 1964 to "open employment
opportunities for Negroes in occupations which have been
traditionally closed to them," but reference to this purpose
cannot adjudicate between broader and narrower readings of
Title VII. On any reading, Title VII "opened up opportunities" for blacks. It is perfectly consistent for Congress to
have had that general aim and for it also to have prohibited any
and all racial preferences in hiring. It is a commonplace to have
an aim and yet not countenance *every* means to that aim. The
general aim of Congress given expression by the words of
Senator Humphrey would support Brennan's position only if
it were combined with further evidence that Congress meant
not to place any limits on means to realizing that aim. The
record of debate provides no such evidence.

Brennan's second argument is equally question-begging. Nothing can be built on Congress's failure to say in Section 703(j) that the Title does not permit as well as does not require preferential hiring. This omission would be significant only if there were reason to believe that Congress thought the issue of permitted preferential hiring were still open at Section 703(j). But it can be argued[3] that the authors of Title VII saw no need to stipulate in Section 703(j) that racial preferences are not permitted since they believed they had already done that in Sections 703(a)–(d). The blanket prohibitions in those sections against the use of race sufficed to make apparent that whatever uses of race were not required by Title VII were forbidden by it. Thus, the only need in Section 703(j) was to make clear what uses of race were or were not required by the Title.

Brennan's reading of the record of debate in Congress in 1964 is tendentious and selective. He quotes Senator Humphrey's general remarks about opening opportunities for blacks, but he omits the Senator's specific remarks about reverse discrimination itself. In responding to those who raised this issue in 1964, Humphrey took up the charge that Title VII would lead to preferential hiring:

Contrary to the allegations of some opponents of this title, there is nothing in it that will give power to the Commission [i.e., the Equal Employment Opportunity Commission], or to any court to require hiring, firing, or promotion of employees in order to meet a racial "quota" or to achieve a certain racial balance.

That bugaboo has been brought up a dozen times; but it is nonexistent. In fact, the very opposite is true. Title VII prohibits discrimination. In effect, it says race, religion, and national origin are not to be used as a basis for hiring and firing.[4]

The Senator's comments make clear that in denying that Title VII requires preferential hiring he was not leaving it open that the Title nevertheless permits it. For Humphrey, the "very opposite" of the Title's requiring preferences is its forbidding them. And it was the "very opposite" which he declared to be true of the Title: "race, religion, and national origin are *not* to be used" (emphasis added).

The floor manager of the Civil Rights Act, Senator Joseph Clark, also addressed the concern that Title VII would countenance preferential hiring. Through a memorandum prepared by the Justice Department for his presentation on the Senate floor, Senator Clark said:

Finally, it has been asserted that Title VII would impose a requirement for a "racial balance." This is incorrect. There is no provision, either in Title VII or in any other part of this bill, that requires or authorizes any federal agency or federal court to require preferential treatment for any individual or any group for the purpose of achieving racial balance. No employer is required to hire an individual because that individual is a Negro. No employer is required to maintain any ratio of Negroes to whites . . . or of women to men. On the contrary, any deliberate attempt to maintain a given balance would almost certainly run afoul of Title VII. . . .[5]

Later Clark repeated this:

There is no requirement in Title VII that an employer maintain a racial balance in his work force. On the contrary, *any deliberate attempt to maintain a racial balance would involve a violation of Title VII because maintaining such a balance would require an employer to hire on the basis of race.*[6]

Like Humphrey, Clark takes it as obvious that in denying that Title VII requires preferences he is also denying that it permits them. Any "hiring on the basis of race" violates the Title. It is evident that Humphrey and Clark believed that the prohibitions of Sections 703(a)–(d) left no room for "permitted preferences."

In a footnote to his opinion, Brennan dismissed the statement by Clark as irrelevant. It speaks only of a prohibition against *maintaining* a racial balance, claimed Brennan, not against achieving one. Thus, it does not militate against reading Title VII to permit bringing about a racial balance by preferential hiring.[7] This is an example of the quality of reasoning to be found throughout Brennan's opinion. What Brennan fails to take note of is the obvious fact that Clark gave a reason why maintaining a racial balance violates Title VII: it involves "hiring on the basis of race." Thus, to the extent that *achieving* a racial balance requires "hiring on the basis of race," it is equally condemned by Clark's remarks. And, of course, Kaiser's attempt to achieve a racial balance in the crafts at its Grammercy plant indeed involved it in admitting on the basis of race.

The *Weber* case provided an opportunity for the Supreme Court to clarify Title VII and to offer a theory to support one of the broader interpretations. It could have settled the confusion about the meaning and scope of remedies under the Title. It could have then established the relevant connections between the preferred conception of remedies and the voluntary actions of employers, so that it would be clear what an employer could do and what he could not do by way of extending racial preferences to blacks. Instead, Brennan with only a casual nod toward argumentation found the Kaiser program within the "spirit" of Title VII. What that "spirit" is was left a mystery, since Brennan refused to "define in detail the line of demarcation between permissible and impermissible" preferential hiring (*Weber* II at 4855). Thus, the legal status of preferential hiring is still muddled since none of the old questions were answered and new ones were raised. It is clear enough that Brennan subscribes to some broader reading of Title VII, but he offers no account of his view and no defense of it. By linking his support of Kaiser's program to its status as a "bona fide affirmative action" program, Brennan presumably meant to indicate that the program was justified as in some sense remedial. However, we still stand in need of a theory of Title VII remedies which makes preferences remedial when they are not directed to the effects of the employer's own discrimination.[8]

ELIMINATING DISCRIMINATION

So far we have concentrated on the second of the two facets of Title VII. We have seen that there are different interpretations about the reach of the remedial aims of the Title. It is widely accepted by the courts that quotas may be ordered as "remedies" on some occasions but they differ in regard to what those occasions are. The same uncertainty extends to which voluntary actions of employers can count as remedial.

What about the first aim of Title VII? Might not the requirement to avoid discriminating on account of race, imposed on the employer by Section 703, actually mandate the use of preferential hiring in certain circumstances? It might seem absurd to think that a form of discrimination would be countenanced by an injunction not to discriminate, but perhaps the absurdity is only apparent. Kenneth Davidson, a commentator on discrimination law, argues against exclusively non-preferential court orders on the ground that they falsely assume that employment selection procedures can be objective and nondiscriminatory.[9] In fact, he claims, they can not be. Thus, court orders which only require seemingly neutral hiring procedures actually allow discrimination to persist.

Let us frame this more fully as an argument. If selection procedures cannot be objective, then supposedly "neutral" approaches to hiring will in fact continue to discriminate against blacks and others. Subjective elements in hiring give play to prejudice and false stereotypes. This non-neutrality is masked by the false assumption that the hiring decisions are objective. The unavoidable non-neutrality of hiring decisions must be recognized and countered by an opposing non-neutrality. Otherwise, employment selection procedures will continue to work against blacks and other minorities. Unlawful discrimination will persist. Consequently, in order to insure that it does not persist — in order, that is, to achieve the first purpose of Title VII — preferential hiring is necessary.

Is this a plausible approach to defending the legality of preferential hiring? If some discrimination against whites will minimize overall discrimination against blacks, then may not an injunction against racial discrimination be viewed as nevertheless justifying some discrimination? What is employment discrimination, anyway? When racial discrimination in employment is forbidden by Title VII, what, specifically, is being forbidden? Can there be a question about what a prohibition of discrimination amounts to?

Incredibly enough, Congress did not define the term "discrimination" in the Civil Rights Act of 1964! This means that it has fallen to the courts and to executive departments to supply, as they interpreted and applied the various titles of the Act, the missing conception of racial discrimination.[10] Since 1964, both the Congress and the courts have come to view employment discrimination as a more complex phenomenon than they orginally thought. It is desirable to pause to understand how employment discrimination has come to be defined.

DISCRIMINATION IN EMPLOYMENT

In 1972, a Congressional committee report, made in conjunction with the consideration of the Equal Employment Opportunity Act which amended Title VII, said this:

During the preparation and presentation of Title VII of the Civil Rights Act of 1964, employment discrimination tended to be viewed as a series of isolated and distinguishable events, due, for the most part, to ill-will on the part of some identifiable individual or organization . . . . Employment discrimination, as we know today, is a far more complex and pervasive phenomenon. Experts familiar with the subject generally describe the problem in terms of "systems" and "effects" rather than simply intentional wrongs . . . . The forms and incidents of discrimination . . . are increasingly complex. Particularly to the untrained observer, their discriminatory nature may not appear obvious at first glance.[11]

In contrast to this 1972 avowal of complexity, the Senate floor managers of the Civil Rights Act in 1964 were more sanguine:

It has been suggested [they said] that the concept of discrimination is vague. In fact it is clear and simple and has no hidden meanings.[12]

By 1972, far from being seen as "clear and simple," with "no hidden meanings," discrimination had come to be viewed as something which the "untrained observer" might not be able to see and which requires "experts" to detect. The crucial factor had ceased to be "intent" and had become "effects."[13]

The bare concept of discrimination is sufficiently elastic to cover a multitude of different acts, practices, episodes, and effects. All they need have in common is that they differentiate or produce differential results. The Congress in 1964 had most clearly in mind such paradigmatic cases of racial discrimination as those involving overt acts of exclusion, overtly racial standards, intentional segregation, and flagrant racial hostility.

An employer who puts a sign in his window, "No blacks hired," is discriminating. So is an employer who segregates his black employees into special all-black departments, limiting the better jobs in his establishment to whites. The distinguishing mark of discrimination here is the employer's use of a facially racial hiring (or job-assignment or promotion) standard. It may well be that the employer is motivated by ill-will or racial hostility, but this is not necessary. The employer's motives for segregation and exclusion can be otherwise: desire not to upset traditional ways of doing things, desire to avoid upsetting white workers, desire to avoid costs of changing, and so on.

An employer may be more subtle. He may adopt facially neutral procedures or standards which nevertheless serve his intention to exclude or limit the number of blacks working for him. For example, if an employer has an all-white work-force, he might adopt a policy that requires every applicant to provide a recommendation from three current or past employers. This policy, though cast in terms that are racially neutral, will effectively assure the employer that there will be few blacks who get hired in his establishment.

I will term instances of discrimination like those just described as *primary discrimination*. Instances of primary discrimination are generally unmistakable. They involve the intent to exclude members of a particular race, or to segregate them, or to deny them benefits accorded to others. And they involve policies, facially racial or facially neutral, which effect this intent.

Since 1971 it has become established law that an employer is engaging in unlawful discrimination under Title VII if he uses any practice or procedure that disproportionately excludes blacks or affects them adversely unless such practice or procedure is a matter of "business necessity,"[14] absolutely essential to the employer's operation.[15] The employer's intending to so affect blacks is no longer a necessary condition of discrimination. (Call this the *Griggs* test.)

For example, if a company uses a standard, professionally developed aptitude test to rank applicants, and the test fails or down-ranks blacks in numbers disproportionately greater than it fails or down-ranks whites, then the company's use of this test constitutes unlawful employment discrimination under Title VII unless the company can demonstrate that the test is a valid and necessary predictor of successful job performance. This is so even if the company has no intention to discriminate and, in fact, makes and has made positive efforts to enhance opportunities for blacks.[16]

Let us call the use of any facially neutral standard or practice which is not designed to carry out an intent to discriminate but which cannot satisfy the *Griggs* test *secondary discrimination.* Combining primary and secondary discrimination, we may say that under Title VII an employer discriminates on the basis of race whenever he (i) uses a facially racial standard or practice to assign jobs, benefits, etc., or (ii) uses a facially neutral standard or procedure to accomplish his intention to assign jobs, benefits, etc., on the basis of race, or (iii) uses a facially neutral standard or procedure which disproportionately and adversely affects members of one race in the assignment of jobs, benefits, etc., and which is not justified by business necessity.

Let us now return to the argument proposed earlier, that preferential hiring is necessary to accomplish the first aim of Title VII, i.e., to prevent further discrimination. Davidson urges this view on the grounds that employment selection procedures cannot be objective. Normal procedures will allow discrimination against blacks to persist unless counter-balanced by explicit racial preferences.

Davidson overstates his case. For many jobs, at least, objective selection procedures are available. In the first place, if an employer uses a selection procedure which disproportion-ately disqualifies applicants who are black, then either his procedure meets the validation and necessitation requirements under the *Griggs* standard or it does not. If it does not, then the employer cannot use the procedure. If it does, then the procedure is not discriminatory. The procedure can be counted as "objective."

If the employer's procedure does meet the validity and necessity conditions, then it either ranks applicants or it does not. If it does rank applicants, the choosing of applicants in rank order will constitute an objective hiring method. If the employer's method does not rank applicants beyond estab-lishing possession of minimal qualifications, then there are several objective (i.e., neutral) devices available to the employer for selecting from the applicant pool. He may rank the applicants according to the order in which they applied, or according to alphabetical order, or according to a lottery, or according to some similar method. All are objective ways of internally ranking the applicants for order of selection.

There are, however, many kinds of jobs in which considerable subjective judgment will remain as part of the selection process. Not all selection techniques can meet the most stringent validation requirements. Managers, executives, professors, actors, and so on, cannot be picked through the use of pencil-and-paper aptitude tests, or even on the basis of educational credentials and accumulated experience. Judgments about suitable candidates must take account of "intangibles" and will nesessarily be subjective to some extent. Davidson's claims possibly have application here.

Let us accept Davidson's contention that to the extent that the selection process remains subjective, it will result inevitably in discrimination against blacks. Does it follow that a counter-balancing preferential hiring is therefore justified by Title VII's aim of eliminating discrimination? Not necessarily.

Davidson's argument, in fact, presents a dilemma for the interpretation of Title VII. On his premises, if we do not use preferential hiring, we permit discrimination to exist. But preferential hiring is also discrimination. Thus, if we use preferential hiring, we also permit discrimination to exist. The dilemma is that whatever we do, we permit discrimination. If Title VII forbids discrimination, then there is nothing we can do in such situations to comply fully with Title VII. It does not follow from this situation that Title VII requires preferential hiring.

If such a dilemma exists for the interpretation of Title VII, it must be resolved by showing that the Title disvalues some discrimination more than it disvalues other discrimination. For example, if it could be shown that when presented with a situation which entails either discrimination against blacks or discrimination against whites Title VII disvalues discrimination against blacks more strongly than it disvalues discrimination against whites, then we could argue that in such a situation, Title VII requires preferential hiring of blacks.

No court has entertained such an argument, and there is little basis for any kind of theory about the relative weights that Title VII assigns to different kinds of discrimination. The Title itself is silent here; the Congress did not anticipate the dilemma suggested by Davidson. One might urge that it was, after all, discrimination against blacks that led Congress to pass the Civil Rights Act of 1964, and this is grounds for claiming that Title VII views discrimination against blacks as the greater evil. It is grounds, but not very substantial grounds. Congress's preoccupation with discrimination against blacks derived from the fact that discrimination against whites was not a problem. It does not follow that Congress meant to approve of discrimination against whites.

Another reply might be considered. It might be claimed that there is clearly a difference under Title VII between unlawful discrimination against blacks and the use of preferential hiring of blacks to remedy this unlawful discrimination. This reply, however, abandons the effort to justify preferential hiring by appeal to the prohibitions in Section 703. It falls back on the arguments discussed above where preferential hiring is defended by appeal to the remedial aims of Title VII. As we have seen in regard to those arguments, there is great unclarity about how much preferential hiring is justified under those remedial aims.

11

Affirmative Action

In the last two chapters the phrases "affirmative action" and "affirmative action plan" have occurred on several occasions. Although affirmative action is much talked about, it is surrounded by a great deal of public controversy and no little confusion. The controversy derives primarily from the character of affirmative action plans which include "goals" and "timetables" for hiring minorities and women. These hiring goals give rise to the widespread opinion that affirmative action plans require preferential hiring and reverse discrimination. The goals are frequently condemned as nothing more than racial or sexual quotas.

Affirmative action plans have become, in the public mind, so thoroughly identified with the hiring goals and the hiring goals so identified with preferential hiring that it has become common to think of affirmative action as meaning preferential hiring.[1] This is partly the consequence of the vigorous criticisms of the plans, criticisms which have succeeded in instilling the belief that preferential hiring is essential to affirmative action. However, it is not only critics who view affirmative action as inherently preferential. Some of its supporters take the same view.[2] Moreover, behavior by those in government charged with the administration and enforcement of affirmative action rules seems, often enough, to corroborate the view that what affirmative action plans aim at is proportional representation through preferential hiring. Government officials offer for public consumption frequent disavowals of this aim, but many people consider these disavowals to be less than honest.[3]

What are affirmative action plans and why is there so much confusion about what they require? The phrase "affirmative action" is used in importantly different contexts. As we have already seen, it occurs in Section 706(g) of Title VII:

If the court finds that the respondent has intentionally engaged in or is intentionally engaging in an unlawful employment practice charged in the complaint, the court may enjoin the respondent from engaging in such unlawful practice, and *order such affirmative action as may be appropriate,* which may include, but is not limited to, reinstatement or hiring of employees, with or without backpay . . . , or any other equitable relief as the court deems appropriate. [42 U.S.C. 2000e—5(g). Emphasis added.]

Here the phrase "affirmative action" occurs in a remedial context. A court might order an offending company to make restitution and to submit a plan detailing the specific steps it intends to take to provide backpay, promotions, and so on, to those it has victimized. The court might also require the company to spell out in the plan how it intends to alter its recruiting and hiring practices to assure there will be no future violations of the law. Thus, an "affirmative action plan" can really be *two* plans, one for making restitution, another for securing nondiscrimination. Thus, although the phrase "affirmative action" occurs in 706(g) hooked to a list of remedies a court might order, it can actually refer not only to remedial actions but to efforts directed toward nondiscrimination as well. This dual reference is responsible for much of the confusion that surrounds affirmative action.

A plan ordered by a court might or might not include hiring goals or quotas. It might generate controversy and further legal challenge. However, the affirmative action plans which have generated so much public dispute are not those occasional plans arising under Title VII but those ubiquitous plans required of every federal contractor under Executive Order 11246, issued in 1965 by President Johnson. The Executive Order, in Part II, "Nondiscrimination in Employment by Government Contractors and Subcontractors," requires that each government contract include the following provision:

During the performance of this contract, the contractor agrees as follows:
(1) The contractor will not discriminate against any employee or applicant for employment because of race, color, religion, sex, or national origin. The contractor will take affirmative action to ensure that applicants are employed and that employees are treated during employment without regard to race, color, religion, sex, or national origin.
. . . . .
(4) The contractor will comply with the provisions of Executive Order No. 11246 of September 24, 1965, and all the rules, regulations, and relevant orders of the Secretary of Labor. [42 U.S.C. 2000e.]

The Secretary of Labor was empowered to "adopt such rules and regulations and issue such orders as he deems necessary and appropriate to achieve the purposes" of the Executive Order.

Here the phrase "affirmative action" occurs in the context of an injunction not to discriminate. Thus, we might expect that the kind of affirmative action typically encountered under Title

VII would have a different emphasis than the kind encountered under the Executive Order. Over the years, however, there has been a tendency to blur the differences between the two kinds of affirmative action.

It is worth noting what a powerful tool this Executive Order can be. Although most, if not all, government contractors fall under Title VII, the enforcement of that Title often requires lengthy and cumbersome litigation. It especially depends upon the initiative of private complainants. Under the Executive Order, each contractor doesn't merely affirm that he will not discriminate, he includes that affirmation as a contractual provision. As a consequence, his discrimination becomes not only a Title VII violation but also a contractual violation or noncompliance. The government may deal with the offending contractor as it deals with any other case of contract violation. It may use various administrative means to bring the contractor into compliance, it may disqualify the contractor from future contracts, or it can go to court to seek an injunction requiring the contractor to fulfill his contractual obligations. All of these things it may do independently of Title VII proceedings. Moreover, the government can periodically inspect the contractor's operation to determine if he is fully abiding by all the "rules, regulations, and relevant orders" promulgated by the Secretary of Labor. And all of this it may do of its own initiative, without depending upon private complaints. The Executive Order thus gives the government a variety of tools it may use to deal with employment discrimination.

The contractual provision is open-ended, requiring the contractor to abide by "all the rules, regulations, and relevant orders of the Secretary of Labor." If the Secretary of Labor can and does issue valid rules that require an employer to prefer minorities and women, then each contractor will have committed himself contractually to do this.

The Secretary of Labor's "rules and regulations" were promulgated in 1972. Revised Order #4, so-called, covered all non-construction contractors.[4] Separate rules were issued for the construction industry.[5] Revised Order #4 defines and describes the affirmative action plans that each contractor is required to submit for approval if his work-force significantly "underutilizes" minorities or women. The plans must include numerical hiring goals and timetables for their achievement.

It is these hiring goals which have been the source of most of the criticism of affirmative action plans and the charges that the plans require preferential hiring. Do the hiring goals require preferential hiring? Why should they be thought to? According to Revised Order #4: "The purpose of a contractor's establishment and use of goals is to insure that he meet his affirmative action obligation. It is not intended and should not be used to discriminate against any applicant or employee because of race, color, religion, sex, or national origin," [41 C.F.R. 60–2.30]. What leads people to dismiss this as empty rhetoric and to view affirmative action as reverse discrimination?

GOALS ARE GOOD AND QUOTAS ARE BAD. BUT WHAT'S THE DIFFERENCE?

Certainly, the requirement that employers adopt and achieve hiring goals by itself raises questions and suspicions. In meeting his goal, must not the employer be prepared to take race (or sex) into account in his hiring? Doesn't this mean that unless his goals are being met otherwise, he will have to hire on the basis of race (or sex)? Aren't hiring goals the same thing as hiring quotas?

One who views affirmative action goals as quotas will hardly be disabused of his opinion by Revised Order #4's own description of the nature and function of goals.

An acceptable affirmative action program must include an analysis of areas within which the contractor is deficient in the utilization of minority groups and women, and further, *goals* and *timetables* to which the contractor's good faith efforts must be directed to correct the deficiencies, and thus to *achieve prompt and full utilization* of minorities and women, at all levels and in all segments of his work force where deficiencies exist. [41 C.F.R. 60–2.10. Emphases added.]

"Underutilization" means the employer has fewer minorities or women in his work-force than "would reasonably be expected by their availability" [41 C.F.R. 60–2.11(b)]. Availability is a matter of the proportion of minorities and women in the relevant labor pool. "Goals, timetables, and affirmative action commitments must be designed to correct any identifiable deficiencies" [41 C.F.R. 60–2.12(g)].

Now, apparently an employer is deficient if his work-force does not reflect the proportion of blacks in the relevant labor pool. The hiring goals are said to be designed to achieve "prompt and full utilization" of blacks. Full utilization means the employer has blacks on his work-force, at all levels, in proportion to their number in the relevant labor pool. Affirmative action plans and their attendant goals look, thus, like a recipe for proportional representation of blacks in the nation's firms and institutions.

If proportional representation ("full utilization") is the aim, and promptness is the requirement, then the employer seemingly will need to hire for reasons of race in order that the aim be accomplished. If the hiring goals are framed with this aim in mind, then surely the hiring goals call for preferential hiring. Nothing depends upon whether they are called goals or quotas. Insisting that there is a significant distinction between them is misleading.

There is support for this picture of affirmative action in Revised Order #4 and in the behavior of those who enforce the Order (some of which will be described below). The Order attempts to forestall this interpretation by declaring:

Goals may not be rigid and inflexible quotas which must be met, but must be targets reasonably attainable by means of applying every good faith effort to make all aspects of the entire affirmative action program work. [41 C.F.R. 60–2.12(e).]

But this effort to distinguish goals and quotas leaves much to be desired. Certainly, the distinguishing characteristic cannot be flexibility. Numerical requirements which are flexible are no less numerical requirements because they are not rigid. What significance is there in attaching the name "quota" to the one and the name "goal" to the other? There is nothing about the ordinary use of these terms which dictates this move. Why can't there be flexible quotas and inflexible goals?[6]

If affirmative action hiring goals require an employer to extend racial preferences, then requiring him to give preferences at a reasonable rate instead of an unreasonable rate does not alter the fact that he is being required to give preferences. Flexibility versus rigidity may be a useful and interesting contrast to draw for some purposes, but the contrast is irrelevant in deciding whether a hiring goal requires an employer to hire on a racially preferential basis.

The use of the phrase "good faith efforts" doesn't clarify matters either. If hiring goals require preferential hiring, then the willingness of an employer to resort to preferential hiring must be counted in determining whether his efforts are in "good faith." So the prior question is, what do the hiring goals require?

Perhaps there is, in the passage quoted from Revised Order #4, a basis for drawing a sound and useful distinction between goals and quotas, but it is not obvious what it is. The suspicions of the critic of affirmative action will not be allayed by the language of the passage. Moreover, the apparent emphasis in the Order on proportional representation ("full utilization") fuels the tendency to see no significant difference between goals and quotas. The disclaimer tagged on at the end of the

Order, as though it were an afterthought, that goals "should not be used to discriminate" can be dismissed as meaningless. Of course the goals are meant to be used to discriminate. What else would they be for?

But goals are *not* quotas, some continue to insist. "Quotas are meant to keep people out. Numerical goals, in contrast, are meant to get people in," claims Rose Coser.[7] But getting people in, where the shape of the "in" is fixed, will be possible only by keeping others out. If an employer hires only a fixed number—say 20—then a goal of 10 blacks "in" (hired) means that any white applicant beyond the 10 whites hired must stay "out." In a medical school class fixed at 100, more blacks means less whites, inclusion of some requires exclusion of others. Coser's distinction is spurious.

Robert O'Neil says: "A goal simply declares an objective which will be met only if a sufficient number of qualified persons apply, while a quota specifies the number to be admitted from a given group regardless of the pool of qualified applicants."[8] But this is not satisfactory, either. Suppose an employer has a superfluity of qualified applicants, say, 100 well-qualified applicants for 20 positions. Suppose that the government tells the employer that he must hire 10 blacks and 10 whites from this pool. Is this a goal? A quota? Does it matter what the government requirement is called?

The former Attorney General of the United States, Griffin Bell, who should know the difference between goals and quotas, if there is any, declared: ". . . I'll tell you the difference. A goal is something you do to alleviate past discrimination and looks to the day the merit system operates."[9] But the Attorney General hasn't told us anything that is useful. He certainly hasn't identified a salient difference between numerical figures which require discrimination and ones which do not. A policy of reverse discrimination might be explicitly adopted to "alleviate (the effects of) past discrimination." Companies might be required to give absolute preferences to blacks until proportional representation is approximated. To insist that these policies involve "goals" rather than "quotas" is to insist upon nothing significant.[10]

Questions about goals and quotas arise in court cases with some frequency, but the courts do no better than Revised Order #4 or the Attorney General in making clear the difference. In *Rios* v. *Enterprise Association Steamfitters Local 638*, frequently cited in other cases, the court said this about goals and quotas:

We use "goals" rather than "quotas" throughout this opinion for the reason that while to some the words may be synonymous, the term "quotas" implies a permanence not associated with "goal." For our purpose the significance of the distinction lies in the fact that once a prescribed goal is achieved the [defendant] will not be obligated to maintain it, provided, of course the [defendant] does not engage in discriminatory conduct. [*Rios* at 628, note 3.]

If the question is whether the hiring goals of affirmative action amount to racially discriminatory quotas, then the rather odd usage of the *Rios* court does not help us. If a process is discriminatory, it does not cease to be discriminatory because it is temporary. The court's ploy here is purely verbal, for nothing of interest is accomplished in distinguishing short-term from long-term numerical requirements. The court merely casts its decision in phrases with less negative overtones. The verbal shift signifies no corresponding conceptual difference.

As often as not, a court will use the term "goal" or "quota" in a decision without offering any definition of it. Other courts deny that any useful distinction between the two can be drawn. One court calls goals the "current pseudonym" for quotas.[11] The court in *Weber* v. *Kaiser Aluminum*, discussed in Chapter Nine, was equally cynical. It declared: "Attempts to distinguish a numerical goal from a quota have proved illusory and most such goals suggested by the OFCC [Office of Federal Contract Compliance, the agency that oversees affirmative action plans] can fairly be characterized as quotas" [*Weber* I at 222].

Yet a third court had this to say:

Ultimately the distinction [between numerical goals and hiring quotas] becomes illusory. As the time nears to reach the goal, a member of the discriminated group must be hired in preference to a majority person as often as is required to meet the goal. A quota, for all its unhappy connotations, is simply a recognition of the reality encountered in reaching the desired goal.[12]

By looking to the courts for guidance about goals and quotas, one finds the courts as confused as everyone else. Some courts recite the language of Revised Order #4, some invent their own distinction as in *Rios*, some use the terms without definition, and others declare that there isn't any real difference between goals and quotas.

Goals versus quotas: we have seen them contrasted as inclusive versus exclusive, flexible versus rigid, reasonable versus unreasonable, temporary versus permanent, aimed at alleviating past discrimination versus not. None of these contrasts goes to the heart of the matter, which is whether affirmative action numerical goals, whatever they are called, lead to reverse discrimination. The effort on every side to distinguish goals significantly from quotas has been such a smashing failure that one must sympathize with the critic of affirmative action who finds the distinction specious. The fact that several courts have found the distinction no more than verbal supports the critic's view. And, finally, there is the testimony of one of the goalmakers, Lawrence Silberman, formerly Undersecretary of Labor:

While serving in the Labor Department, I helped devise mandatory employment goals for government contractors.

I now realize that the distinction we saw between goals on the one hand, and unconstitutional quotas on the other, was not valid. Our use of numerical standards in pursuit of equal opportunity has led ineluctably to the very quotas, guaranteeing equal results, that we wished to avoid. [13]

Is it not, then, as Sidney Hook says, "as obvious as two plus two equals four that a numerical goal and a quota are synonymous. Why do they insist that there is a difference?" [14]

The critic of affirmative action is prompted to view it as fostering reverse discrimination partly because he sees its hiring goals as racial quotas. But there is yet other evidence that may support the critic's view.

In 1972, Stanley Pottinger, Director of the Office of Civil Rights (DHEW), the agency responsible for overseeing affirmative action plans in higher education, sent a letter to college and university presidents to explain affirmative action and to assure them that it did not require reverse discrimination. But in explaining the meaning of affirmative action, Pottinger ironically provided the critic with grounds for believing that the assurance was empty. Pottinger attempted to clarify the meaning of affirmative action this way:

Executive Order 11246 embodies two concepts: nondiscrimination and affirmative action.

'Nondiscrimination' requires the elimination of all existing discriminatory conditions, whether purposeful or inadvertent.
. . . . .
'Affirmative action' requires the contractor *to do more than ensure employment neutrality with regard to race.* . . . [15]

This passage seems to belie Pottinger's assurance that affirmative action is nondiscriminatory. Surely the heart of racial discrimination is non-neutrality with regard to race. The most natural account one could give of nondiscrimination is to say that it is racial neutrality. How, then, can affirmative action be consistent with nondiscrimination if it requires "more than neutrality"?

What does being more than neutral mean? Can it mean anything besides being non-neutral? If an employer makes a racially non-neutral hiring choice, how can this fail to be racially discriminatory? The critic of affirmative action would argue that it can't be. He would see in Pottinger's letter to the presidents conceptual evidence that his own view of affirmative action hiring goals is correct. Hiring goals do impose reverse discrimination because they are in the service of a policy that abandons racial neutrality.

Many view affirmative action as the critic does. If not outright hostile, they are suspicious and skeptical. There is enough in the language of Revised Order #4 and in the official explanations of affirmative action to give credence to the critic's view. His belief that official claims of nondiscriminatory purpose and effect are empty rhetoric, window-dressing designed to obscure the essentially preferential thrust of affirmative action, cannot be dismissed as groundless. The *Weber* I court itself could not make sense of Revised Order #4's disclaimer of discrimination:

Goals for hiring and promotion must be set to overcome any 'underutilization' found to exist [said the court, paraphrasing the Order]. The regulation then *confuses* things mightily by declaring that a goal shall not be considered a device for instituting quotas or reverse discrimination . . . [*Weber* I at 222. Emphasis added.]

The court, as we saw, went on to insist that no real distinction could be drawn between goals and quotas. Thus, the court itself seemed to join the critic in giving little standing to the claim in Revised Order #4 [at 60-2.30] that affirmative action hiring goals are not to be used to discriminate. The court found the claim anomalous in light of the implications of the rest of the Order. As we saw above, some friends of affirmative action concur in dismissing the disclaimer of discrimination as mean-ingless.[16] Thus, the critic can hardly be faulted if he does the same.

A NONDISCRIMINATORY INTERPRETATION OF AFFIRMATIVE ACTION

Must we accept the critic's view? Or can we take seriously the assertion in Section 60-20.3 that hiring goals must not be used to discriminate? Must we simply dismiss this section as "dust in our eyes," thrown to obscure our vision of the true nature of Revised Order #4?

There are numerous official statements affirming allegiance to nondiscriminatory affirmative action. From the President down to the lowest functionary, officials have constantly repeated that government supports goals but not quotas. John Powell, then-chairman of the EEOC, in testimony before the O'Hara Committee in 1974, disavowed any preferential impli-cations of affirmative action. "The object of [Executive Order] 11246 is to eliminate discrimination and you don't achieve it by discriminating against white males. . . ."[17] And as I mentioned in the last section, Stanley Pottinger, at that time Director of the Office of Civil Rights (DHEW), sought in 1972 to assure university and college presidents that Revised Order #4 did not require preferential hiring.

In this section I will offer a theory of affirmative action which is nondiscriminatory. Whether those who enforce Revised Order #4 perceive affirmative action in this way is a question I shall not fully pursue. The theory I offer shows that affirmative action can be viewed as nondiscriminatory and that it has a value which is not threatened by any legal decision against preferential hiring.

After Stanley Pottinger described affirmative action as "going beyond neutrality," he went on to say:

The premise of the affirmative action concept of the Executive Order is that unless *positive action is undertaken to overcome the effects of systematic institutional forms of exclusion and discrimination,* a benign neutrality in employment practices will tend to perpetuate the 'status quo ante' indefinitely.[18]

Although this is not itself terribly clear, I think we can see in it the leading idea of affirmative action: positive action to overcome systematic (or systemic) institutional discrimination. The issue is not one of non-neutrality as opposed to neutrality in matters of race. The issue, rather, is one of activity as opposed to passivity in accomplishing the desired neutrality in employment practices. To characterize the issue, as Pottinger does, as one of neutrality and more than neutrality is infelicitous.

Let me distinguish between *passive nondiscrimination* and *active nondiscrimination.* In passive nondiscrimination, an employer says: "If any blacks apply, I will treat their applications without prejudice." In active nondiscrimination, an employer says: "If any blacks apply, I will treat their applications without prejudice, and I will go out of my way to encourage and facilitate black applications and to make sure my recruiting methods do not limit or exclude black candidates." In passive nondiscrimination, the employer says: "I will use neutral standards in rating and promoting and discharging my employees." In active nondiscrimination, the employer says: "I will use neutral standards in rating, promoting, and discharging my employees; and I will thoroughly examine and overhaul my employee practices to make sure that they are genuinely neutral, not just apparently so."

The point is this: passive nondiscrimination fails to be really nondiscriminatory. The problem of discrimination is not merely located at the level of conscious, explicit racial bias. Although discrimination of this sort still exists, the broader problem is the inertial weight of decades and decades of institutional habits, procedures, and reflexes which, though apparently neutral, have the effect of unnecessarily excluding blacks and limiting their opportunities. What is needed to achieve genuine racial neutrality in employment is a disruption of habitual ways of doing things, a restructuring of activities so that systemic and largely invisible barriers are eliminated.

Habits are automatic and unreflective ways of acting. When one acquires a bad habit, breaking it requires the person to regain awareness of the specific tasks usually done without attention. The throwing motion of a baseball pitcher is largely automatic, habitual. His paying attention to his pitching usually impedes his effectiveness. But if the pitcher falls into a bad habit in his delivery, then he must reassert an awareness, a consciousness of the entire process, so that he can discover the fault in his motion and consciously adjust for it. Affirmative action works this way. It is a device for making the employer conscious of all of the elements of his employment practices and of their impact upon blacks. By means of a specific set of steps and instructions, including the hiring goals, affirmative action forces the employer to re-examine his recruitment and selection procedures to see that no element unnecessarily disadvantages blacks.

Affirmative action requires the employer to become aware fully and continually of the racial make-up of his work-force. It makes him pay close attention to the racial impact of each of his business practices. It forces him to become aware of the proportion of blacks in the labor pool. Affirmative action requires the employer to advertise jobs widely, to use recruitment procedures which will maximally include applications from all races. Affirmative action requires the employer to display publicly his welcome of black applications and his commitment to consider them on a nondiscriminatory basis.

All of this is directed toward achieving nondiscrimination: the affirmative action is "to ensure that applicants are employed without regard to race. . . . "[19] In order that there be nondiscrimination in employment, it is necessary to adopt mechanisms which force continual monitoring and re-examination of recruitment and selection procedures. This is so because our institutions are permeated with habits and reflexes which have the effect, unintended for the most part, of especially burdening blacks.

What is the role of the hiring goals and timetables in this process of affirmative action? They serve as automatic monitors. An employer is supposed to evaluate his recruitment and selection procedures and to appraise the labor pool from which he recruits. His aim is to be nondiscriminatory. What would his selection profile look like assuming nondiscrimination? It is this question that should underlie the establishment of hiring goals. The employer should set his goals at that figure one would expect to be realized under nondiscrimination. In an article derived from his letter to the university presidents, Pottinger made this clear:

> Universities are required to commit themselves to defined, specific steps that will bring the university into contact with qualified women and minorities and that will ensure that in the selection process they will be judged fairly on the basis of their capabilities. Universities are also required to make an honest prediction of what those efforts are likely to yield over a given period of time, assuming that the availability of women and minorities is accurately approximated, and assuming that the procedures for recruitment and selection are actually followed.
>
> This predictive aspect of Affirmative Action could be called any number of things. . . . They happen to be called "goals."[20]

Here we have the basis for distinguishing affirmative action "goals" from "quotas." The so-called goals are *predictions* of the number of blacks that will be hired under assumed nondiscrimination. The so-called quotas represent *intentions* or *aims* to hire a certain number of blacks. In the first instance, the employer aims at true neutrality and uses the predicted outcome as a standard against which to measure his achievement of his aim. In the second instance, the employer aims directly at achieving the desired number. The effective difference between goals and quotas thus distinguished can be illustrated by the following two cases.

Case 1: *I aim to adopt a neutral selection procedure.* I choose to select employees by a coin-flip. Suppose half of the applicant pool is white and half black. I can surmise that over a period of time, half my employees should be black and half white. Suppose that at the end of a significant period I find that 60% of my employees are white and 40% black (or vice versa). This failure of actual outcome to match expected results may cause me to wonder about the coin I am using. Perhaps it is "biased"—unbalanced in such a way that it will keep coming up more heads than tails. If I discover that this is so, I will throw out the coin and use another one. Suppose, however, I determine that the coin is true. Then, I continue to use it, and I dismiss the 60-40 ratio in my work-force as a fluke.

Case 2: *I aim to have a work-force 50% white and 50% black.* (Again, the relevant applicant pool is assumed to be half black and half white.) I elect to use a coin-flip as an efficient way to realize my aim. Suppose that after a significant period of time, my work-force consists of 60% white and 40% black. Even if I determine that my coin is a true one, I will abandon my method of selection because I am not getting the results I aim for. I will turn to explicit hiring of more blacks until the 50/50 ratio I seek is accomplished.

The numerical ratio "50% whites/50% blacks" figures into both cases but in different ways. In the first case it is an expectation. Failure to meet the expectation caused me to re-examine the coin. However, once I was satisfied, the disparity between actual results and expected results ceased to have any further significance for me and did not cause me to alter my procedure. On the other hand, I did alter my procedure in the second case. This was because the ratio was not an expectation but my actual aim. Even though the coin proved to be true in the second case, I was unwilling to accept the deviations from 50/50 generated by the coin-tossing.

The distinction we can draw between nondiscriminatory "hiring goals" and discriminatory "quotas" does not lie, thus, in common usage or even in lexicographical meaning. A goal, according to the dictionary, is an aim; it is "that toward which effort is directed." One could easily direct one's efforts toward the promotion and realization of a quota, "a proportional part or share of a total."[21] Since we want to draw a distinction in which goals are associated with nondiscrimination and quotas with discrimination, the dictionary meanings cannot guide us. There is no significant difference between aiming to hire a fixed number of blacks and aiming to hire a ratio or proportion of blacks.

The real issue has to do with a difference in aims and intentions. The view of nondiscriminatory hiring goals I am offering sees them as predictions of what will happen when an employer pursues the independent and primary aim of nondiscrimination. The "hiring goal," thus, is not a genuine goal at all, since *it* is not "that towards which effort is directed," but only the expected concomitant of that toward which the employer's effort is directed: nondiscriminatory employment practices.[22] The affirmative action hiring goals are, consequently, badly misnamed. They easily mislead us into thinking they are what the employer must be aiming at.

If my aim as an employer is to make racially neutral hiring choices, then abandoning racial neutrality cannot be a means to my aim. Predicting that my neutral hiring will result in 10 blacks hired does not commit me to hiring 10 blacks because it does not involve me in intending to hire 10 blacks.[23] I intend to be neutral and I expect 10 blacks will be hired as a result.

If I aim to hire 10 blacks, plain and simple, then I must be prepared to extend racial preferences if this is necessary, or I must be prepared to give up my aim. When such an aim is imposed upon me from outside by court order or government regulation, I do not have the second option. I must anticipate that abandoning racial neutrality can (and perhaps must) be a means to my aim. Thus, whether racial neutrality is or is not to be abandoned depends on my aim. The difference, accordingly, between "goals" and "quotas" has to do with the differing intentions that lie behind them.

It should be apparent that the ideas of flexibility and rigidity have nothing to do with whether something is a goal or quota. The distinction between flexible versus rigid might mean a wider versus a narrower aim or it might mean a conditional versus an unconditional aim. I can aim to hire 8 to 12 blacks or I can aim to hire precisely 10. Whatever interesting differences there might be between these two aims, there is nothing that distinguishes the one as nondiscriminatory and the other as discriminatory. Likewise, I can aim to hire 10 blacks no matter what or I can aim to hire 10 blacks on condition they are all minimally qualified. One aim is unconditional, the other conditional. As I have defined a quota, there can be flexible and inflexible ones and conditional and unconditional ones. What remains constant is that there is an aim to hire a certain (fixed or range) number of blacks (conditionally or unconditionally) and thus a commitment to giving racial preferences when this is necessary.

It is useful for an employer to state hiring goals, i.e., to frame predictions, in an affirmative action plan because they serve as one check of the success of his efforts to promote racial neutrality in his employment practices. He can measure his actual results against his predicted results. If he does not meet the predicted figure, then he needs to re-examine his hiring procedures and his affirmative action plan. Why were his actual hiring results not as predicted? Could it be that despite his best efforts his procedures still contain undetected exclusionary elements? It is important to see that if on re-examination the employer shows that his procedures are genuinely free of discrimination we can judge the employer's efforts a success even though the predicted figure was not met. We can do this because his efforts were directed toward being nondiscriminatory.

When a court imposes a quota, it imposes an aim on the employer to meet the figures in the quota. Failure to meet the quota is always failure to carry out the required aim. There may be acceptable excuses for this failure, but the disparity between required outcome and actual outcome must be viewed as a deficiency of achievement. This is equally true if the employer sets the aim for himself rather than having it imposed on him.

The distinction I have been making between nondiscriminatory goals and discriminatory quotas can be summarized. Using the figure "10 blacks hired" and the time frame "one year," the distinction can be represented this way:

Quota: real aim–10 blacks in one year; not getting 10 blacks represents failure.
Goal: real aim–nondiscrimination; predicted outcome of discrimination–10 blacks in one year; not getting 10 blacks
  (i) represents failure if due to discrimination
  (ii) does not represent failure if due to factors other than discrimination.

DIVERGENCE BETWEEN THEORY AND PRACTICE

The critic of affirmative action might concede that we can, after all, draw a theoretically sound and useful distinction between "goals" (predictions) and "quotas" (aims or intentions), but nevertheless insist that in practice the distinction is bound to collapse. Under the pressure of government oversight, employers will treat their affirmative action goals as real goals, as themselves the objects of effort. They will aim directly at achieving the hiring goals in order to avoid unpleasant entanglements with government contract enforcement agencies. The employer will soon realize that if his hiring results at the end of the prescribed period match or exceed his affirmative action goals, government agencies will leave him alone. On the other hand, if his results fall short of the goals, the employer knows that he must account for this and must do so under the threat of possible sanctions should his explanation fail to satisfy the government. The employer will soon see that his safest course lies in meeting his goals, and he will make this his aim, even if he has to discriminate in reverse.

Thus, even if a nondiscriminatory theory of Revised Order #4 is available, affirmative action hiring goals are bound to be subject to abuse, argues the critic. They ought to be eliminated because even where there is a minimum of confusion and a maximum of understanding about affirmative action, employers will have incentives to treat their goals as quotas, that is, they will have incentives to abandon nondiscrimination.

I believe we must unquestionably accord considerable force to the critic's charge. The threat of involvement with government scrutiny and possible adversary proceedings will incline some employers toward an insurance strategy. They can insure noninvolvement with the government by "meeting" their affirmative action hiring goals. Now, it might be argued that if the employer's goals *qua* predictions are accurate assessments of what can be expected from his nondiscriminatory hiring, then he will certainly not have to resort to reverse discrimination to "meet" his goals. The problem with this response is that predictions about the results of nondiscriminatory hiring can be only rough and ready at best. They will seldom be very accurate. This is because no one can accurately predict the behavior of various job markets over 5 and 10 year periods. That behavior is influenced by unpredictable changes in national and local economic conditions, unexpected trends in education and training, complex changes in family life and cultural norms, international events beyond our control, and so on. The calculating employer can reasonably believe that it will not be unlikely that he will find his time period expiring and his goals "unmet" despite his best efforts to eliminate discrimination in hiring. Seeing that this can lead to costly involvement with government agencies, he will be tempted to assure that his goals are "met" and to use racial preferences if necessary.

It would be naive to deny that some employers will face and succumb to such temptations.[24] Nevertheless, there may be less to the critic's charge than he believes. The fact is, the success rate of employers in meeting their affirmative action goals is pretty low. We would expect otherwise if we believed employers are universally ready and willing to resort to reverse discrimination to keep the government out of their hair.

Nevertheless the critic is correct in seeing a considerable potential for abuse of hiring goals. Is he also correct in drawing the conclusion that the hiring goals ought to be eliminated? The critic points to certain inevitable evils attendant upon the use of goals. These evils would be sufficient grounds for eliminating the goals only if there were not other evils attendant upon the not using of goals. Because systemic discrimination is so deeply and pervasively entrenched in American institutions, a check is needed against which both the employer and the government can evaluate efforts to achieve real racial neutrality. This check (the goals *qua* predictions) may create abuse: there is the risk that some employers will resort to reverse discrimination. But the absence of the check will likewise allow abuse: there is the risk that many employers will diminish their (costly) efforts to detect and eliminate those deep and nonobvious elements of their practices which produce discriminatory impact. If affirmative action goals are eliminated, one sort of abuse risks being replaced by another sort. The critic of hiring goals, in order to justify their abolition, must show that their abuse will outweigh the abuses that would occur without them. It is not likely he can make a strong case here.

Without the hiring goals and the government scrutiny they make possible, there will be little effective pressure on employers to take the time extensively to examine and revise their employment practices. Even the employer with the best will, who does not need government pressure, still needs goals *qua* predictions so that his own efforts are not blind. The critic must show that affirmative action can be more than a paper program if it dispenses with hiring goals. Or else he must be prepared to reject the principal idea behind affirmative action: that passive neutrality will not end discrimination.

12

Nondiscriminatory Versus Preferential Affirmative Action

A DEFENSE OF THE NONDISCRIMINATORY INTERPRETATION

In the previous chapter, I offered an interpretation of the aims and language of Revised Order #4 which viewed it as mandating positive efforts by employers to assure that their employment practices are and remain truly racially neutral. The role of hiring goals in the employer's affirmative action plan is to provide a convenient check against which he and the government can assess the success of his efforts. Affirmative action plans are not, on this view, schemes for preferential hiring.

This interpretation takes as its touchstone the declaration of Revised Order #4 at 60–20.3 that affirmative action goals "should not be used to discriminate against any applicant or employee because of race, color, religion, sex, or national origin." A problem for this interpretation is Section 60–2.10, which describes the employer directing his efforts toward goals designed to "achieve prompt and full utilization of minorities" where "deficiencies exist." This passage certainly lends itself to a preferential interpretation.

Suppose an employer has 10 blacks on a work force of 250. He draws from a labor pool that is and has been 20 percent black. According to the Revised Order, he "underutilizes" blacks. He would be "fully utilizing" them if he had 50 blacks in his employ instead of 10. The employer is not expanding his work force and has a turnover rate of only 10 workers a year. If each year he hires 2 blacks and 8 whites—roughly what would be expected from nondiscriminatory hiring—then it would be twenty years before 50 of his employees were black—before, in other words, "full utilization" would be accomplished.

If the employer must submit an affirmative action plan with "[g]oals, timetables, and . . . commitments . . . to correct any deficiencies" (60—2.12[g]), a plan designed to achieve "prompt and full utilization of minorities and women" (60–2.10), what will his hiring goals be? If his affirmative action plan has a 5 year duration, then it appears that his hiring goals for those years must be sufficient to correct his "underutiliza-tion" of blacks. Given a 5-year timetable, this means that his goal must be 8 blacks a year.

If the employer's affirmative action hiring goal is set at 8 blacks a year, then he will have to hire blacks at a rate greater than would occur under racially neutral selection. Thus, his goal cannot constitute a *prediction* of what will occur when he uses nondiscriminatory hiring. The affirmative action plan requires of him not nondiscrimination but proportional repre-sentation of blacks; the goals are means to this; and they will require him to extend racial preferences except under the most unusual circumstances.

This, or something like it, is what many, both friends and foes, see affirmative action to be all about. Much of the talk in Revised Order #4 about "correcting underutilization" lends itself to the belief that proportional representation is the chief aim of affirmative action. This aim is a quite different one from the aim of nondiscrimination.

If this is the appropriate understanding of 60–2.10 and similar sections of Revised Order #4, then there is no way to reconcile these sections with 60–2.30 which says that goals are not to discriminate; no way, that is, unless we are willing to accept some very tendentious definition of "discrimination." If we take the nondiscriminatory view of affirmative action, then we will have to find some reading of the "prompt utilization" talk which does not imply that an employer must act as the one just described.

There are sources outside Revised Order #4 which lend support to the nondiscriminatory interpretation. In the first place there is the text of Executive Order 11246 itself. Since the Revised Order is supposed to elaborate and implement the Executive Order, it seems reasonable to accept the rule that any interpretation of the Revised Order which unequivocally contradicts the text of the Executive Order ought to be rejected. Now, the Executive Order requires each contractor to affirm that he will hire "without regard to race."[1] To read Revised Order #4 as mandating preferential hiring is quite clearly to read it as permitting or requiring employers to hire "with regard to race." Thus, we ought not to read the Revised Order this way.

This may seem an excessively literalistic reading of the Executive Order and one which doesn't give due weight to the Order's charge to the Secretary of Labor to offer suitable interpretations of its language. Let us turn, then, to the new Uniform Guidelines on Employee Selection, issued in August 1978. These Guidelines "incorporate a single set of principles . . . designed to provide a framework for the proper use of tests and other [employment] selection procedures" (Section 1, B). They supersede previous rules and will guide the Justice Department, EEOC, Department of Labor, and Civil Service Commission in the application of federal law, including Title

VII and E.O. 11246. In that they speak for the Secretary of Labor, the Uniform Guidelines count as his latest gloss on Revised Order #4. Section 4, E, of the Guidelines says this:

In carrying out their obligations, the Federal enforcement agencies will consider the general posture of the [employer] . . . with respect to equal employment opportunity for the job or group of jobs in question. Where [an employer] . . . has adopted an affirmative action program, the Federal enforcement agencies will consider the provisions of that program, including the goals and timetables which the [employer] . . . has adopted and the progress which [he] . . . has made in carrying out that program and in meeting the goals and timetables. While such affirmative action programs may in design and execution be race, color, sex, or ethnic conscious, selection procedures under such programs should be based upon *ability or relative ability* to do the work. [43 *FR* 38298. Emphasis added.]

What do the Guidelines mean by saying that affirmative action programs may be racially conscious? This is explained in Section 1, C:

These guidelines apply only to selection procedures which are used as a basis for making employment decisions. For example, the use of recruiting procedures designed to attract members of a particular race . . . which were previously denied employment opportunities or which are currently underutilized, may be necessary to bring an employer into compliance with Federal law, and is frequently an essential element of any effective affirmative action program; but recruitment practices are not considered by these guidelines to be selection procedures. [43 *FR* 38296–38297.]

An employer's recruiting aim is to generate a pool of applicants that is racially representative. Thus, his recruiting needs to be racially conscious in the sense that he takes special pains to disseminate job information so that it reaches black audiences. In this sense, his entire affirmative action program must be racially conscious. The employer should be constantly aware of the racial impact of any of his practices.

The Guidelines seem quite clear about employment selection itself: it is to be racially neutral. Selection procedures under affirmative action programs should be based on "relative ability." The matter is made clearer yet later in the Guidelines. In Section 13, those employers not required under E.O. 11246 to have affirmative action plans are encouraged to develop programs on their own. The Guidelines there commend to all private employers the Equal Employment Opportunity Coordinating Council's 1976 "Policy Statement on Affirmative Action for State and Local Government Agencies," which says this:

Selection under such plans should be based upon the ability of the applicant(s) to do the work. Such plans should not require the selection of the unqualified, or the unneeded, *nor should they require the selection of persons on the basis of race, color, sex, religion, or national origin.*" [43 *FR* 38309. Emphasis added.]

As regulatory jargon goes, this seems quite plain in its meaning. It supports the nondiscriminatory interpretation of affirmative action.

THE REMEDIAL ELEMENT OF REVISED ORDER #4

The nondiscriminatory theory of affirmative action under Executive Order 11246 would, I believe, be difficult to dispute were it not for an aspect of Revised Order #4 that I have neglected to discuss. It is the "remedial" aspect, and it opens the door to all the complexities and confusions that surround the interpretation of Title VII. At 60–2.1(b), the Revised Order reads: "Relief for members of an affected class who, by virtue of past discrimination, continue to suffer the present effects of that discrimination shall be provided. . . ." Thus, if a complaint has been made against a contractor and he has been found by the appropriate contract compliance agency to have discriminated, or if on-site inspections or reviews give evidence of past discrimination, the contractor can be asked to provide relief as part of his affirmative action program. Those who are members of the "affected class," entitled to relief, are those employees who suffered from the employer's discrimination.[2] The aim of the relief is to move them to their "rightful places" in the employer's organization.[3]

This limited conception of remedies poses no problem for the nondiscriminatory interpretation of affirmative action. In the first place, as I have already pointed out in connection with Title VII remedies, making a victim of discrimination "whole" or moving him to his "rightful place," even when this means jumping him over other employees, does not amount to giving a racial preference. Secondly, such internal adjustments by an employer are separate from his hiring goals, which ought to remain unaffected by his remedial efforts. If the remedial reach of Revised Order #4 were no greater than this, we would have no problem in maintaining the nondiscriminatory theory of affirmative action.

However, despite the language of the Revised Order, the government's actual interpretation of remedial affirmative action is very broad indeed. The Kaiser program challenged by Brian Weber was an affirmative action plan developed under government pressure and defended by the government before the Supreme Court. The government follows policies which encourage, pressure, or require employers to engage in preferential hiring in the name of affirmative action "remedies." The doctrinal basis for these policies is laid out in the EEOC's "Guidelines on Affirmative Action Appropriate Under Title VII," published on January 19, 1979 (44 FR 442). These Guidelines seek to immunize employers from reverse discrimination suits by recognizing as an adequate defense the fact that the employer was following an affirmative action plan under E.O. 11246. And what would be acceptable in those plans is indicated by the nature of the "remedial" plans which the EEOC urges employers not covered by the Executive Order to adopt voluntarily. Those plans

> may include interim goals or targets. Such interim goals or targets for previously excluded groups may be higher than the percentage of their availability in the workforce so that the long term goal may be met in a reasonable period of time. In order to achieve such interim goals or targets, an employer may consider race, sex, and/or national origin in making *selections* from among qualified applicants. [44 *FR* 4425. Emphasis added.]

Moreover, it is made explicit that the benefits of the "remedies" may fall on those who are not members of the "affected class."[4] The "affected class" has been transformed into the "underutilized class." Remedy is associated with eliminating the effects of past discrimination and this idea is taken broadly enough to extend beyond those effects suffered by the victims of the employer's own discrimination.

The Guidelines on Affirmative Action (1979) say that race may be considered in employment selections in order to meet "interim goals," and the Uniform Guidelines (1978) say that although race may be used in recruitment it cannot be used in selection. Is the government in flat contradiction with itself? The Uniform Guidelines, upon which we relied for the nondiscriminatory interpretation of affirmative action, contain a catch which resolves the apparent conflict. After insisting that selection procedures must be neutral, the Uniform Guidelines, in Section 13(a), provide this exception: "Nothing in these guidelines is intended to preclude the use of lawful selection procedures which assist in remedying the effects of prior discriminatory practices, or the achievement of affirmative action objectives" [43 *FR* 38300].

And what constitutes a "lawful selection procedure" for

remedying the effects of prior discrimination? In the Guidelines on Affirmative Action, the EEOC makes clear it will view accelerated hiring of blacks as a "lawful procedure," and will protect any employer from reverse discrimination suits who gives preferences pursuant to an approved "remedial" affirmative action plan.

Thus, so long as the government is prepared to interpret remedies in the broadest fashion, as encompassing any effort to eliminate any effect of historical discrimination, both Title VII and E.O. 11246 affirmative action plans may well include preferential hiring quotas, by whatever name they are called. "Prompt utilization" of underrepresented minorities is, indeed, the key factor. The "prompt utilization" talk in Revised Order #4 occurs in sections not addressing matters of remedy. Nevertheless, once remedies come to be viewed in a broad fashion, "prompt utilization" can itself be viewed as a form of remedy. The difference between policies of restitution to those victimized by the employer's discrimination and policies of quickly achieving racial proportionality in the employer's work force are simply covered over by the larger view of remedies.

Is, then, affirmative action discriminatory or nondiscriminatory? As I pointed out at the beginning, affirmative action refers to two different things. It refers to those efforts which aim to secure nondiscriminatory hiring, and it refers to those efforts which are directed toward "remedying the effects of past discrimination." If the concept of "remedies" is taken broadly, detached from restitution to the individual victim, and if the remedial aspect becomes dominant, then affirmative action plans and affirmative action "hiring goals" will indeed involve preferential hiring.

Just as with the parallel evolution of the idea of remedies in Title VII litigation, we will not find in government regulations any theory which explains and justifies turning "make whole the victim of the employer's discrimination" into "make the employer's work force racially balanced." The latter policy may indeed be desirable and defensible on its own merits. But for those who believe otherwise, the government's use of the remedial provisions of Revised Order #4 (and Title VII) to pursue a policy of racial balancing is going to seem like the arbitrary use of government power rather than a lawful course of action.

GOVERNMENT POLICY AND PRACTICE

I leave aside further questions of justifying a policy of "remedial" affirmative action aimed at "prompt utilization" of minorities and women and requiring the use of racial and sexual preferences as means. What bears noting here is that by acting on the more expansive view of "remedial" affirmative action, the government truly puts itself in the position of dissimulating about the nature of affirmative action hiring goals. Under the broad remedial approach, the interim and long-range hiring goals are genuine goals, not predictions. Quite clearly the aim of the employer is to raise the number of blacks in his employ. The aim of the Kaiser program was to have 39% of its craft workers be black. It carried out the aim by selecting one black for each white selected. This one-for-one ratio certainly constitutes no prediction about what would happen under nondiscriminatory selection. In fact, it was expressly instituted to surpass what would happen under nondiscrimination.

By continuing to use the term "goal" to refer to two quite different things—predictions and aims—the government manages to confuse itself, the courts, the public, and both the friends and foes of affirmative action. And it manages, unwittingly or not, to offer some very shoddy and disingenuous defenses of its practices. Perhaps the best example of the full degeneration of language as a means of clear communication is to be found in the affirmative action plan developed by AT&T under government prodding and threats.

The AT&T case was the first instance of coordinated action

between the Equal Employment Opportunity Commission (EEOC) and the Office of Federal Contract Compliance Programs in the Labor Department. In proceedings before the Federal Communications Commission, American Telephone and Telegraph Company was accused of employment discrimination under both Title VII and E.O. 11246. However, the charges were not litigated in court. Instead, the government and the company negotiated a settlement, incorporated in a Memorandum of Agreement, which was approved in January 1973 by the U.S. District Court for the Eastern District of Pennsylvania. Affecting 767,000 workers, the consent decree required AT&T to set goals to rapidly overcome "deficiencies in utilization" of women and minorities and to give priorities to members of these groups in order to meet the goals.

Accordingly, AT&T formulated a Model Plan of Affirmative Action to effectuate the requirements of the conciliation agreement. We need quote only a small portion in order to exhibit the extreme schizophrenia of the Plan:

Section IA. The . . . Company's Affirmative Action Plan is a set of specific and result oriented procedures to which the Company is committed. The procedures coupled with good faith efforts will insure *equal employment opportunity.* (FEP 431:82. Emphasis added.)

Section IB. An integral part of this policy is to provide *equal employment opportunity* for all persons . . . and to recruit . . . *without discrimination* because of race, color, religion, national origin, sex or age. (FEP 431.82. Emphasis added.)

Section IC. The Equal Employment objective of the Bell System is to achieve, within a reasonable time, an employee profile, with respect to race and sex in each major job classification, *at a pace beyond that which would occur normally; to prohibit discrimination* in employment because of race, color, religion, national origin, sex or age; and to have a work environment free of discrimination. (FEP 431:82. Emphasis added.)

If the objective of the Bell System was to achieve a sexually and racially representative employee profile "at a pace beyond that which would occur normally," how could this be done without discrimination, i.e., without sexual and racial preferences? That it obviously couldn't be done is revealed by Section IV which describes the "Affirmative Action Override":

. . . to the extent any Bell System operating company is unable to meet its intermediate targets . . . the Decree requires that . . . selections be made from among any at least basically qualified candidates for promotion and hiring of the group or groups for which the target is not being met. . . .

The . . . Companies shall employ the affirmative action override . . . (a) at any point in a quarter when they conclude that such is necessary to meet intermediate targets or (b) in quarters following the end of any quarter when a Company is failing to meet any intermediate target . . . and until such target is being met for the year. (FEP 431: 124g.)

The "affirmative action override" was to be used to meet "targets" both in new hirings and in promotions and transfers. In 1976, the third year of the Plan, of 61,000 promotions and new hirings at Bell, 39,000 went to women and 5,000 went to minority men. Among 18,500 new hirings, "affirmative action override" was used 1,650 times.[5] This means that in 1,650 instances in 1976, Bell companies hired a lesser qualified person over a more qualified one of the wrong race or sex.

The Model Plan avowed that:

The . . . Company recognizes that all goals, intermediate targets and time frames explained in this section . . . are neither rigid nor inflexible quotas, but objectives to be pursued by mobilization of available company resources for a "good faith effort." (FEP 431:91.)

Quotas are bad, so the Model Plan offered instead "goals," "targets," and "objectives." There is no conceptual clarity gained by this semantic fastidiousness. It is evident that the main aim of the plan was to bring about faster than normally could be expected an increase in minorities and women on the job. Moreover, the aim clearly embraced the possible use of direct racial and sexual preferences as means. Thus, the "goals," "targets," and "objectives" functioned altogether differently than predictions would have functioned in the plan.

It is of no consequence what aims and predictions are called, but they ought to be called by different names in order that the differences between them are not obscured. Unfortunately, by attaching the term "goal" to both predictions and *flexible aims* and by reserving the word "quota" for *inflexible aims,* the government covers over a real distinction and invents a useless one.

The consent decree signed by AT&T and the consequent Model Plan were upheld by the federal courts when it was subsequently challenged by several unions.[6] The AT&T case did not involve a company being ordered to adopt quotas after being found guilty of discrimination. Rather, the requirement for the Bell companies to meet sexual and racial quotas derived not from a court order but from the conciliation agreement entered into by AT&T, EEOC, and the Secretary of Labor. There was no trial, no finding of discrimination, and no admission of guilt by the Company. Nevertheless, the court assimilated the AT&T case to the body of Title VII cases involving court-ordered preferential hiring. It found the consent decree sufficient to justify the preferential hiring required of AT&T.[7]

That the court found the consent decree and the Model Plan consistent with Title VII is of less interest to us here, however, than its finding that the Model Plan was also consistent with E.O. 11246. Since the Plan explicitly called for preferential hiring whenever necessary to meet its "targets," how could it be found compatible with Revised Order #4 and E.O. 11246? The court relied on the rule established in *Contractors Association of Eastern Pennsylvania* v. *Secretary of Labor,* one of the first rulings under E.O. 11246, that "more than ordinary deference" is owed by the court "to an administrative agency's interpretation of an Executive Order or regulation which it is charged to administer" (*Contractors* at 175). Accordingly, since the Secretary of Labor avowed to the court that the Model Plan was within the law, the court deferred to the government's own interpretation and held that "affirmative action override" was consistent with the Executive Order.[8] To the degree that courts take this approach to government action under E.O. 11246, there is going to be little judicial resistance to even the most expansive and preferential interpretations offered by government of "remedial" affirmative action.

It is evident that the Model Plan aimed at increasing the representation of minorities and women in the different job classifications in the Bell companies.[9] The aim of achieving "prompt utilization" approximating proportional representation is increasingly a part of government policy in both Title VII and E.O. 11246 proceedings. This is seen from the Kaiser program, from other massive settlements on the order of the AT&T agreement,[10] and from the EEOC's promulgation of guidelines to protect companies who, taking hint from these settlements, voluntarily adopt their own "remedial" quotas before the government turns its attention their way.

THE MORAL AUTHORITY OF THE LAW

At the end of Chapter Eight, we turned to an examination of statutes and rules and cases because of the possibility that we could accord to the law a certain moral authority in the debate about reverse discrimination. Where the application of general moral principles does not pick out a clear solution to a problem, we may give moral weight to the actual policy decided upon by a representative, deliberative body authorized to decide. If the body promulgates a choice that is clear and defended by publicly comprehensible reasons which go to the merits of the choice, then we may be satisfied to defer to this course.

It is apparent, however, that anti-discrimination law, at least in regard to the question of reverse discrimination, does not meet any of the conditions which would induce us to defer from independent moral judgment. Instead of being clear, the law is a confused mass of interpretations by the courts, the government, and legal commentators. It is full of unresolved controversies. Since 1965, there is a clearly discernible evolution from a modest interpretation of "remedies to discrimination" under both Title VII and E.O. 11246 to a very broad and aggressive interpretation that virtually turns "remedial action" into a policy of proportional representation. The evolution has been characterized by the use of vague concepts, by an absence of solid argumentation, and by a lack of bureaucratic candor. Neither the courts nor the government departments have been able to articulate a clear, principled, and publicly comprehensible theory to underlie and support this evolution. Congress has carefully avoided having to face up to the problems in the law. Thus, representation of the public in this evolution in the meaning of the law has been quite minimal.

We have already noted that Congress did not bother to define the crucial notion of "discrimination" in its major anti-discrimination legislation, the Civil Rights Act of 1964. As a consequence, there has been considerable confusion in the law about "discrimination" and even more about "reverse discrimination." The situation is even worse in regard to "equal opportunity." Time after time courts, government officials, and commentators, in need of a justification for one or another of their interpretations of the law, will fall back on a reference to equality of opportunity. No definition of equality of opportunity is offered, as if this notion were self-evident in its meaning. Yet, as we have seen in previous chapters, there is not an obscurer idea in our political vocabulary.

All of those interpretations of affirmative action which push for hiring women and minorities at rates greater than their proportions in the relevant labor pools in order to "promptly achieve full utilization," though they invoke the idea of equal opportunity, have the most disputable connection with such a goal. If they can claim any underlying conception of equal opportunity at all, it is the idea of Actuarial Equal Opportunity. But this conception, as we saw in Chapter Ten, is a pseudo-conception of equal opportunity. It is really a conception of equal results applied to groups. The court in *Germann* v. *Kipp* was more candid than most government rhetoric in exposing the real rationale for its defense of preferential affirmative action: "Properly applied, affirmative action seeks not just equality as a right and a theory but equality as a fact and equality as a *result*" (*Germann* at 1341).

The extensions, expansions, reinterpretations, and shifts of the law since 1964 and 1965 have resulted not from forceful argument among representative bodies but from judicial decisions and bureaucratic initiative. Yet, the outcome is law very different from that foreseen by Congress in 1964. To interpret Congressional legislation promoting "equal opportunity" as a mandate to pursue, through reverse discrimination if necessary, the goal of "equality of result" is not merely to extend or develop or interpret Congressional intent but to substitute one distinct substantive aim for another.

Because the law is inchoate and has developed without debate and reveals no articulate principled foundation, we cannot attach to it a moral authority which would guide us in reaching a conclusion about the rights and wrongs of reverse discrimination. Law which represents no more than mere power to enforce a policy never has moral authority.

But suppose all were otherwise. Suppose statutes and regulations and interpretations added up to a body of clear and cogent law supporting preferential hiring. There would still remain a legal and moral problem. Under the American political-legal system, legislation which violates the Constitution is not law at all. Thus, even if Congress tomorrow legislated unequivocally in favor of preferential hiring, we could not say that preferential hiring is legal until we had satisfied ourselves that it is constitutional. Thus, it is time we turned to the question of race and the Constitution.

13

Discrimination and the Constitution

Does the Constitution permit preferential hiring? Does it prohibit all discrimination on the basis of race? Does it guarantee equality of opportunity? Does it provide a right to equal consideration in employment (RTEC)?[1]

The Fourteenth Amendment to the Constitution guarantees to each person "the equal protection of the laws."[2] This Amendment, which is the only place in the Constitution where equality is spoken of, has been used by the Supreme Court, beginning with the watershed decision in *Brown* v. *Board of Education* in 1954, to attack the whole structure of racial distinctions and preferences that permeated American law and social practices. As far back as the 19th century, however, Justice Harlan had urged the view that the Amendment forbade racial distinctions of the sort not struck down until the 1950s and 1960s. In his famous dissent in *Plessy* v. *Ferguson* in 1896, he had said: "Our Constitution is color-blind, and neither knows nor tolerates classes among citizens."[3]

If the Constitution is color-blind and the Fourteenth Amendment does not tolerate racial distinctions, what then of court orders and consent decrees and federal regulations which require or permit racially preferential hiring? In handing down their orders and in defending their decrees, the lower courts have seen the need to make at least some passing attempt to square their decisions with the Constitution, but their efforts have been half-hearted and have not been notably successful in clarifying the principle of equal protection. One court in 1967 tried to set matters straight this way:

The Constitution is both color-blind and color-conscious. To avoid conflict with the equal protection clause, a classification that denies a benefit, causes a harm, or imposes a burden must not be based on race. In that sense the Constitution is color-blind. But the Constitution is color-conscious to prevent discrimination being perpetuated and to undo the effects of past discrimination. The criterion is the relevancy of color to a legitimate governmental purpose.[4]

This leaves something to be desired as a clarification.

Although the Supreme Court has decided a great many cases dealing with race, it has never decided a constitutional challenge to the practice of preferring blacks in hiring. Thus, the lower courts have had to undertake the defense of racial quotas without benefit of a direct authoritative precedent. By and large, the individual courts devote little effort to the constitutional question; they are content to rely upon a small number of appellate decisions which are invariably cited as proof of the constitutionality of their orders. These influential decisions, however, are themselves unpersuasive and badly argued.[5] The need for the Supreme Court to directly address the constitutionality of preferential hiring is pressing. In the meanwhile, we must try to draw constitutional inferences from the Court's other equal protection decisions.

THE SUPREME COURT AND THE FOURTEENTH AMENDMENT

What does "the equal protection of the laws" command? It cannot command that the laws treat all (literally) equally. Such a command would subvert the very process of legislation. "The legislature, if it is to act at all, must impose special burdens upon or grant special benefits to special groups or classes of individuals."[6] To interpret "equal protection" so that it would, for example, prohibit legislating tax relief for the elderly would be absurd. Thus, however we are to understand it, constitutional equality must be compatible with laws which impose differential obligations and confer differential rights.

Perhaps, then, equal protection commands not that all be treated equally but that all who are equal be treated equally. This might be taken two ways. We might take it to mean that government should treat similarly all the members of a class defined by legislation. However, since the legislature can define statutory classes as narrowly or broadly as it pleases, this way of understanding equal protection emasculates it as a standard for evaluating the validity of legislation. Thus, it is better to take the command to treat equally all who are equal to mean that the government should treat similarly those who are similarly situated with respect to legislative goals.[7] With some qualifications, this is, indeed, essentially the standard used by the Supreme Court. It applies a "rational basis test" to most legislation, asking if a legitimate state purpose is served by the statute under review and if the classification embodied in the statute is reasonably related to that purpose.[8] The classification, however, need not perfectly include all of those similarly situated with respect to the purposes of the statute nor perfectly exclude all those dissimilarly situated.[9] Moreover, it is a well-established rule that Congress may attack one part of a problem without attacking all parts.[10]

When the Court applies the rational basis test, it seldom invalidates the legislation it is reviewing. It will sustain all but the most capricious and patently arbitrary classifications; "a discrimination will not be set aside if any state of facts reasonably may be conceived to justify it."[11] "[W]e will not overturn . . . a statute," the Court has written, "unless the varying treatment of different groups or persons is so unrelated to the achievement of any combination of legitimate purposes that we can only conclude that the legislature's actions were irrational."[12] It is quite evident that if the equal protection clause of the Fourteenth Amendment demanded no more than that legislatures make classifications that are reasonably related to their purposes, the standard of equal protection would place only the weakest of checks on governmental discrimination.

The equal protection clause has been used by the Court, however, to strike down countless state and federal laws which discriminated against blacks. It is clear that on some occasions the Court requires more of a legislated discrimination than that it serve more or less effectively some conceivable public purpose. If certain "triggering" factors are present in a challenged legislative classification, the Court will impose "strict scrutiny."[13] The triggering factors are of two sorts. First, the legislation under challenge may touch upon a "fundamental interest" or "fundamental right."[14] Second, the legislation may employ a "suspect classification."[15] If either triggering factor is present, the Court will require the legislation to meet a more stringent standard of justification than usual.

Consider, first, the approach to that legislation which bears unequally upon our fundamental interests. Many of our basic interests as persons and citizens are explicitly recognized and protected in the Bill of Rights—our interests in unrestricted speech, choice of religious worship, freedom from arbitrary search and seizure, and so on. However, the Supreme Court has also found in the Constitution other "fundamental interests," or rights, deserving protection against state interference. For example, the Court has discerned a right to privacy although neither that word nor a synonym is mentioned in the Constitution.[16]

The Court has struck down several statutes in Fourteenth Amendment cases because they unequally affected other fundamental interests that it has found in the Constitution. Found to be fundamental are interests in voting *(Reynolds v. Sims, Harper v. Virginia Board of Elections)*, interstate travel *(Shapiro v. Thompson, United States v. Guest)*, access to criminal appeal procedures *(Griffin v. Illinois, Bounds v. Smith)*, procreation and family companionship *(Skinner v. Oklahoma ex. rel. Williamson, Weinberger v. Wiesenfeld)*.

When a discriminatory policy touches upon a recognized fundamental interest, it cannot be justified unless the state can demonstrate that the policy is indispensable to the promotion of a "compelling state interest."[17] When the Court imposes this standard of justification, challenged legislation is not likely to survive.[18]

Why have interests in travel, voting, procreation, and so on, been identified by the Court as deserving special protection against legislated inequality? It is hard to find a rationale in the Court's decisions. Many have criticized the Court's willingness to raise certain interests to the status of constitutional rights for no other apparent reason than that it deemed them very important. In a 1969 dissent, Justice Harlan argued that "when a statute affects only matters *not* mentioned in the Federal Constitution and is not arbitrary or irrational . . . I know of nothing which entitles this Court to pick out particular activities, characterizing them as 'fundamental', and give them added protection under an unusually stringent equal protection test" *(Shapiro v. Thompson* at 662). In a 1973 decision the Court appeared to take this criticism seriously. Writing for the majority in *San Antonio v. Rodriguez,* Justice Powell declared: "It is not the province of this Court to create substantive constitutional rights in the name of guaranteeing equal protection of the laws" *(San Antonio* at 33). He denied that "importance" of an interest was a criterion of fundamentality and that the Court had ever "made up" rights not already found in the Constitution. Although Powell's avowals may have signaled a drawing back of the Court from the development of the fundamental interest approach to equal protection, they left unclear how the recognized fundamental rights are to be accounted for.

In any case, what is important for our immediate purposes is that the Court has never recognized any fundamental rights to employment or employment opportunities. There is no constitutionally protected right like RTEC. The Court has been quite willing to uphold legislation which established employment favoritism or preference. For example, in *Kotch* v. *Pilot Commissioners,* it held that a Louisiana law which allowed state-appointed river pilots to "select their relatives and friends as the only ones ultimately eligible for appointment as pilots" did not violate the Fourteenth Amendment. The Louisiana practice, held the Court, "is not without relation to the objective of securing . . . the safest and most efficiently operated pilotage system practicable" (*Kotch* at 553). The Court reasoned that

the advantages of early experience under friendly supervision in the locality of the pilot's training, the benefits to morale and *esprit de corps* which family and neighborly tradition might contribute, the close association in which pilots must work and live in their pilot communities and on water, and the discipline and regulation which is imposed to assure the State competent pilot service after appointment, might have prompted the legislature to permit Louisiana pilot officers to select those with whom they would serve. (*Kotch* at 563.)

The Court offered this as a conceivable set of facts that connected the practice to legitimate aims of safety and efficiency. That this was sufficient to justify the practice indicates that the Court applied the very weakest test to the challenged statute, not the kind of stringent standard called for when a statute touches upon a fundamental interest.

That employment interests have never been accorded the

status of constitutionally fundamental is quite evident from the long history of legal acceptance of veteran's preference in public employment. Giving preferences to veterans has been a feature of public employment for most of this century, and it has been subject to many legal challenges. These challenges have typically invoked the equal protection clause. In a recent case, the plaintiff urged that a provision of the Pennsylvania Veteran's Preference Act which granted a ten-point bonus to the score of any veteran passing the state civil service examination violated the Fourteenth Amendment rights of non-veterans, in particular the "right to be fairly considered in public employment" (*Feinerman* v. *Jones* at 257). The court conceded that the practice of preferring veterans denied the plaintiff "the opportunity to be considered equally with veterans," but denied "that the abstract right to be fairly considered for public employment is a fundamental right for the purposes of equal protection analysis."[19] The right to fair or equal consideration in employment was not among the fundamental rights discoverable in the Constitution.[20]

Now, if as a matter of constitutional law the government need not be fair or equal in its own hiring practices (subject to qualifications about suspect classifications to be discussed shortly), then it will surely be difficult to infer from the Constitution any general right of an applicant to be given a job if he is demonstrably the best qualified for it. Nothing like RTEC has constitutional recognition under the regnant doctrine of equal protection. Employment practices which may seem unfair to those excluded from effective competition may serve social goals. This should be enough to defend those policies under the rational basis test. Government policies which result in employment preferences for some will not trigger strict scrutiny by the Supreme Court—not unless the policies touch upon some other interest which the Court has designated as fundamental or unless they use *suspect classifications*.

SUSPECT CLASSIFICATION APPROACH

Generally, the Supreme Court will ask of a legislative classification whether it is reasonably related to a state purpose. Some classifications, however, have been identified as inherently questionable, as "suspect." When legislation employs a "suspect classification," the state must carry a "heavy burden of justification";[21] such a classification must serve a "substantial regulatory interest,"[22] "an appreciable public interest,"[23] or "some overriding statutory purpose."[24] Although suspect classifications must stand against a heightened judicial scrutiny, the Court has never made precise the more stringent standard to be used, adopting different phraseology in different decisions. In *San Antonio* v. *Rodriguez* (1973), the Court appeared to assimilate the test for suspect classifications to the test for legislation touching upon fundamental interests: the classification must be necessary to serve some compelling state interest (*San Antonio* at 17–18).

The primary suspect classification is race (*McLaughlin* v. *Florida, Loving* v. *Virginia*). Other classifications that are suspect, or virtually so, are those based on national origin (*Hernandez* v. *Texas, Korematsu* v. *United States*), alienage (*In re Griffiths, Sugarman* v. *Dougall, Graham* v. *Richardson*), illegitimacy (*Levy* v. *Louisiana, Glona* v. *American Guar. & Liab. Co.*). Sex has not yet been firmly established as a suspect classification; Supreme Court decisions are undecided on this. Nevertheless, classifications based on gender are subject to heightened scrutiny and must meet more than the rational basis test.[25]

The Supreme Court, then, will approach constitutional questions raised by preferential treatment of blacks in employment by way of its suspect classifications doctrine rather than by way of its fundamental interests doctrine. If Title VII or E.O. 11246 actually permit or require the use of racial preferences, how might we expect the Court to respond to a constitutional challenge?

RACE AND THE CONSTITUTION

The state's use of a racial classification will be viewed with special severity by the Court. Critics of reverse discrimination would urge the Court to prohibit any use of race by the state. They are fond of quoting Justice Harlan's famous remark in *Plessy* v. *Ferguson* that the Constitution is color-blind. They take this to mean that the equal protection clause categorically forbids the use of race. Any use of racial quotas is unconstitutional.

Although this view is popular, it does not square with the Supreme Court's own decisions. It has never said that the use of race is by itself always unconstitutional. On several occasions it has permitted the explicit use of race (although none of these uses touched on employment). In *Swann* v. *Charlotte-Mecklenburg Board of Education,* the Court upheld a plan whereby children were assigned to schools within the school district on the basis of race. The aim of the plan was to bring about a racial balance in the schools of a previously segregated system. Similar plans involving racial assignments and busing have been sustained by the Court.[26]

A more recent case was *United Jewish Organization of Williamsburgh, Inc.* v. *Carey.* In order to achieve full compliance with the Voting Rights Act of 1965, the New York State legislature redrew legislative districts in Kings County to enhance black voting strength in the districts. The Supreme Court sustained the New York plan, agreeing that the state's purposeful use of race to comply with the Voting Rights Act did not violate the Fourteenth Amendment (*United Jewish* at 1009–1010).

Finally, in the recent, much-publicized decision in *Regents of University of California* v. *Bakke,* the Court, although invalidating the specific racially preferential admissions procedure used by the Medical School at Davis, appeared to approve of some uses of race in admitting candidates into professional schools. In three different ways, then, the Court has permitted race to be used as a factor in government action: in assigning children to public schools, in fixing the boundaries of voting districts, and in selecting applicants for admission to institutions of higher education.

If the Constitution permits some use of race, what is the principle that distinguishes permissible from impermissible uses? How are we to fit different cases into the Court's analytic framework? In looking at the Court's decisions, we find uncertainty here. The standard against which racial classifications are to be judged remains vague.

In *Bakke,* Justice Powell declared that when political policies "touch upon an individual's race or ethnic background, he is entitled to a judicial determination that the burden he is asked to bear is precisely tailored to serve a compelling governmental interest" (2753). Now, this is the standard that, when deployed in fundamental interest cases, invariably proves "insurmountable" (in the words of Chief Justice Burger). If the standard is one of such extreme stringency, then our expectation would be that when it is applied to racial classifications the use of such classifications will never surmount the standard either, except in extreme or emergency situations.[27]

However, it would be a mistake to stand on that expectation. The standard is too vague for us to conclude that the state interests to be served must be *literally* compelling. In the *Bakke* case, for example, Justice Powell held that "the interest of [student body] diversity is compelling in the context of a university's admissions program" (2761). He held against the preferential admissions scheme at Davis not because he judged the school's use of race to serve no compelling interest but because, in his view, its use of racial preferences was unnecessary (2761-2764).

Other goals the university might have had, such as producing more minority doctors or increasing the number of doctors who practice in minority communities, were found by Powell not to be "compelling" (2757-2761).[28] It would seem, on the face of it, that these goals are intrinsically more valuable than the goal of an "ethnically diverse student body." What raised this relatively modest interest (among a university's many interests) to a higher significance was the fact that it attached to the university's interest in shaping the quality of its educational offering, this latter being an interest protected by the First Amendment. Even under such an umbrella, however, it is difficult to understand what is "compelling" about the interest in student diversity.

It is a mistake to look for literalness in the Court's expressions of its standard for judging suspect classifications. For example, in *Bakke* Justice Powell first expressed his standard of review as requiring that a racial policy be "precisely tailored to serve a compelling governmental interest," then re-expressed the same standard as requiring that such a policy be "necessary to promote a substantial state interest" (2764). The phrases that occur in the Court's many decisions— "compelling state interest," "substantial state interest," "appreciable public interest," "overriding legislative purpose," and so on—must not be viewed as descriptions of a test but as alternative designators for a test whose character remains largely opaque. We can say that a state interest has to be non-trivial in order to justify a racial classification, but the exact threshold of seriousness is left mysterious.

The vagueness of the standard for reviewing racial classifications is due partly to the particular history of its development. From 1954, when the Court began to use the Fourteenth Amendment extensively in attacking racial segregation, until 1971, every racial classification that came before the court was found unconstitutional. In dealing with a vast array of segregation legislation, the Court felt no need, one surmises, to be precise about its standard of review because it could not conceive of any discrimination against blacks which might pass the test. It is only in the past half-dozen years that the Court has begun to encounter uses of race to benefit blacks rather than harm them, and it has not succeeded in making clear the principles underlying its responses to these cases. *Swann* and *United Jewish Organization* turned primarily on the need for public agencies to bring themselves into compliance with the law. Only the *Bakke* decision attempts to spell out the nature of the general standard to be applied to racial policies which benefit blacks, and it does not succeed in clarifying the matter.

The vagueness of the standard of review used in *Bakke* (and in other cases) is troubling. It calls forth a question: in what circumstances would legislation which favored whites over blacks pass constitutional muster? Could there be circumstances in which a college could exclude blacks in order to attain diversity? If the race of a black can be considered a positive factor in some decisions, can it not be a negative factor in others? If the standard of review is terribly vague, how can the Court know it is applying the standard consistently?

These problems in describing the standard of review in cases like *Bakke* are generated by the fact that racial classifications apparently require "strict scrutiny" and thus must be tested more stringently than ordinary legislation. But why must all racial classifications be subject to strict scrutiny? Why may not racial classifications which benefit blacks be viewed with less hostility than those which harm them?

This is what the University of California tried to persuade the Court to believe in *Bakke*. It urged that strict scrutiny should be reserved for legislative classifications and state policies that disadvantage minorities (2747). When the use of race disadvantages only some members of a majority, the Court should apply the same test it applies in most cases: the rational basis test. Not all uses of race should be viewed as "suspect."

This position would make it easy constitutionally to justify some forms of reverse discrimination. But it faces one obvious objection: it seems to make the equal protection clause express a double-standard. How can it be plausible to interpret a principle of equality in this paradoxical way?

Special Protection. One way might be to argue that the Fourteenth Amendment must be interpreted in light of its original purpose, which was to accord special protection to the rights and liberties of the newly freed blacks. In the *Slaughter-House Cases* of 1873, five years after the Fourteenth Amendment was adopted, Justice Miller wrote that

in light of . . . events, almost too recent to be called history, but which are familiar to us all; and on the most casual examination of these amendments, no one can fail to be impressed with the one pervading purpose . . .; we mean the freedom of the slave race, the security and the firm establishment of that freedom, and the protection of the newly made freeman and citizen from the oppression of those who had formerly exercised unlimited dominion over him.

Miller went on to predict: "We doubt very much whether any action of a state not directed by way of discrimination against negroes as a class, or on account of their race, will ever be held to come within the purview of this provision" (referring to the enforcement clause of the Fourteenth Amendment).[29]

Some modern commentators have similarly urged that the interpretation of the equal protection clause be governed by the intent and purposes of the framers of the Amendment. One, for example, indicates that the "dominant purpose of the framers was to achieve for blacks and other minority groups . . . freedom from their racial underclass status by obtaining their equality with whites," and argues from this that the Amendment "must be construed in light of the social ends which the framers sought to achieve."[30] To so construe the Amendment would, presumably, allow us to treat racial preferences asymmetrically. Whereas white-favoring policies would be subject to strict scrutiny, black-favoring policies would not, since the latter could often serve the "social ends which the framers sought to achieve."

Does this line of argument overcome the paradox inherent in interpreting equal protection as permitting a racial double-standard? There is no question that the Fourteenth Amendment was framed in light of the special problems facing the newly emancipated blacks and that it was aimed at protecting their rights. This does not require, however, that we view the Fourteenth Amendment as limited in its purpose to protecting the rights of blacks (Justice Miller's view), nor that we read the Amendment as expressing a double-standard, nor that we restrict its interpretation to the intentions of the framers.

In light of the history of Supreme Court decisions under the Fourteenth Amendment, such views are not plausible. Justice Miller's prediction has not been borne out. The Fourteenth Amendment has been applied to issues and classifications having nothing to do with race. For example, the Supreme Court has applied the equal protection clause to the rights of women,[31] to legislative apportionment,[32] and to the rights of criminal defendants.[33] Achieving equality for women was not among the "social aims" of the framers, nor was interference with the manner in which states drew their electoral districts or organized their criminal procedures.

Moreover, it is even dubious that the racial equality envisioned by the framers was the same as the racial equality today protected by the Court. Indeed, when in 1953 the Supreme Court asked the parties to *Brown* v. *Board of Education* to submit briefs on the history of the debate on the adoption of the Fourteenth Amendment, the NAACP found that there was little evidence of a uniform understanding at the time of adoption that the Amendment would imply the integration of schools. In fact, there was evidence that many of the framers believed that the Amendment would not require black and white children to attend school together.[34] Given the prevailing social beliefs in the 1860s, there is no reason to believe that those who wrote, debated, and adopted the Fourteenth Amendment shared the same view of racial equality as that possessed by modern Americans.

The Supreme Court is justified in not hewing slavishly to the framers' intent because whatever their specific and multiple purposes, the framers cast the Amendment in perfectly general language. [35] Unless we judge that they did not understand what they were doing, we must assume that their choice of broad, sweeping language was deliberate and that they were willing for future generations to construe that language on its own terms.[36] An interpretation of equal protection must stand on its own, deriving its persuasiveness from the cogency and power of the conception of equality which it expresses. Without some more compelling ground than appeal to what the framers had in mind, it is objectionable to construe the principle of constitutional equality as a principle of unequal protection!

Insular Minorities. The University of California presented a different argument for the Court's adopting a double-standard of scrutiny for racial classifications. It relied not on the framers' intent but on a prior characterization by the Supreme Court of the Fourteenth Amendment as a tool to combat "prejudice against discrete and insular minorities . . . which tends seriously to curtail the operation of those political processes ordinarily relied upon to protect minorities, and which may well call for a correspondingly more searching judicial inquiry."[37] Since the racial preferences at Davis, argued the University of California, did not adversely affect any "insular minority," they did not require a "more searching judicial inquiry" (*Bakke*, 2747–2748).

Justice Powell rejected this argument. "Racial and ethnic distinctions of any sort are inherently suspect," he wrote, "and thus call for the most exacting judicial examination" (2749). Historically, the Court has viewed equal protection rights as individual rights (2748);[38] it has treated the guarantees of equal protection as universal in their application (2750); and it has consistently viewed racial classifications with suspicion. "It is far too late," concluded Powell, "to argue that the guarantee of equal protection to *all* persons permits the recognition of special wards entitled to a degree of protection greater than that accorded others" (2751).[39]

Apart from these considerations, Powell noted one further difficulty with what he termed the "two-class theory" of the Fourteenth Amendment. This theory requires that we be able to distinguish those minorities which deserve special protection from those which do not. But, Powell points out:

There is no principled basis for deciding which groups would merit "heightened judicial solicitude" and which would not. Courts would be asked to evaluate the extent of the prejudice and consequent harm suffered by various minority groups. Those whose societal injury is thought to exceed some arbitrary level of tolerability then would be entitled to preferential classifications at the expense of individuals belonging to other groups. Those classifications would be free from exacting judicial scrutiny. As these preferences began to have their desired effect, and the consequences of past discriminations were undone, new judicial rankings would be necessary. (2751–2752.)

The weight of the Court lies against the double-standard interpretation of equal protection.

THE BRENNAN-WHITE THESIS

The rejection of the double-standard approach does not, however, exhaust the possibilities for viewing some uses of race with less hostility than other uses. There are real distinctions to be made among different uses of racial preferences. There is no *a priori* reason why every racial classification should receive the same response or even be tested against the same standard. Unless the "compelling state interest" test is actually a sliding scale of standards, one may ask why it should be the sole test of racial classifications. There is an alternative approach which is at least as cogent and which seems to me more desirable.

Justice White, writing the majority opinion in *United Jewish Organization*, said:

There is no doubt that . . . the State [of New York] used race in a purposeful manner. But its plan represented *no racial slur or stigma* with respect to whites or any other race, and we discern no violation of the Fourteenth Amendment. . . . (*United Jewish* at 1009–1010. Emphasis added.)

In a separate, concurring opinion Justice Brennan made the same point. He held that equal protection was not violated because New York's actions were made "in a remedial context with respect to a disadvantaged class rather than in a setting that *aims to demean or insult any racial group.*" Had the state's behavior been "motivated by racial animus," the Court, claimed Brennan, would have come to a different conclusion (*United Jewish* at 1012; emphasis added).

Brennan advanced a similar argument, concurred in by White, in *Bakke*. Although the Court invalidated the particular admissions scheme used by the Medical School at Davis, "this should not and must not," urged Brennan, "mask the central meaning of today's opinions: Government may take race into account when it acts not to demean or insult any racial group, but to remedy disadvantages cast on minorities by past racial prejudice . . ." (*Bakke* at 2766).

Implicit in these assertions is the idea that racial classifications can be either demeaning or non-demeaning and that non-demeaning uses of race are more tolerable than demeaning uses. There is the idea that, although all uses of race require heightened judicial scrutiny, stigmatizing uses of race must be measured against a more stringent test than other uses. Not every use of race is suspect, although every use must meet more than the rational basis test. When classifications express an official hostility or antipathy toward a race or foster stigmatizing racial stereotypes, they are particularly pernicious.[40] When a use of race is non-stigmatizing and when it does not harm a relatively powerless minority, the use should be measured against a lesser test than the "insurmountable" compelling state interest test. Instead, the state should be required to show "an important and articulated purpose for its use" of race and must show a "substantial relationship" between the use and the purpose (*Bakke* at 2785).

Brennan and White (along with Justices Marshall and Blackmun) found the admissions scheme at the Davis Medical School to be constitutionally acceptable. Although the scheme arguably excluded Allan Bakke because of his race, the Medical School policy did not "stigmatize" Bakke with the badge of racial inferiority. The policy was aimed, moreover, at increasing the number of black professionals, an aim of no small importance for our society.

The Brennan-White approach, thus, allows some uses of race to meet a lesser judicial test. When a racial classification stigmatizes or implies state antipathy, it must be shown to be utterly necessary to a compelling state need. When a racial classification does not stigmatize or imply hostility, it must be shown to serve an important state interest, one with which the classification is substantially connected. Some uses of race might meet this test.

Justice Powell included the Brennan-White approach under his condemnation of the "two-class theory" (*Bakke* at 2751, note 34). However, he is mistaken in viewing it as another double-standard interpretation. On a double-standard approach there is more than one standard of constitutional review, and what determines the strength of the standard to be used to test legislation which racially discriminates against an individual is the individual's race. On the Brennan-White thesis (as I have construed it) there are likewise multiple standards of review, but the criterion for applying one standard rather than another is racially neutral. It is the effects of the tested legislation which are relevant. Legislation which stigmatizes any individual, black or white, must meet one test, legislation which does not must meet another. The Brennan-White approach merely elaborates the already standard approach of the Court in applying the rational basis test to some legislation and one or more stronger tests to other legislation. There is no reason why the Court may not use various judicial tests. So long as the application of the tests is not geared to the racial identity of individuals, the use of multiple tests involves no racial double-standard.

However, the use of the Brennan-White approach will produce outcomes not dissimilar to those produced by the use of a double-standard. That is, it will tend to treat discrimination against whites less harshly than it has treated past discrimination against blacks. This does not reflect, however, the use of a double-standard; it simply reflects that as a matter of fact past discrimination against blacks has been stigmatizing, demeaning, and motivated by racial antipathy, while as a matter of fact recent discrimination against whites has not. Powell's strictures against the double-standard interpretation of equal protection do not tell against the Brennan-White thesis.

CONCLUSIONS

I suggested that the Brennan-White approach to the use of race is more promising than Powell's. This may be a mistake. It may be that the same results gotten from the Brennan-White approach can be gotten from the proper application of the compelling state interest test. Or, it may be that the proper application of the Brennan-White test should condemn racial schemes like the one at Davis, just as the compelling state interest standard would. What makes this so speculative is that neither approach is articulated with enough precision to generate deductive consequences. As a result, it is far from obvious what conclusions should be drawn on either approach.

To think that things have been made clearer by speaking of "important interests" and "substantial connections" rather than "compelling interests" and "necessary connections" is to be mesmerized by word-play. We can, at least in the context of

Bakke, see that Brennan's group is willing to view "benign" racial classifications with more tolerance than "malign" ones. We may presume that Powell does not view the two uses of race as on par, but he nevertheless appears to be more hostile toward even "good" uses of race than the Brennan group. This much, of course, is obvious from the opinions in the case. I believe that we can say very little more about the exact differences between the standards they used in their opinions.

This much, I think, can be said. The Court's past decisions on equal protection do not constrain it to reject a multiple approach to race like that suggested by the Brennan-White thesis. There is much to be said for avoiding a rigid or clumsy standard of review in dealing with racial policies because the factors that make one use of race an affront to equality may not be present in another use. Clearly the moral quality of racial preferences designed to help minorities victimized by past discrimination is different from the moral quality of racial preferences designed to oppress them. There is room in the Court's opinions to take an approach to racial classifications which reflects this moral difference. There is, in its doctrine, room for the Court to approve a program like the one which excluded Brian Weber or the one which excluded Allan Bakke.

As a matter of fact, the Court did not approve of the program at the Medical School at Davis. The *Bakke* decision, however, cannot be considered the last word about the constitutionality of racial preferences. In that decision, only five justices examined the constitutional question, and four of them were disposed to approve the Medical School's use of race (Brennan, White, Marshall, and Blackmun). The other four justices (Stevens, Burger, Stewart, and Rehnquist) found the Medical School program illegal under Title VI of the Civil Rights Act of 1964. Thus, the constitutional disapproval of the California program rested on the singular judgment of Justice Powell.

14

Moral and Constitutional Equality

INTRODUCTION

Even if the Supreme Court can find within its past decisions a constitutional justification for some reverse discrimination, the moral authority for such a holding will be insecure. This is because the Court is vague about its standards of review and has not articulated the underlying principles which organize and unify them. The basic grounds for protecting some interests against inequality remain obscure. The basic principles which make all racial classifications questionable and some of them intolerable are undeveloped. When the members of the Court fall into disagreement, there is no ready body of doctrine with the power to resolve the differences.

If the critic of reverse discrimination persists in believing that all racially preferential policies are unconstitutional, he must do so because he has some idea of basic equality which the use of race violates. If the Court finds some racial classifications permissible, this must be because it presupposes some idea of equality compatible with some uses of race. The dispute between the critic and the Court about the constitutionality of racial preferences cannot be answered, then, without asking which conception of equality is to be preferred. Do the Court's decisions flow from a rich, powerful, and defensible view of equality—a view which it has not yet successfully articulated—or from one that is confused and inadequate?

To seek to unify the Court's decisions under a plausible and attractive conception of equality is to return to moral theorizing. This brings us full circle. Earlier, in Chapter Nine, we broke away from moral investigations because they seemed to lead us into controversies we could not solve. We turned at that point to the law, with the hope that there we might find at least a clear expression of public will. This has turned out to be a vain hope. The law is confused, unclear, its interpretation muddled and frequently arbitrary, its enforcement uneven. Far from representing public debate and public consensus, much of the law has been "made" by courts, executive departments of government, and other nonrepresentative agencies.

Neither have we found constitutional interpretation to be the hoped-for alternative to moral theorizing. On the contrary, it is now apparent that moral notions such as equality are deeply implicated in interpreting and applying the Fourteenth Amendment and that interpretations which stop short of laying bare their moral bases will fail to satisfy. If we are to resolve the constitutional debate between the critic and the Court, we have to ask which overall moral view of equality is to be preferred, how this view is to yield a constitutional principle, and how this constitutional principle can justify the Court's decisions.

MORAL EQUALITY

Nearly every moral theory seeks in some way to give recognition to a *basic moral equality among persons*. Different theories explain this equality in different ways and translate it into different social and political demands.

One view of basic equality underlies the social utility approach to policy applied to preferential hiring in Chapter Eight. Under this approach, political decisions are defended by reference to the public interest. The negative and positive impacts of alternative policies on members of the community are weighed and the policy having the most favorable overall effect is preferred. Underlying this approach is the idea that in calculating the effect on people's interests of alternative policies, "each person is to count for one and none for more than one." Moral equality is taken to require that, when policy is justified by a summation process in which positive and negative effects on people are aggregated into a total, the interests of each person contribute in the same way to the summation.[1]

A society could fail to act according to this principle of moral equality. If it chose policies on the basis of their calculated capacity to promote welfare, but systematically failed to include the interests of certain individuals in the calculation, or systematically undervalued their interests, it would not treat all of its members as moral equals. Some people and their interests would simply count for less, not in the sense that their interests could be overridden by the combined greater interests of others but by the fact that their interests would not count at all or would not count the same.

Even when "equality in counting" is preserved, however, it is still the case that the interests of some can be outweighed by the interests of others, just as in a vote some can be outvoted by others. The whole society might be made better off by making some of its members relatively worse off. Where the social utility approach is the only guide to policy, it is possible that an individual could find his most pressing claims and most intense preferences continually defeated. Groups of individuals could find themselves in the same position, permanently outvoted in the calculation of maximum utility. Policies that promote total welfare will not always, or even usually, satisfy in the same way or to the same degree the desires of everyone. Consequently, the moral equality presupposed by the social utility approach is compatible with varying kinds of *unequal treatment*.

The fact that a principle of equality tolerates unequal treatment should not be objectionable by itself. Strictly equal treatment in every regard is impossible in organized society and, if possible, would be undesirable. There are countless ways in which government legitimately distinguishes among its citizens, classifying, sorting, registering, separating, labeling, certifying, and licensing them for differential obligations, rewards, penalties, and so on. Any feasible principle of moral equality will allow some unequal treatment. Even so, the idea of moral equality that underlies the social utility approach seems too permissive of inequality. In principle, at least, "equality in counting" is compatible with unacceptably extreme sacrifices being imposed upon some of us for the benefit of all the rest.

It is not surprising, therefore, that the social utility approach is hedged about—both in political theories and in the constitutions of actual states—by systems of personal rights which limit the reach of social utility justifications. From such systems we quite naturally derive the idea of "equal rights." For example, we believe that all persons ought to be equal before the law. There should be no person or group formally excluded as not deserving due process, access to legal proceedings, benefit of counsel, and so on. Likewise, we would reject the idea of denying the franchise to some adults simply because it is socially beneficial to do so. There are limits to inequality of treatment. In some cases, treating people unequally will be wrong not because it diminishes social utility but because it violates moral equality itself.

If we believe this, then we must believe in some conception

of moral equality stronger than "equality in counting." The task is to give an account of this stronger moral equality and to explain its bearing on constitutional questions about racial preferences. In what follows, I shall sketch an account of a stronger conception of equality which is rooted in widely shared beliefs.

We can begin from the idea that the stronger moral equality will require some kinds of equal treatment as a matter of principle. A constitutional canon of equality must express the social implications of this moral requirement. But, because there are two distinct sources of equality, there are two different but complementary accounts we can give of a constitutional expression of moral equality.

BEING TREATED AS AN EQUAL

Consider first one motivation that leads us generally to approve limitations on social utility justifications of policy. We approve constraints, in the form of rights, which protect us against certain state incursions upon our persons, our property, and our liberty. Take an obvious example. No social system, merely because the balance of utility favors it, should be able to conscript a person's body for dangerous medical experimentation. Such conscription would surely be, in Kant's apt phrase, using a person "as a mere means," not "as an end in himself." To the extent that each of us desires to be treated as "ends" and not as "mere means," we each have a motive for approving of general moral principles against practices which threaten our bodies and liberties in ways that jeopardize our capacities to lead lives of our own making.

No person should be wholly at the disposal of the community to use as it will. A system of rights to personal liberty, bodily integrity, privacy, freedom of conscience, and so on, protects the dignity of the individual by identifying certain fundamental interests of persons and immunizing them against

direct state injury or invasion. A just constitution will give
legal protection to these "human rights." To the extent that
this "human rights" morality expresses a conception of moral
equality among persons, a just constitution will contain,
implicitly if not explicitly, a principle of equality.

Now, this "human rights" approach gives us one way of
understanding moral equality, of understanding what it is to be
treated as a moral equal. "Moral equality" means "equality of
human rights." The equality of rights is entailed by the very
form of the human rights themselves: they are universal in
scope, applying to everybody.

For example, any just constitution ought to contain an
explicit or implicit prohibition against the state's use of torture
to obtain criminal confessions. Suppose a state nevertheless
tortures an individual. We can say, then, that the right not to be
tortured is being violated. But we can also say something else:
we can say that the victim is *not being treated as an equal* in that
he is not being treated as immune from torture, as *all individuals ought to be treated*! Because the human right against being
tortured is universal in scope, a constitutional expression of the
right must apply equally to each individual within the state's
jurisdiction.

We may say, then, that in torturing an individual the state
violates moral and constitutional equality (assuming its constitution is just). This is equality understood in a *non-
comparative* way.[2] The violation of equality in the case of the
tortured individual lies not in the fact that he is tortured when
others are not but in the fact, simply, that he is tortured. The
state does not relieve its violation of equality in this case by
proceeding to torture every criminal suspect; it only multiplies
the violation.

The fundamental moral equality of persons, then, may mean
just that there are certain universal human rights which ought
to be part of the structure of any just state. "Being treated as a
moral equal" comes to "being treated as required by one's

human rights." On this view of moral equality, an explicit rule of constitutional equality, such as the equal protection clause of the Fourteenth Amendment, does not *add* anything distinct from and independent of the other rights (to liberty, security, due process, etc.) already enumerated in or implied by other provisions of the constitution. Since these other constitutional rights apply to all citizens, their form already entails their equal application. The explicit principle of constitutional equality serves only a rhetorical purpose, reminding us of the nature of other constitutional principles.

If strong moral equality is to be understood in this non-comparative way, then the "fundamental interests" approach to the Fourteenth Amendment is obviously primary. The Supreme Court serves "equal protection" when it correctly identifies rights explicitly or implicitly assigned by the Constitution and then applies those rights in their full universality.

This conception of moral equality as "equality of human rights" seems a desirable advance over "equality in counting." Our next step would appear to be to apply this strong conception of moral equality to the constitutional questions about preferential hiring. However, before we do so we should discuss a possible dimension of moral equality not captured in the human rights account.

On the latter view, the constitutional principle of equality requires equal treatment—i.e., equal application of rights—for the sake of liberty, or personal security, or due process, or bodily integrity, or some other similar individual value. The equal treatment is never required simply for the sake of equality itself. But there can be principles of equality which have equal treatment as their content, not as merely an implication of their form. These principles are egalitarian in nature; they are principles of *comparative* equality. Comparative equality necessarily makes reference to the way individuals are treated in relation to one another. An example of a comparative principle is one requiring equal incomes. Equality is violated if different persons make different incomes, even if each earns an amount amply sufficient to maintain a high standard of living.

In applying this principle of incomes, we cannot know whether it is violated by knowing only the income of one person. We must know how others are faring as well. This is unlike the case with non-comparative equality. There, we can identify a violation without knowing how others are treated in relation to the victim. When a person is being tortured, we know there is a violation regardless of whether others are similarly tortured or not.

When a principle of comparative equality is being violated, the violation can be remedied by eliminating the relevant *differences* in treatment. For example, if C earns less than A and B, this violation of the incomes principle is relieved equally by lowering A and B to the level of C as by raising C to the level of A and B. As we have already remarked, the situation is different with non-comparative equality; when an individual is tortured, things are not made better by extending torture to others.

EQUALITY AND CITIZENSHIP

Does the moral equality of persons have a comparative dimension? Our intuitions on this matter would suggest so. Under a just constitution, each person must be accorded *equal standing* as a citizen. There is no place for second-class citizenship. Full citizenship, moreover, involves comparative as well as non-comparative equality.

What do I mean by equal standing? What I have in mind is illustrated in the operations of clubs and fraternal organizations. An individual is admitted into *full membership* in a club when he has the right to participate fully both in the primary activities and benefits of the club and in those special forms and rituals through which members symbolically acknowledge each other as equals—as "brothers" and "sisters." Junior or associate or auxiliary membership is typically signified by exclusion from full participation. Auxiliary or associate members do not have the same standing as full members; and this inequality of standing derives from the inequality in participation.

It is the same with citizenship. Full citizenship means the right to full social participation. This means more than the right to vote or hold office; it means the right to participate in the dominant cultural, religious, and educational activities in society. If playing in major symphony orchestras, starring in Hollywood productions, participating in major league baseball, attending Ivy League colleges, piloting jet fighters, exhibiting in important museums and galleries, and so on, are barred to a group, then the group is truly excluded from full participation in American life.

Now, it can be argued that laws which exclude people from major areas of social life violate their basic liberties and that the right to full participation just consists in these non-comparative liberties. Nothing said so far suggests that full participation implies any comparative equality. What makes the right to full participation a matter of comparative as well as non-comparative equality is the symbolic dimension of social practices. Full membership in a club includes full participation in those rituals which symbolize equality of standing. Similarly, full citizenship requires comparative equality in those matters where inequality symbolizes the "second-classness" of some.

This point can be illustrated by one of the features of racial segregation in our recent past. Blacks were required to drink at different water fountains from whites. Now, why was this inequality offensive? It is true that water fountains reserved for blacks were fewer in number, less conveniently located, or less desirable than those reserved for whites. Even so, the inequality produced by water fountain segregation caused blacks no great injuries *in terms of water consumption.* The losses of liberty, taken by themselves, were not significant.

That water fountain segregation violates constitutional equality cannot be explained solely in terms of non-comparative rights. There is no basic right—moral or constitutional—to drink from a particular water fountain or from any water fountain at all. We can imagine circumstances, perhaps involving health or safety considerations, which would justify government regulation of the use of water fountains. The deprivations of liberty involved in such regulation would likely be trivial. What made the *racial* segregation of water fountains significantly objectionable was its symbolism. Making blacks use separate water fountains was a public, official way of saying that blacks were inferior to whites and were not to be allowed to associate with them on terms of equality.

Social and legal practices which officially, publicly symbolize inequality and exclusion are the reverse of those rituals and practices in clubs which symbolize equality and fraternity. Full citizenship means that such social and legal practices are forbidden and prevented. Full citizenship requires that in those symbolically important practices, citizens are to be treated the same way. Everybody—black and white—must be allowed to drink at the same fountain or none must be allowed to drink there. Either way can relieve the violation of equality entailed by the racial segregation. What is important in this situation is the comparative similarity of treatment. Thus, not being allowed to drink at a water fountain on account of race is not like being tortured. There is only one way to relieve the violation of equality involved in torture.

Comparative equality is an element of full citizenship. A constitution containing only non-comparative principles of equality does not take account of the symbolic function of social practices. A just constitution needs a principle of equality which is comparative. Such a principle will not be rhetorical but substantive; it will add something to the list of non-comparative principles in the constitution.

What will it add? What forms of dissimilar treatment violate the right to full social participation? Those forms which independently violate non-comparative constitutional rights are identifiable through the contents of those rights. As for those forms which are violations solely because they are vehicles of symbolic stigmatization, they cannot be specified *a prior*. Why does racial segregation of water fountains symbolize inequality and exclusion? It does so in the context of American history because it is part of a pattern of exclusion and stigmatization.

The symbolic value of practices depends upon shared conventions and understandings.[3] It depends upon the role they play in larger patterns and systems. Conventions and roles can vary from time to time and place to place. What symbolizes exclusion in one circumstance need not symbolize exclusion in a different circumstance. Thus, a constitutional principle of comparative equality can indicate only in the most general way the forms of equal treatment it requires. In the words of Kenneth Karst, it will be a principle which "guarantees to each individual the right to be treated by organized society as a respected, responsible, and participating member."[4] No further specification of the principle is possible at the constitutional level.

If an acceptable conception of moral equality entails both constitutional rights of a non-comparative sort and a general constitutional principle of comparative equality (a principle of full citizenship), we are brought to ask: Does moral equality so conceived forbid racially preferential hiring? This question divides into two.

1. Does every differentiation based on race violate the Karst principle? More particularly, do employment decisions giving racial preferences violate the principle?

2. Is there a principle of opportunity among the basic "human rights" which entails that employment decisions based on race are always impermissible? More particularly, is RTEC a right implied by moral equality?

In the remainder of this section, I will address the first question.

Uses of race which violate the Karst principle will be those which imply racial disrespect, foster unacceptable racial stereotypes, and/or promote racial exclusion from full participation. Specific practices or policies will offend against the Karst principle, in the usual case, because of the role they play in larger patterns of practices. Thus, to use the example of water fountain segregation again, the exclusion of blacks from drinking at "whites only" water fountains has no special significance, taken in isolation. It takes on its significance when seen as part of a general pattern of exclusion and hostility toward blacks. In looking to apply the Karst principle, then, what we want to look for are patterns of exclusion and disrespect and the connection specific policies have to these patterns.

Now, we can certainly conceive of uses of race which are not parts of patterns of racial exclusion and not expressions of racial antipathy or disrespect. Where such uses of race secure some important public good and violate no non-comparative rights, they constitute no violation of comparative moral equality. It is possible, thus, that some racial preferences in employment are acceptable from both a moral and constitutional perspective. A theory of the "color-blind" constitution would, in fact, misunderstand the nature of constitutionality equality and its relation to racial preferences.

This conclusion must deal with the following objection. We have said that moral equality requires among other things that individuals be free of the burden of disabling stereotypes. But this means—so runs the objection—that moral equality requires that we treat individuals "as individuals." It is the essence of racial standards that they treat persons as representative types rather than as distinct, unique individuals. Thus, the use of racial standards of any sort violates moral and constitutional equality.

The idea of "being treated as an individual" is important and has universal appeal. One of the commonest objections against the use of race is that it doesn't treat people as individuals. It was on such grounds, for example, that Justice Powell in his *Bakke* opinion commended as an alternative to the racial quotas at Davis the admissions program at Harvard University, which takes race into account as but one factor in admissions decisions. "This kind of program," he thought, "treats each applicant as an individual in the admissions process" (*Bakke* at 2763).[5]

There is doubtless some connection between being treated as an individual and being treated as an equal. But being clear about this connection requires our being clear about what it means "to be treated as an individual." Those whites excluded from desirable positions when blacks are given racial preferences may indeed feel that they are not being treated as individuals. Allan Bakke, for example, may have felt that what he valued and considered significant about his life—its history of effort and attainment reflected in his test scores and educational experience—counted for nothing when he was rejected for admission at the Davis Medical School because he was a representative of a particular race. By the same token, however, an applicant who performs poorly on admissions tests may feel that basing school admissions on mechanical and objective tests fails to treat him as an individual, fails, that is, to take account of the many dimensions of his life which could make him a successful student and productive professional.

In fact, any person may feel he is "not being treated as an individual" when he is denied a benefit as a result of a process he views as too shallow to give full accord to the dimensions of his life and character he considers most significant. If we are looking for an interpretation of "being treated as an individual" which expresses the demands of moral equality, we must look for an objective foundation instead of looking to the subjective responses of different individuals to social policies. Finding an objective foundation is not easy. One strategy that suggests itself is to rely upon the idea of a social contract.

The essential idea of the social contract is that independent, individual persons unanimously agree to the common rules under which they will be governed. The individuality and equality of persons is built into the very foundation of the process which determines the basic principles of justice. The individual contractor will agree only to that contract which preserves in society the essence of his equality of standing as a party to the contract. Thus, any social structure that would have been chosen by the contractor can be said to "treat him as an individual" even in circumstances where legitimate social policy subjects him to mechanical or impersonal processes or subordinates his interests to the public welfare. For we may suppose that in agreeing that some matters of social choice will be decided in these ways, the contractor has accepted this as compatible with his true individuality and his deeper interests.

The most recent and sophisticated version of the social contract view is the theory of John Rawls, already discussed in some detail in Chapter Eight. In his theory, persons are imagined in an Original Position in which they must agree to general principles for designing and criticizing the basic institutions under which they live. They must choose these principles behind a "veil of ignorance," that is, without knowledge of their personal qualities or their particular desires or values.

Each contractor is concerned to protect what is fundamental to his life; but because he chooses from behind the veil of ignorance he does not know the details of his specific lifeplan. Thus, he is reduced to aiming at maximizing for himself—

through the contractual agreement—those goods like general liberties, opportunities, powers, and wealth which are useful for living any kind of life. According to Rawls, the contractors would settle on these three principles:

1. Each person is to have an equal right to the most extensive total system of equal basic liberties compatible with a similar system of liberty for all (Equal Liberties Principle);
2. Social and economic inequalities are to be arranged so that they are both:
   (a) to the greatest benefit of the least advantaged . . . (Difference Principle), and
   (b) attached to offices and positions open to all under conditions of fair equality of opportunity (Equal Opportunity Principle). (*TJ*, 302.)

These principles supply the basis for assigning rights and privileges in society.

Rawls indicates that content can be provided to the very general principles chosen in the Original Position by imagining a series of subsequent choice situations: a constitutional stage which sets out the political organization of society and formulates a bill of rights; a legislative stage in which policies are devised and laws made; and a judicial stage in which specific statutes and regulations are applied to particular cases. The veil of ignorance is progressively lifted at each stage.

The Equal Liberties Principle—the principle with greatest priority, according to Rawls—gives to the contractors at the constitutional stage a basis for enumerating in the constitution specific liberties such as freedom of speech, freedom of worship, freedom from compelled self-incrimination, freedom from arbitrary search and seizure, and so on. To these non-comparative rights, the Equal Liberties Principle also provides a basis for adding a constitutional principle of comparative equality. Underlying the entire apparatus of the contract itself is the background equality of the contractors themselves. Although they are prepared to agree to the existence of some social inequalities when all are thus made better off, none is inclined to agree to a social system which can make him a second-class citizen, stigmatized as inferior and denied significant participation in social life.

The Karst principle would commend itself to the contractors at the constitutional stage since it expresses the demand of equal citizenship which is implicit in the making of the contract itself. Once the Karst principle is added to the non-comparative rights flowing from the Equal Liberties Principle, there is no reason why the contractors should add further constitutional stipulations against racial discrimination or policies using racial preferences. Those uses of race which are intolerable from their point of view are forbidden by the Karst principle itself. The wisdom and desirability of other uses of race in social policy are better left to the informed political judgments of the legislative stage.

If these comments are sound, then the Karst principle can be taken as the appropriate "objective" interpretation of "being treated as an individual." Only on this interpretation is being treated as an individual to be identified with being treated as a moral equal. It is, thus, no compelling objection against the use of racial standards that they do not treat a person as an individual in *some other sense,* for example, in the sense that racial standards fail to cognize those characteristics about a person he is likely to count as most significant about himself. I conclude that basic moral equality, understood comparatively, does not forbid all uses of race without qualification. Some forms of preferential hiring of blacks need not violate the Karst principle since they need not imply any kind of racial disrespect nor be part of a pattern of racial antipathy. If preferential hiring, done in furtherance of reasonable prospects of maximizing social welfare, violates constitutional principle, the principle must be some non-comparative one. Let us now inquire if there is such a principle.

EQUAL OPPORTUNITY AND RACE

The second of the two questions we want to answer is this: Is there a principle of equal opportunity among the basic, non-comparative "human rights" which entails that employment decisions giving racial preference are always impermissible? In Chapter Two, we took note of the implied claim by 125 professors opposed to reverse discrimination that there is such a constitutional right. They argued that no civil libertarian would countenance a "temporary suspension" of the right to counsel or the right to a fair trial; thus, it would be inconsistent for a civil libertarian to countenance a temporary suspension of the right to equality of opportuntiy.

What is the right to equal opportunity assumed by the 125 professors? Comparing it with a right to counsel or a right to a fair trial implies it has similar constitutional standing. Moreover, it must be a right which is violated by a single instance of preferring a black applicant over a better qualified white applicant. Otherwise, some preferential hiring could be compatible with it. The right must be, then, more or less the right to equal consideration for a job (RTEC), discussed in earlier chapters. This is the right of an individual to be hired if he is the most qualified of all the applicants for the job being offered.[6] To prefer an applicant because of his race would, where race is not a job-related qualification, violate other applicants' rights to equal consideration. The 125 professors are right in believing that if RTEC is a constitutional right like the right to a fair trial, then there is no warrant for "temporarily suspending" it no matter what the public benefit. To allow it to be set aside for some individuals would be to violate moral and constitutional equality in at least the non-comparative sense.

How plausible is it to assert that RTEC is or ought to be a constitutional right? It may be a generally desirable ideal that hiring practices conform to the merit principle embodied in RTEC. Under some circumstances it is surely the best policy.

However, RTEC is too rigid and specific to be a desirable constitutional principle. It would make into constitutional violations instances of behavior which seem unobjectionable. Suppose, for example, that an employer had two well-qualified applicants for a position, the slightly better qualified applicant already having a good, secure job, the other being unemployed. If the employer hired the unemployed applicant, would he have violated a constitutional principle? A moral principle? If the state adopted a policy requiring the employer to hire the unemployed applicant, would it be violating a constitutional right of the other applicant (the employed one) in the way that it would be violating an individual's right if it denied him counsel? To suggest that it would be is, to me anyway, strongly counter-intuitive.

I am not arguing that need or desert or other similar factors, excluded by the merit principle, ought to be taken into account in hiring situations. There may be good reasons why, normally, it is good policy to hire the best qualified and bad policy to consider factors such as need in making hiring decisions. But what may be generally good policy may under special circumstances be less desirable. There may be circumstances where deviation from strict merit hiring would produce a great deal of good without producing very much suffering. To deviate from merit hiring in such circumstances does not seem unreasonable, and seems hardly to constitute a violation of constitutional principle.

Frequently enough, considerations of competition and efficiency will motivate firms and institutions to hire by qualification in any case. Where social trends develop which produce harmful deviations from merit hiring, various legislative responses could restore the situation to the desired practice. Where minor but beneficial deviations from merit hiring were possible, without permanently diminishing the opportunities of some, it is hard to see the value of a constitutional principle of equal opportunity which would block policies encouraging such deviations.

The parties to Rawls' social contract choose a principle of equal opportunity: economic and social positions must be open to all on the basis of fair equality of opportunity. The non-specificity of this principle reflects that in choosing behind the veil of ignorance the contractors can characterize opportunities only in the most general way. Moreover, this principle, along with the Equal Liberties Principle and the Difference Principle, is chosen to apply to evaluation and criticism of basic institutions, not to evaluation of specific social policies or individual distributions of opportunities. Consequently, the emphasis of the Equal Opportunity Principle is on how the overall operations of the social structure affect total life prospects.

The principle of equal opportunity chosen in the Original Position does not describe any specific goals for which opportunity must be equalized, nor any specific obstacles which must be made the same. In fact, it is not altogether clear to whom the principle is supposed to apply. At one place, Rawls says that his principles refer to "representative persons" in the various social classes. This suggests that the Equal Opportunity Principle is to be construed somewhat along the lines of AEO, making reference to "average" or "typical" opportunities for different social stations. The ultimate principle of opportunity might not even apply to individuals. Rawls suggests at another place, however, that it is only the Difference Principle which refers to representative persons, implying that the Equal Opportunity Principle refers to the opportunities of individuals (*TJ*, 64).

This implication suggests that the Equal Opportunity Principle, leaving aside its institutional application, is more akin to LEO #2, expanded to include not only employment but all important educational, economic, and political opportunities. In any case, the Principle is nothing like RTEC. Moreover, as we noted in Chapter Eight, the contractors do not rule out all inequalities of opportunity: some may be justified if they enhance the opportunities of those with the least (*TJ*, 302–303).

Although Rawlsian contractors do not choose RTEC in the Original Position, would they choose it at the constitutional stage or the legislative stage? There seems no reason to suppose the contractors would choose RTEC as a constitutional principle. It would make no sense for them to adopt a principle which would block inequalities of opportunity designed to help out, at little cost, those with least opportunity since they have already agreed in the Original Position that such deviations from equal opportunity may be acceptable. It is not even likely that the contractors would formulate a distinct principle of equal opportunity in the constitution (aside from the Karst principle). The Equal Opportunity Principle might be satisfied simply by the way political and economic institutions are arranged under the constitution, making it unnecessary that it be expressed in an independent constitutional rule.

At the legislative stage, where policies are made in light of full social knowledge, matters might be otherwise. Under most conditions, fair and impartial legislators might prefer explicit and specific equality of opportunity policies. It is plausible that under many circumstances they would favor an employment policy which embraced much of the substance of RTEC. It is also reasonable to think that sometimes they would embrace other policies.

To sum up: In this chapter I have explored the most basic notions of moral equality that might underlie and inform a theory of constitutional equality. If moral equality among persons means no more than "equality in counting," then constitutional equality should not bar those uses of race which are utility maximizing for society as a whole. If moral equality is extended to include "equality of human rights," there appears to be no argument for concluding that every racial preference in employment violates non-comparative constitutional equality, since there is no reason to number RTEC among the "human rights" a just constitution must protect.

Suppose moral equality also contains a comparative dimension. It is conceivable that comparative constitutional equality could require strict nondiscrimination; but given the grounds we adduced for thinking a just constitution should contain a principle of comparative equality, we have no reason to think the principle can be any less general than the Karst principle. This means that constitutional equality in its comparative form requires that social policies not deny to anyone his status as a "respected, responsible, and participating member" of society. Policies which permanently damage the opportunities of some for a decent life violate this principle; so do policies which impose injuries to opportunities as a way of stigmatizing persons as inferior. Policies which temporarily and in very limited ways deviate from merit hiring in order to solve serious social problems are of a different stripe altogether. I do not see how they would obviously violate the basic equality of standing among its citizens that a society must preserve.

15

Conclusions

A UTILITARIAN ARGUMENT

Although many take it for granted that preferential hiring of blacks must violate a basic principle of equality, we have found no convincing argument for believing this. Neither have we found a plausible conception of constitutional equality which absolutely bars the use of race to promote desirable social goals. Are we to conclude that no moral principle stands in the way of at least some employment preferences for blacks?

Before we do, there is at least one further argument to consider. It accepts the conclusion that RTEC is too strong to be an acceptable constitutional principle. A constitutional RTEC would prevent us from adopting as occasions warranted certain forms of favoritism—for example, favoring of the handicapped, the unemployed, the especially needy or deserving, the Vietnam veteran, and so on. However, there are other kinds of favoritism that we want to block—favoritism based on race, for example. Thus, we want at the constitutional level not RTEC but a principle specifically prohibiting racial preferences of any sort. So goes the argument.

238

But here is the problem. A principle against racial preferences is necessarily derivative. Racial preferences must be related in some fashion to harms or denials of rights or violations of justice in order to account for their evil. Otherwise, it would be inexplicable why racial discrimination is always prohibited. This was the purpose of asserting RTEC: it provided us with a principle from which we could derive the conclusion that racial preferences in employment are always wrong. Preferential hiring violates equality. If we conclude that RTEC is not a suitable constitutional principle, then from what do we derive a principle against all racial preferences?

An option to basing such a principle on equality is to base it on utility. In the preceding chapters, I have avoided identifying the social utility approach to policy with the moral theory known as *utilitarianism*. This theory, given its classical expression in the 19th century by Jeremy Bentham, John Stuart Mill, and Henry Sidgwick, views the rightness of any action or policy as resting ultimately on its contribution to general welfare. It would seem that such a theory necessarily recommends the social utility approach, that is, the approach that has us balance the foreseeable and measurable costs and benefits of alternative programs and choose the program with the most favorable balance. Some utilitarians might indeed endorse this approach, applying the general welfare standard directly to all policy questions. However, this does not seem to be a necessary implication of utilitarianism.

Some utilitarians hold that we ought not apply the general welfare standard directly to some controversies. They believe that when we directly apply the standard in those situations, gains in general welfare are lost. This belief might seem paradoxical. How can we fail to get the most general welfare just by aiming at it? Consider a simple illustration where aiming at something is not the way to get it. If you are running a boat across a river with a strong current, you do not want to set out aiming directly at the point on the farther shore where you wish to land. If you do, you will end up downstream of that point. You get to your destination by aiming at a point upstream—in short, by aiming at something else.

There may well be circumstances where aiming directly at the general welfare is not the best way to promote it. These may be circumstances where there are special dangers of error in calculating the welfare benefits of various policies or where there is special liability of corruption of presumably welfare maximizing policies. Adopting and acting upon inflexible general rules may prove the wiser course. There can thus be utilitarian reasons for refusing to consider utility in certain decisions.

Such might be the case in regard to using race to promote social goals. There are cases where using race would pretty clearly produce foreseeable and measurable benefits outweighing any attendant foreseeable and measurable evils. Nevertheless, we ought not to resort to race in these cases, it might be argued. The use of race is a dangerous business; it lends itself to great abuses. If we allow policymakers to use race, we open the way to policies which do good but we necessarily also open the door to inevitable abuses which in the long run will outweigh all the good. Over the long run, general welfare is best served by our adopting an absolute prohibition against the use of race.

How does this argument differ from a social utility argument? Why can't the corruptibility of policies, the liability to abuse, the probability of error, and so on, enter directly into social utility calculations? They can. What results, however, is a recommendation for or against a specific policy. The conclusion derived from a social utility calculation does not apply to other times, other places, and other policies. The utilitarian argument, on the other hand, is an argument founded in utility for recognizing and honoring a *principle,* one which is to be applied always and everywhere. Thus, the argument relies upon the consideration of utilities viewed over the longest run and entails that welfare over the longest run is maximized in some cases by our always acting on a principle rather than calculating utilities anew for each policy decision.

The present argument, then, is one for never directly applying the general welfare standard in certain kinds of cases, namely those where use of race is a policy option. In these cases, a utilitarian might argue, we should apply instead a principle of nondiscrimination absolutely and without exception. Although this principle of nondiscrimination is not fundamental, it is nevertheless a moral principle. It is derived from the general welfare standard by considering that standard in conjunction with the supposed inevitable corruption of race-conscious policies. If we were persuaded by the argument, we would have reason to oppose racially preferential hiring as a matter of principle, much as if we held RTEC.[1]

The trouble is that the argument does not seem fully persuasive. It urges us to recognize a principle forbidding any uses of race because of alleged long-term evils. If these were foreseeable and measurable evils which outweighed any good, the use of race would be condemned by the social utility approach itself, condemned in each instance by the direct application of the general welfare standard. Thus, the argument for not applying the welfare standard to cases of using race must rest upon consequences which can't be captured in the social utility approach, that is, consequences not directly foreseeable or measurable.

At this point the utilitarian argument faces a dilemma. If the alleged long-term evils of the use of race cannot be factored into individual social utility calculations, this suggests that our knowledge or expectation of these evils is tenuous, not empirically secured, not strongly founded in any science or discipline. In this case, what is the warrant for shaping so much of our moral decisions on the basis of such expectations? On the other hand, if the expectations are well-defined and well-supported by common sense, social science, or whatever, why can't they count as part of the foreseeable and measurable consequences which any social utility calculation embraces? The point is this: either these long-run expectations are clear enough and well enough grounded to include straightforwardly in social utility calculations, or they are so nebulous that there is no reason to have confidence in them.

NO PRINCIPLE BARS PREFERENTIAL HIRING

I conclude that the utilitarian argument does not successfully establish a principled prohibition against all racial preferences. I also conclude that moral equality itself does not necessarily bar all preferential hiring of blacks. Racial preferences need not violate basic moral principles or the rights that derive from them.

I offer a second conclusion: the Social Utility Argument constitutes the best kind of defense of preferential hiring. Despite its indeterminacy, it has the greatest likelihood of showing some forms of employment preferences to be morally justifiable. The Compensatory Justice Argument and the Distributive Justice Argument cannot, in my estimation, provide adequate support for any general scheme of preferential hiring which is insensitive to specific personal desert.

In denying the force of the Compensatory Justice Argument, I have not denied the validity of claims to compensation by black individuals injured by past discrimination. I have denied, rather, that realistic and feasible forms of preferential hiring truly answer to these claims. Nothing I have said in this book denigrates any genuine attempt to compensate victims of discrimination for their injuries. Quite the reverse. In using the simple model of compensation in my arguments, I have committed myself to accepting any scheme which meets its terms.

In denying that the Distributive Justice Argument is successful, I have not denied that discriminatory practices—

reverse or otherwise—raise elemental questions of justice. Any discrimination that denies an individual a basic right or which denies his status as an equal is deeply unjust. Our primary concern, as a matter of fact, has been with whether principles of distributive justice (specifically, principles of equal opportunity) are *violated* by preferential hiring. Little attention has been given to constructing an argument *for* preferential hiring, aside from sketching the Unjust Advantage Argument in Chapter Seven.

One reason for this neglect is the feature of distributive justice principles already noted: their vagueness and disputability. A forceful Distributive Justice Argument for preferential hiring would have to show that blacks have rights to be preferred over whites, rights not deriving from compensatory justice. Or, it would have to show that in refusing to extend preferences to blacks we treat them as less than equals. Now, what sorts of considerations could show one or the other of these things? I suppose that the considerations would appeal to the poverty or need of blacks. But by appealing to poverty or need, we get an argument not for preferring blacks but for preferring the poor and needy. There are more poor and needy whites than there are poor and needy blacks.

Suppose we appeal instead to some conception of equality. As we have seen in regard to the concept of equal opportunity, there are many possible conceptions of equality. Those that gain the most consensus are usually also the most general and vague. Those that are highly specific are usually most debatable. Moreover, it is likely to be the case that in putting forth a conception of equality specific enough to require as a matter of justice that blacks be preferred in employment, the same conception will entail that it is wrong to discriminate against (at least some) whites on account of their race. For, what index of equality will the conception be guided by? Equality of income? Equality of power? Equality of status? Any such index is general and applies to whites as well as blacks. Equality is not promoted by preferring a poor (powerless, low-status) black over a poor (powerless, low-status) white.

This is not to say that there is no conception of equality which could require preferring blacks in employment. Of course there is. For example, the notion of Actuarial Equal Opportunity discussed in Chapter Eight, which calls for equalizing group success rates in getting jobs, gets us started toward a defense of job preferences for blacks. Such strong conceptions of equality, however, do not have the same plausibility as the broad and general notions of equality embodied in "equality in counting," "equality of human rights," or the Karst principle. The broad notions, on the other hand, seem at most to permit rather than require preferential hiring. To the extent that they permit preferences, the justification for actually resorting to them must come from the good they do. This brings us back to the Social Utility Argument.

THE SOCIAL UTILITY DEFENSE AND POPULAR ARGUMENTS

The argument for the superiority of the Social Utility Defense is partly negative. It rests on the fact that the other defenses encounter troubles which seem to disqualify them. As with any negative argument, it is incomplete. It is always possible that there is some variation of one of the other defenses which will be free of the objections I have noted. I think this is unlikely, but it is a possibility I have not ruled out. There is, however, also a positive argument for the superiority of the Social Utility Defense, an argument that points to the "fit" between the practice being defended and the defense of it. I have already spoken of this. It is important to remember that the sorts of racially preferential practices we are talking about are blind in a particular way. Racial quotas, whether absolute or conditional, will ask about the color of job applicants, not about their personal desert. What quotas will accomplish, then, is not genuine restitution but integration. And this accomplishment should be, in my judgment, the major line of defense of preferential hiring.

Nevertheless, popular defenses of preferences tend to personalize the issue. Popular arguments from compensation or restitution especially do this, since in genuine cases of compensation everything turns on the personal desert of the injured and the personal culpability of the injurer. When transformed into a *general* defense of preferential hiring, this line of argument implies that those whites who suffer as a result of preferences given to blacks deserve to lose out. And on the other side, this defense implies that those blacks who gain from preferences deserve their gain. They are more deserving than the whites they are preferred over. Since the whites affected by preferences are affected at random, the implication is that all whites deserve to lose out. And since the blacks benefited by preferences are benefited at random, the implication is that all blacks are more deserving.

One reason why many whites oppose preferential hiring is that they resent the implication that they are all personally less deserving than blacks. Are they justified in resenting this implication? Does each black deserve some special benefit at the expense of some white? What would account for this fact? In Justice Marshall's mind the matter is simple enough. Preferential treatment is justified because all blacks have been victims of racism (*Bakke* at 2805). But this is insufficient. The question is not whether every black has been touched in one way or another by discrimination but whether and in what ways he has been injured by it. Has each black suffered the same injuries, to the same degree? Has each black suffered injuries that give him a moral claim to be preferred over any similarly qualified white?

There is no question that many blacks have suffered tangible and serious injuries from employment discrimination, injuries which do give rise to various moral claims. When a court seeks to identify victims of an employer's specific acts of discrimination and to restore the victims to their "rightful places" in the employer's organization, it attends to those claims. Doing so is a matter of justice. Generalizing from this situation to a defense of preferential hiring, however, requires premises which are counterfeits of the originals. In *Bakke,* Justice Brennan claimed that if there had not been past societal discrimination the blacks admitted to Davis would have beaten out Bakke without any special treatment. To his thinking, Davis' preferences amounted to putting these blacks in their rightful places. Brennan presumed a kind of "cosmic rightful place" theory, but unlike the real thing it is spurious.

In genuine attempts to put an individual in his rightful place, there are real efforts to identify the specific acts that can be pointed to in support of the counterfactual claim that the individual "would have been in a better position but for. . . ." The specific acts and their context establish that it was a wrongful deed and not something else which caused the individual to be in his present position. On Brennan's cosmic theory, no specific acts affecting specific individuals are pointed to. He adduces no facts about the histories of the individual blacks admitted in the special admissions program at Davis. Instead, he invokes an amorphous phenomenon called "societal discrimination" which is supposed to be sufficient.

The Marshall generalization and the Brennan theory are bogus attempts to lead us to believe that those who are being preferred deserve it.[2] The generalization and the theory leech off of a kind of argument in which personal desert plays a crucial role; yet they are offered in defense of preferences which do not discriminate on the basis of personal desert but on the basis of color. Brennan and Marshall try to associate color with personal desert so that racial quotas can be made to look like standard cases of compensation. This association won't do and whites are not amiss in resenting blanket claims that they are less deserving, that all blacks who get preferences are morally more deserving than they.

On the Social Utility Defense, personal desert never enters the picture. The black who receives a preference doesn't (necessarily) deserve it. It just happens that giving him the preference works to the social good. The white who loses out doesn't (necessarily) deserve to. It just happens that it is convenient to impose upon him the cost of producing the social good. It is like the military draft in wartime. There is a social need to be met; an army must be raised. This means inducting into service the young and the fit. We clearly misunderstand what is going on if we think that the young and the fit are more obligated to serve the nation than the old and the unfit. It is, rather, a matter of efficiency that they are taken. Utility demands that the burden of national defense fall upon them.

I make these points for a reason. If, as I have argued, the moral acceptability of a scheme of preferential hiring depends upon the good it does, then one part of such a scheme which can itself produce good or bad consequences is the public justification given it. The effects of a particular public defense might themselves make the difference of whether the overall impact of preferential hiring is good or bad. Justifications which unnecessarily raise resistance to preferential hiring create conditions which work against its overall success. I think it is an advantage of the Social Utility Argument that as a public justification of preferential hiring it will likely create less resistance among whites. Individuals, of course, are seldom keen to bear a sacrifice which falls on them impersonally in the name of the general welfare. But individuals are even less ready to accept sacrifices imposed upon them on grounds of desert which they believe to be false and unfounded.

SUMMARY

Those who believe that preferential hiring is morally wrong might do so on one of two grounds: (i) they might believe that it denies basic rights or violates fundamental principles, or (ii) they might believe that the social welfare is best served by strict nondiscrimination. In this book I have tried to identify the rights or principles which might stand in the way of prefer-

ences. One candidate was an equal opportunity right—
RTEC—but we could not find adequate grounds for believing
it to be a constitutional or moral right. Another candidate was a
strict principle against any use of race in policy. Such a
principle must be derivative, and we could not successfully
derive it either from a strong conception of moral equality or
from considerations of long-range utility. Thus, the first
ground for opposing preferential hiring seems insubstantial.

The second ground offers greater prospects. The balance of
social utility may well lie against the use of racial preferences in
employment. There are a number of obvious risks which
attend the use of preferential hiring. Although it may serve, by
integrating more blacks into the various occupations and
professions, to work against racial stereotypes, it may have the
reverse effect as well. It can work to reinforce stereotypes of
black inferiority by fostering the idea that "blacks can't make it
on their own." Blacks who have been recipients of preferences
frequently face the attitude on the part of whites that they must
be second-rate. Recipients of preferences are even led to
question their own ability and worth. Because preferential
hiring easily generates such attitudes, many blacks oppose it
for this very reason. However true it may be that the use of
preferences need not strictly imply the inability to compete on
even terms, the implication is going to be drawn anyway, by
recipient and non-recipient alike.

Another danger is this. "Temporary" racial preferences can
easily become permanent. Almost without fail, those who
defend hiring quotas see them as temporary. But why should
we expect that quotas, once established on a wide scale, can
easily be abandoned after several years? Privileges once created
are hard to undo. Their existence creates a constituency with an
interest in their maintenance. Blacks may come to see quotas as
assuring them their "fair share" of jobs. If eliminating quotas
means that representation of blacks in good jobs begins to
erode, there will be pressure to reinstate or continue them.

In their recent book on the *Bakke* case, Joel Dreyfuss and Charles Lawrence dismiss this possibility. "The prediction," they write, "that preferred minorities would want to retain their advantage [is] no doubt an accurate assessment of human nature. But the advantages bestowed by the majority on a minority can easily be taken away."[3] It is naive to think it is as simple as that. It is commonplace that well organized political minorities can block policy changes which would eliminate special privileges. The object lesson here is veteran's preference. Here is a form of preferential treatment that has outlived its justification, yet the veterans' lobby is politically powerful enough to block any changes in federal or state law. The Carter Administration's efforts in 1978 and 1979 to impose some limitations on the preference in federal jobs met abject defeat. The political pressure on Congress made the issue too touchy to deal with.

Thirty-five years after V-J Day, veterans of World War II are still enjoying employment preferences in state and federal governments. Because of this, women are effectively barred from holding many top level civil service jobs. Here is a preferential program that tolls a substantial cost in the frustrated aspirations of many non-veterans and which effectively discriminates against women; yet, although once given by a majority, the program is a privilege the majority cannot now easily eliminate. The danger that racial preferences will become similarly entrenched should be taken seriously.

Those who favor preferential hiring also seek justification on one of two grounds: (i) they believe that those who receive preferences deserve them as a matter of justice, that preferences are "restitution" received as a matter of right, or (ii) they believe that social welfare is best served by the temporary use of preferences. I have argued in this book that defenses founded on the first ground are flawed and that the best line of defense lies with the second ground.

The Social Utility Defense has both welcome and unwelcome aspects. On the one hand, it does not rest upon attributing to all whites personal guilt or liability for past discrimination, and it does not require questionable assumptions about the personal deservingness of each black recipient of preferences. On the other hand, the defense is made possible by concluding that there is not any absolute bar to the use of race to promote important social goals. This means not only that some racial discrimination against whites may be acceptable but that under conceivable circumstances some racial discrimination against blacks likewise may be morally tolerable.

It is not hard to think of great goods that preferential hiring might accomplish. To a very considerable extent, this is still a divided nation. Genuine racial integration is still a pressing national need. It can be argued that whatever serves integration serves the national welfare. Preferential hiring can offer itself as an effective mechanism for speeding the inclusion of representative numbers of blacks in all levels of the nation's economy. It is unfortunate that what might be a useful tool for gradually bringing racial harmony is also a breeder of racial antagonism. Thus, the good that preferential hiring might do does not clearly outweigh the harm that it might do.

Here, I submit, is a common ground upon which proponents and opponents of preferential hiring can join argument. Focusing on the contribution to or diminution of the public welfare expected to derive from preferential hiring can make the debate about reverse discrimination less polemical and move us closer to a reasoned consensus on one part of the reverse discrimination controversy.

*   *   *

What I have said in connection with preferential hiring of blacks obviously has application to controversies about other forms of preferential treatment of blacks such as preferential admissions to professional schools. It also has obvious applications to controversies about sexual and ethnic preferences. Nevertheless, some of the arguments in this book require modification when applied to a context different from preferential hiring of blacks, and the conclusions to be drawn in those different contexts may not always coincide with the conclusions to be drawn about preferential hiring.

Notes

PREFACE

1. N. J. Block and Gerald Dworkin, eds., *The I. Q. Controversy* (New York: Pantheon Books, 1976), xiii.

CHAPTER ONE

1. Public Law 95–28, 91 *Stat.* 116 (1977).
2. Full citation of court cases is given in the List of Cases at the end of the book. Cases are referred to in the text and notes by name only.
3. The latter charge was made in a pamphlet distributed in the spring of 1978 by the Montclair State College Committee Against Racism.
4. Theodore St. Antoine, "Affirmative Action, A 'Heroic' Measure," *The New York Times,* November 26, 1976, Op-Ed page; William F. Harvey, "Some Different Thoughts About Bakke," *National Review,* 30 (February 3, 1978), 151–152, 171.
5. Kenneth Tollet, "What Led to Bakke," *The Center Magazine,* 11 (January–February 1978), 3.
6. Quoted in *The Chronicle of Higher Education,* 16 (July 3, 1978), 12.
7. *The American College Dictionary* (New York: Random House, 1962).
8. The equivocation: X distinguishes in favor of or against implies X discriminates (in the neutral sense). X discriminates (in the non-neutral sense) implies X is wrong. But: X discriminates (in the neutral sense) does not imply that X discriminates (in the non-neutral sense).
9. See, e.g., the testimony of Cesar Sereseres, in *Federal Higher Education Programs Institutional Eligibility.* Hearings Before the Special Subcommittee on Education, U. S. House of Representatives, 93rd Congress, 2nd Session, August–September 1974 (Government Printing Office, 1974), Part 2A, 275. (Hereafter referred to in the text and notes as O'Hara Hearings.) Notice as well the multiple uses of "discrimination" in the testimony of Mary Gray and Carolyn Polowy, O'Hara Hearings, 579–591.

An example of an explicit non-neutral definition of discrimination is this: "As the term is used here, discrimination is differential treatment with insufficient reason. . . ." Evan Simpson, "Discrimination as an Example of Moral Irrationality," in Paul Welsh, ed., *Fact, Value, and Perception: Essays in Honor of Charles Baylis* (Durham, North Carolina: Duke University Press, 1975), 107.

10. This formulation of the principle goes back to Aristotle, *Ethics*, Book V, III, 1131a–1131b.

11. Andreas Auer, "Public School Desegregation and the Color-Blind Constitution," *Southwestern Law Journal*, 27 (August 1973), 477.

12. I take this last example from George J. Alexander, "Forward: Symposium–*Bakke* v. *Board of Regents*," *Santa Clara Law Review*, 17 (1977) 272. See *Powell* v. *Texas*.

13. Thomas Nagel, "Equal Treatment and Compensatory Discrimination," *Philosophy & Public Affairs*, 2 (Summer 1973), 348.

14. Although I will later examine the arguments for considering race as a qualification, it is worth noting here that as a matter of law, Title VII of the Civil Rights Act of 1964 does not recognize race as a genuine job-related qualification. This point will be emphasized later. See Section 703(e) of Title VII which does recognize sex, religion, and similar statuses as possible "bona fide occupational qualifications." See also O'Hara Hearings, 84, and Barbara Babcock, Ann Freedman, Eleanor Norton, and Susan Ross, *Sex Discrimination and the Law: Causes and Remedies* (Boston: Little, Brown and Company, 1975), 230–231. See Chapter Six, below, for further discussion of qualifications.

CHAPTER TWO

1. Irving Thalberg, "Reverse Discrimination and the Future," *Philosophical Forum*, 5 (Fall - Winter 1973–1974), 300.

2. Just as Allan Bakke urged that racial preferences in the admissions procedures at the University of California Medical School at Davis violated his Fourteenth Amendment rights.

3. *The New York Times*, February 9, 1978, A16.

4. "Manifesto to the White Christian Churches and the Jewish Synagogues in the United States of America and All Other Racist Institutions," presented by James Forman at the National Black Economic Development Conference, Detroit, Michigan, April 1969. Included as an appendix to Boris Bittker, *The Case for Black Reparations* (New York: Vintage Books, 1973), 159–175. The quoted passages are from Bittker, 168. For two careful discussions of the Black Manifesto, see Hugo Bedau, "Compensatory Justice and the Black Manifesto," *The Monist*, 56 (January 1972), 20–42, and Merle Longwood, "Justice and Reparations: The Black Manifesto Reconsidered," *Lutheran Quarterly*, 27 (August 1975), 203–219.

5. Lewis D. Solomon and Judith S. Heeter, "Affirmative Action in Higher Education: Towards a Rationale for Preference," *Notre Dame Lawyer,* 52 (October 1976), 67.

CHAPTER THREE

1. A fuller account of corporate associations is contained in Chapter Five.

2. ". . . white males as a class have benefited from . . . systematic discrimination [against blacks]. The notion that these workers are innocent and blameless is a myth, and we categorically reject this notion." Speech by Herbert Hill, June 28, 1977, in St. Louis to the NAACP. Reported in *The New York Times,* June 29, 1977, A14.

3. Judith Jarvis Thomson, "Preferential Hiring," *Philosophy & Public Affairs,* 2 (Summer 1973), 383–384.

CHAPTER FOUR

1. Thomson, "Preferential Hiring," 378. Subsequent page references are given in parentheses in the text.

2. Although Thomson does not assume RTEC specifically, she does assume that job candidates have a "right to an equal chance for a job" (377). This would seem to encompass a right to be considered fairly for a job.

3. One might urge that despite what I have said there is a real conflict of rights in the hiring case, a conflict between W's right to equal consideration (RTEC) and B's right to a fair share of society's resources (or some such right). Notice that this claim amounts to abandoning the Argument from Compensatory Justice, since B's alleged right in this case is not a compensatory right but one which derives from some other sphere of justice. One might consider, when we examine principles of distributive justice, whether conflicts of this sort arise.

4. In *McAleer* v. *American Telephone & Telegraph Co.,* a ruling by a federal district court seemed to offer this possibility. AT&T had been placed under an order by a federal court in Pennsylvania requiring the company to give preferences in promotions and hiring to females and minorities. (See Chapter Twelve, below, for a full account.) McAleer sued in federal court in the District of Columbia, claiming he had been denied promotion on grounds of race. The court refused to overturn the protested promotion, made pursuant to the order of the other court, but it did order AT&T to pay McAleer damages. The court referred to the Supreme Court's decision in *Franks* v. *Bowman Transportation Company* in which Chief Justice Burger (at 1272), both dissenting and concurring, spoke of the possibility of compensating with monetary damages those innocent employees adversely affected by an employer's corrective efforts.

5. The right to a fair trial does not lend itself naturally to this kind of solution.

6. See Robert Simon, "Preferential Hiring: A Reply to Judith Jarvis Thomson," *Philosophy & Public Affairs*, 3 (Spring 1974), 315–316.

7. See Robert Simon, "Preferential Hiring," 315–316, and Alan Goldman, "Reparations to Individuals or Groups?" *Analysis*, 35 (April 1975), 168–170.

CHAPTER FIVE

1. Robert Simon, "Preferential Hiring," 314. Simon is not a supporter of the position he is describing.

2. George Sher, "Groups and Justice," *Ethics*, 83 (January 1977), 176.

3. Alfred Blumrosen, "Quotas, Common Sense, and Law in Labor Relations: Three Dimensions of Equal Opportunity," *Rutgers Law Review*, 27 (Spring 1974), 683.

4. Michael Bayles falls into the same error when he writes: "By using the characteristic of being black as an identifying characteristic to discriminate against people, a person wronged the group, blacks." ("Reparations to Wronged Groups," *Analysis*, 33 [June 1973], 183.) By using a characteristic to discriminate against people, I injure the people I discriminate against. By discriminating against one black, I do not (necessarily) injure another black, just as by discriminating against one smelly person, I do not (necessarily) injure another smelly person.

5. Kenneth L. Karst and Harold Horowitz, "Affirmative Action and Equal Protection," *Virginia Law Review*, 60 (October 1974), 960.

6. The points in the preceding two paragraphs owe much to discussions with Steven Davis. I also learned much from an advanced look at David Copp, "Collective Actions and Secondary Actions," *American Philosophical Quarterly*, 16 (July 1979), 177–186. See also Rolf Gruner, "On the Action of Social Groups," *Inquiry*, 19 (Winter 1976), 443–454. An article bearing directly on this issue but published too late to be taken into account here is Peter French, "The Corporation as a Moral Person," *American Philosophical Quarterly*, 16 (July 1979), 207–215.

7. Cornelius Golightly, "Justice and 'Discrimination For' in Higher Education," *Philosophic Exchange*, 1 (Summer 1974), 6.

8. See, for example, the Supreme Court's interpretation of Title VII of the Civil Rights Act of 1964 in *City of Los Angeles Department of Water* v. *Manhart* at 1372.

9. See *Shelley* v. *Kraemer* at 22. Under American law, Indian tribes do constitute separate "nations" and have special legal relations with the United States Government.

10. Referred to in Ewart Guinier, "Review: *The Case for Black Reparations* by Boris Bittker," *Yale Law Journal*, 82 (July 1973), 1721. See Robert

S. Browne and Robert Vernon, *Should the U. S. Be Partitioned Into Separate and Independent Nations—One a Homeland for White Americans and the Other a Homeland for Black Americans?* (New York: Merit Publishers, 1968).

11. Gidon Gottlieb, "Comment," in Eugene V. Rostow, ed., *Is the Law Dead?* (New York: Simon and Schuster, 1971), 202, 203, 204. Consider also:

> A fifth type of public policy would redefine and restructure fundamental constitutional relationships between racial groups . . . [O]ne demand might be for constitutional recognition of the unique Black position in American society. In that case we might see the development of Black collectivity rights that would be constitutionally defined and protected.

Marguerite Ross Barnett, "A Theoretical Perspective on American Racial Policy," in Marguerite Ross Barnett and James A. Hefner, eds., *Public Policy for the Black Community: Strategies and Perspectives* (Port Washington, New York: Alfred Publishing Company, 1976), 29.

12. For ideal and practical arguments against such "corporatism," see Nathan Glazer, *Affirmative Discrimination: Ethnic Inequality and Public Policy* (New York: Basic Books, 1975). See also the concerns about the implications of "recognition of peoplehood of Blacks for reparations" expressed by Henry J. Richardson III, "Black People, Technocracy, and Legal Process: Thoughts, Fears, and Goals," in Barnett and Hefner, *Public Policy for the Black Community*, 174–175, 185ff. On the economic viability of separatism, see Gary Becker, *The Economic Approach to Human Behavior* (Chicago: University of Chicago Press, 1976), Chapter Two.

13. See Stanley French and Andres Gutman, "The Principle of National Self-Determination," in Virginia Held, Sidney Morgenbesser, and Thomas Nagel, eds., *Philosophy, Morality, and International Affairs* (New York: Oxford University Press, 1974), 139.

CHAPTER SIX

1. My information about the Philadelphia construction industry comes from *Contractors Ass'n of Eastern Pennsylvania* v. *Secretary of Labor* at 164–165.

2. See, in this regard, the discussion by Nathan Glazer, *Affirmative Discrimination;* for some other costs associated with preferential hiring, see Virginia Black, "The Erosion of Legal Principles in Creation of Legal Policies," *Ethics,* 84 (January 1974), 93–115.

3. For an argument of this sort applied to university hiring, see Sidney Hook, "Discrimination, Color Blindness, and the Quota System," in Barry Gross, ed., *Reverse Discrimination* (Buffalo, New York: Prometheus Books, 1977), 84–87.

4. See Title VII and the case law based upon it, especially *City of Los*

Angeles Department of Water v. *Manhart* at 1375: "Even a *true* generalization about the class is an insufficient [legal] reason for disqualifying an
individual to whom the generalization does not apply." Emphasis added.
The Court is not talking about all generalizations, but generalizations framed
in terms of race, sex, color, and the like.

   5. I borrow this particular example from Mary Vetterling, "Some Common Sense Notes on Preferential Hiring," *Philosophical Forum*, 5 (Fall -
Winter 1973–1974), 321.

   6. See *Griggs* v. *Duke Power Company*.

   7. Report of the Council Commission on Discrimination, AAUP, 1973,
in O'Hara Hearings, 570–571. All emphases added.

   8. Graham Hughes, *The Conscience of the Courts: Law and Morals in
American Life* (Garden City, New York: Anchor Press/Doubleday, 1975),
269.

   9. *Porcelli* has not served as a precedent for interpreting Title VII
otherwise.

   10. For a discussion of some the points in this paragraph, see Sara Ann
Ketchum and Christine Pierce, "Implicit Racism," *Analysis,* 36 (January
1976), 92.

   11. Onora O'Neill, "Efficiency and Equal Opportunity," unpub., 3.
Quoted with permission.

   12. O'Neill, "Efficiency and Equal Opportunity," 11.

CHAPTER SEVEN

   1. Friedrich A. Hayek, *The Constitution of Liberty* (Chicago: Henry
Regnery and Company, 1972), 99-100, 230.

   2. See the discussion of the precepts of justice in Joel Feinberg, *Social
Philosophy* (Englewood Cliffs, New Jersey: Prentice-Hall, Inc., 1973),
Chapter Seven. Hayek identifies distributive justice with the precept:
Reward according to merit. It is because he thinks it impossible objectively to
determine merit that he thinks distributive justice to be a dangerous idea.

   3. Quoted in Lewis Solomon and Judith Heeter, "Affirmative Action in
Higher Education," 67.

   4. For versions of this argument, see George Sher, "Justifying Reverse
Discrimination in Employment," *Philosophy & Public Affairs*, 4 (Winter
1975), 159–170; Kenneth Strike, "Justice and Reverse Discrimination,"
University of Chicago School Review, 84 (August 1976), 516–537; and
Bernard Boxill, "The Morality of Reparation," in Richard Wasserstrom,
ed., *Today's Moral Problems* (New York: Macmillan Publishing Company,
1975), 209–217.

   5. The next several paragraphs rely upon Charles Frankel, "Equality of
Opportunity," *Ethics*, 81 (April 1971), 191–211; Onora O'Neill, "How Do

We Know When Opportunities Are Equal?" in Mary Vetterling-Braggin, Frederick A. Elliston, and Jane English, eds., *Feminism and Philosophy* (Totowa, New Jersey: Littlefield, Adams and Company, 1977), 177–189; Onora O'Neill, "Opportunities, Inequalities and Education," *Theory and Decision,* 7 (October 1976), 275–295; John Rawls, *A Theory of Justice* (Cambridge, Massachusetts: Harvard University Press, 1971), 72–89; Feinberg, *Social Philosophy,* 12–14; and especially T. D. Campbell, "Equality of Opportunity," *Proceedings of the Aristotelian Society,* 75 (1974–1975), 51–68.

6. Campbell, "Equality of Opportunity," 56. When we speak not so strictly, we often interchange "opportunity" and "chance."

7. An example of confusing equal opportunity with equal chance occurs in Hank Greely, "The Equality of Allocation by Lot," *Harvard Civil Rights-Civil Liberties Law Review,* 12 (Winter 1977), 122, where the author argues that "random selection is the only allocative method which honestly can claim the objective of equality of opportunity" because "equality of opportunity . . . parcels out equal chances to receive a good." If equality of opportunity to have a good were equality of chance to have it, Greely would be justified in preferring a random selection method of allocation, but equality of opportunity to have a good is *not* simply an equal chance to have it. Allocation by lot does not secure equal opportunity; it may even defeat it by nullifying the effects of effort and choice.

Equality of opportunity might be analyzed in terms of equal chances *given* equal choice *and* equal effort *and* equal luck (see Rawls: "those who are at the same level of talent and ability, and have the same willingness to use them, should have the same prospects of success regardless of their initial place in the social system," *A Theory of Justice,* 73), but this would not call for allocation by lot either.

8. By being limited, they minimize possible conflicts with other principles of justice or liberty.

9. O'Neill, "How Do We Know When Opportunities Are Equal?" 179.

10. We must assume some way of quantifying and summing opportunities.

11. O'Neill, "How Do We Know When Opportunities Are Equal?" 179.

12. The seminal case regarding employment tests which produce a "disproportionate impact" on blacks is *Griggs* v. *Duke Power Company.* But see also *Washington* v. *Davis.*

13. John Rawls *appears* to build his preferred conception of equal opportunity in this way. He says: "The liberal interpretation . . . tries to correct for this [i.e., the arbitrariness of starting points] by *adding to* the requirement of careers open to talents the further condition of the principle of fair equality of opportunity." *(A Theory of Justice,* 73. Emphasis added.) I suggest, below, that contrary to these words, Rawls' favored view of equal opportunity is not just an "add-on" to FEO.

CHAPTER EIGHT

1. O'Neill, "How Do We Know When Opportunities Are Equal?" 181–182.

2. Whites represent four-fifths of the labor (applicant) pool, blacks one-fifth. Whites get four-fifths of the jobs, blacks one-fifth. This means that 2 out of every 5 whites get jobs and that 2 out of every 5 blacks do too. Their rates of success are the same.

3. Earlier, in connection with the initial examination of FEO, I described a scheme of proportional hiring designed to make the total actual opportunities equal for each individual. Here, the proportional hiring aims only at making group averages equal.

4. "It is important," says Rawls, "to distinguish that sense of equality which is an aspect of the concept of justice from the sense of equality which belongs to a more comprehensive social ideal," John Rawls, "Justice as Fairness," *Philosophical Review*, 67 (April 1958), 165. The failure to distinguish the different roles equality may play in a social theory is the source of many bad arguments.

5. Henceforth cited in the text and notes as *TJ*.

6. *TJ*, 302. Rawls speaks of his "two principles," but since the second principle is a conjunction, I will refer to the principles by the names I have given in parentheses ("Difference Principle" is Rawls' own name), or as "the three principles."

CHAPTER NINE

1. Public Law 88–352, 78 *Stat.* 240 (1964).

2. Public Law 92–261, 86 *Stat.* 103 (1972).

3. The numbers in brackets refer to sections in the United States Code.

4. "Section 703, which defines unlawful employment practices, *does not limit* judicial remedies which are governed by the broad language of section 706(g) authorizing 'such affirmative action as may be appropriate'." *Weber* v. *Kaiser Aluminum & Chemical Corp.* at 223. Emphasis added.

5. *Albemarle Paper Company* v. *Moody* at 417–418. See also *Franks* v. *Bowman Transportation Company* at 1253: "Federal courts are empowered to fashion such relief as the particular circumstances of a case may require to effect restitution, making whole, insofar as possible, the victims of racial discrimination in hiring." See the discussion of compensation in Chapters Two and Three above.

6. Here is a great problem in understanding the law and judicial decisions: courts use no common vocabulary. One court might deem the order to hire Jones preferential while another would not. This makes the case law difficult to interpret and it makes the use of precedent treacherous. The dangers of equivocation are magnified. The reader must be warned that in reading court cases and in comparing them to my interpretations, he must translate the

courts' terminology into my own. Some of my conclusions may seem at variance with what a court actually says until the terminological differences are taken into account.

7. For expressions of the "rightful place" theory and for further citations, see *International Brotherhood of Teamsters* v. *United States,* esp. at 371–377; *United States* v. *Bethlehem Steel Corp.;* and *United States* v. *N. L. Industries, Inc.,* esp. at 374. The seminal early case here was *Quarles* v. *Phillip Morris, Inc.*

8. See *Chance* v. *Board of Examiners.*

9. The court found the examination discriminatory on the ground that it disproportionately disqualified black and Spanish-surnamed applicants and could not be shown by the state to be validly job-related under the standard established in *Griggs* v. *Duke Power Company.* A fuller discussion of this standard is found in Chapter Ten.

10. *Germann* at 1333, quoting from the Code of General Ordinances of Kansas City, Missouri, No. 42406.

11. The court went on to say:

Title VII outlaws preferences for any group, minority or majority, if based on race or other impermissible classifications, but it does not outlaw preferences favoring victims of discrimination. A minority worker who has been kept from his rightful place by discriminating hiring practices may be entitled to preferential treatment "not because be is Black, but because, and only to the extent that, he has been discriminated against."

(The court was quoting *Chance* v. *Board of Examiners.*) Notice that the court speaks of restitution provided to the victims of discrimination as "preferential treatment" whereas I do not.

12. "Our response is that unless a preference is enacted to restore employees to their rightful places within a particular employment scheme it is strictly forbidden by Title VII" *(Weber* I at 225). This would apply against both *Germann* and *Boston Chapter.*

13. For example, in the past most large companies routinely used employment tests held to be invalid in the 1971 *Griggs* decision.

14. The *Boston Chapter* II court argued that 703(j) did not apply when the imbalance was due to the employer's *own* past discrimination. The implication is that 703(j) does apply in the absence of the employer's own discrimination.

15. In a muddled passage in his *Bakke* opinion, Justice Brennan speaks as if this were not so. In talking about Title VI (rather than Title VII) and the University of California's self-imposed admissions quota at the Medical School at Davis, he said:

It would be inconsistent with . . . the emphasis of Title VI and HEW regulations on voluntary action, however, to require an institution wait to be adjudicated in violation of the law before being permitted to voluntarily undertake action based upon a good faith and reasonable belief that the failure of certain ethnic minorities to satisfy entrance requirements is not a measure of their ultimate performance as doctors but a result of the lingering effects of past societal discrimination. *(Bakke* at 2780.)

This is puzzling to me. To speak of an institution awaiting to be adjudicated in violation of the law for the effects of *someone else's* discrimination implies that an institution need not be guilty itself of discrimination in order to be in violation of the law. I can find no possible ground in either the texts of Title VI or Title VII or the voluminous case law for such an idea.

16. *United States* v. *Chesapeake and Ohio Ry.* at 593.

17. 118 *Cong. Rec.* 7166, 7168 (1972).

18. 44 *FR* 4422, 4427 (January 19, 1979). Since these affirmative action plans may include hiring "goals" and since these "goals" for "previously excluded groups may be higher than the percentage of their availability in the workforce," the "opportunities" spoken of in the passage mean "preferential opportunities."

CHAPTER TEN

1. At 1027, including *Rios* v. *Enterprise Association Steamfitters Local 638* and *Carter* v. *Gallagher,* two frequently cited cases.

2. See *Patterson* v. *American Tobacco Company.*

3. As did Justice Rehnquist in his dissent to *Weber* II at 4865.

4. 110 *Cong. Rec.* 6549 (1964).

5. Argument by Senator Clark Against Senator Hill, 110 *Cong. Rec.* 7207 (1964).

6. 110 *Cong. Rec.* 7213 (1964). Emphasis added.

7. *Weber* II at 4855, note 7.

8. Ronald Dworkin, in "How to Read the Civil Rights Act," *New York Review of Books,* 26 (December 20, 1979), 37–43, which appeared as this book was going to press, presents an interesting thesis about the nature of legislative intent and applies it to the majority and minority opinions in *Weber* II. I do not here have the space to do justice to Dworkin's complex analysis, but a few remarks are in order.

Dworkin would have a judge interpret the meaning of Title VII (as it pertained to the issue raised in *Weber)* without referring to Congressional intent. The judge should do this because Congress did not utilize a conventional means (e.g., a committee report accompanying the legislation) to express an institutional opinion on the issue, and because the scattered remarks of Senators Humphrey, Clark, and others do not constitute evidence about the mental states of most Representatives and Senators at the time of the vote on Title VII. The judge instead must offer an interpretation of the Title in light of its aim, an interpretation which is "consistent with the provisions of the statute and finds substantial support in the political climate of the times." (41).

Dworkin goes on to reconstruct Brennan's first argument along these lines. The argument, as simplified by me, is this:

(B1) Title VII aimed to ameliorate the economic inferiority of blacks.
(B2) Kaiser's policy advances this aim.
(B3) Thus, Kaiser's policy is permitted by Title VII.

As I pointed out in the text, B1 does not adjudicate between different interpretations of *how* this aim of Title VII is to be promoted unless it is to be taken wholly without qualification or unless its qualifications are specified.

Justice Brennan indicates that he would not find lawful under Title VII a company's voluntarily firing white workers in order to replace them with black workers (*Weber* II at 4855). Yet he is not unaware that such replacements would "ameliorate the economic inferiority of blacks." Thus, he is prepared to find some means to this end to be in violation of Title VII even when these means are not forbidden by other statutes or laws. The problem for Brennan is to explain why he will allow some means but not others. More particularly, how does Brennan defend his position against someone who believes that Title VII permits firing white workers so they can be replaced by blacks? Given that Brennan and his critic rely on the same putative aim of Title VII, I do not know how they can resolve their differences by offering theories about the aims of the legislation. It seems to me that Brennan can defend himself only by pointing out that Congress surely did not intend for Title VII to allow companies to fire whites so they could hire blacks. Reference to Congressional intent seems unavoidable.

If we cannot avoid recourse to Congressional intent, regardless of how feeble the evidence for a specific intent is, then, in regard to the debate between Brennan and Rehnquist, we are left with the question: which man gives a better account of Congress' intent. Perhaps, however, Dworkin can show this conclusion mistaken and can show how Brennan can answer both his critic from the right and his critic from the left without appealing to Congressional intent.

9. Kenneth Davidson, "Preferential Treatment and Equal Opportunity," *Oregon Law Review*, 55 (1976), 68.

10. Much of the division of opinion in the Supreme Court's *Bakke* decision turned on the proper interpretation of the term "discrimination" in Title VI.

11. House Report No.92-238, Report of the Education and Labor Committee on the Equal Employment Opportunity Act of 1972, *U.S. Code, Cong. & Ad. News* 2137, 2143–2144 (1972).

12. Interpretative Memorandum on Title VII, 110 *Cong. Rec.* 7212, 7213 (1964). Senators Clark and Case, the floor managers, went on to say: "To discriminate is to make a distinction, to make a difference in treatment or favor. . . . " But this definition corroborates rather than rebuts the charge that discrimination is a vague concept!

13. In spite of its realization that understanding of discrimination could now be a matter of controversy, Congress still did not define "discrimina-

tion" in the 1972 Act nor add comments which would allow precise application of the term.

14. *Griggs* v. *Duke Power Company* at 431: "The touchstone is business necessity."

15. See *United States* v. *St. Louis-San Francisco Railway Co.* at 308, and *Robinson* v. *Lorillard Corp.* at 798.

This is not the standard of discrimination under the Fourteenth Amendment. In the case of *Washington* v. *Davis,* the Supreme Court upheld a test used to select policemen in the District of Columbia which it would have invalidated had it been in use in a state. Because the issue arose in the District of Columbia, it had to be adjudicated under constitutional standards rather than under Title VII standards. The Court held that "a law is not unconstitutional solely because it has a racially disproportionate impact regardless of whether it reflects a racially discriminatory purpose; [and] that the disproportionate impact of the test, which was neutral on its face, did not warrant the conclusion that the test was a purposely discriminatory device . . . " (*Washington* v. *Davis* at 2041).

16. The "valid and necessary" rule was first established by *Griggs*. The most recent standards of test validation are provided in Uniform Guidelines on Employee Selection Procedures, 43 *FR* 38290 (1978). These Guidelines govern the decisions of EEOC, the Civil Service Commission (now the Office of Personnel Management), the Justice Department, and the Office of Federal Contract Compliance in the Department of Labor.

CHAPTER ELEVEN

1. "Preferential treatment for women and minorities is usually referred to as affirmative action. . . . " *The New York Times,* May 1, 1977, 33.

2. "The whole theory of affirmative action is to give preference to women and minorities to overcome the detrimental effects of past discrimination. That is, affirmative action is the practice of reverse discrimination." These remarks were made by a strong supporter of affirmative action (as she understood it), Kathleen Fisher, in a letter to Congressman James O'Hara, O'Hara Hearings, 1218, 1220. See also the testimony of Cesar Sereseres, O'Hara Hearings, 274.

3. Affirmative action "in effect calls for race and sex preferences in recruitment and hiring, and . . . the government's occasional disclaimers or denunciations of 'reverse discrimination' are disingenuous." Theodore St. Antoine, "Affirmative Action: Hypocritical Euphemism or Noble Mandate?" *University of Michigan Journal of Law Reform,* 10 (Fall 1976), 32. St. Antoine supports affirmative action understood as "preferences in recruitment and hiring." Robert F. Sasseen agrees that affirmative action is "simply and overall a preferential policy of proportional employment" clothed in the rhetoric of "nondiscrimination" and "equal opportunity," and for this

reason opposes it. Robert F. Sasseen, "Affirmative Action and the Principle of Equality," *Studies in Philosophy and Education*, 9 (Spring 1976), 282, 283.

4. This order is codified at 41 C.F.R. 60-2. Future references are included in parentheses in the text.

5. 41 C.F.R. 60. These rules are in the form of separate region-wide plans. Authority for enforcing the affirmative action rules for both construction and non-construction contractors lies with the Office of Contract Compliance in the Department of Labor. Until recently, this authority was delegated to contract compliance offices in each department. (In DHEW, enforcement is lodged in the Office of Civil Rights.)

6. A long distance swimmer declares: "My goal is to swim from Cuba to Miami and I will settle for nothing less." Rigid or flexible? A sales manager informs his salesmen: "This month's sales quota is 20 to 25 units." Rigid or flexible?

7. Rose Coser, "Affirmative Action: A Letter to a Worried Colleague," *Dissent*, 22 (Fall 1975), 366.

8. Robert O'Neill, *Discriminating Against Discrimination: Preferential Admissions and the DeFunis Case* (Bloomington, Indiana: Indiana University Press, 1975), 68.

9. Griffin Bell, quoted in Victor Navasky, "The Greening of Griffin Bell," *The New York Times Magazine*, February 27, 1977, 44.

10. Perhaps the most tendentious definition is the one offered by the University of California in *Bakke:* "Petitioners [i.e., University of California] define 'quota' as a requirement which must be met but can never be exceeded, regardless of the quality of the minority applicants." (*Bakke* at 2748, note 26.) On the basis of this definition it is not difficult to show that the special admissions system at Davis did not involve a quota since very bright minority applicants could be admitted through the regular system!

11. *Cramer* v. *Virginia Commonwealth University* at 679.

12. *Bridgeport Guardians, Inc.* v. *Bridgeport Civil Service Commission* at 798.

13. Lawrence Silberman, "The Road to Racial Quotas," *Wall Street Journal*, August 11, 1974, 12.

14. O'Hara Hearings, 464.

15. *37 FR* 24687 (1972). Emphasis added.

16. See the comments by Theodore St. Antoine and Kathleen Fisher quoted at the beginning of this chapter, notes 3 and 4.

17. O'Hara Hearings, 22. Powell went on to say:

It is commonly thought that the goal of the Equal Employment Opportunity Commission and other agencies that are concerned with elimination of barriers is to see to it there are a specific number of women, a specific number of minorities in jobs. . . .

The goal, the objective is to eliminate barriers to equal employment opportunity, a convenient benchmark is the number of women who are qualified. . . . I am sure the Harvard Universities, the Yale Universities, the Stanfords, the General Motors and General Electric are aware that they don't have to hire *x* number of women, *x* numbers of blacks or *x* numbers of Spanish-surnamed people.

There is no necessity to do it. . . . Statistics must be seen as a guidepost. The objective is to see to it that a qualified person, whether he be white or black or female or male, is accorded that degree of consideration commensurate with his or her qualifications. (23–24.)

18. *37 FR* 24687 (1972). Emphasis added.
19. Executive Order 11246 (1965), 42 U.S.C. 2000e.
20. Stanley Pottinger, "The Drive Toward Equality," in Babcock, Freedman, et al, *Sex Discrimination and the Law*, 516.
21. *American College Dictionary*.
22. But see Revised Order #4, 41 C.F.R. 60—2.14, where it speaks of the employer's "good faith efforts to make his program work *toward* the realization of the program's *goals* within the timetables set for completion." (Emphasis added.) The language of Revised Order #4 is thoroughly confusing on this matter and exhibits no clear conceptual grasp of the differences I am depicting between nondiscriminatory "goals" and discriminatory "quotas."
23. By the same token, if I expect 10 whites will be hired, that does not commit me to hiring 10 whites.
24. Consider the following colloquy between Congressman O'Hara and Bernice Sandler, Association of American Colleges:

O'Hara: If the employer knows or suspects that he will be called down to justify hiring decisions that don't lead him toward a numerical goal and that he will not be called upon to justify decisions that do lead toward numerical goals, many employers—I think wrongfully—will find it easier to sacrifice someone else's rights in order to avoid trouble for themselves.
Sandler: I can't quite see people saying, well, I will hire one woman and one black to get HEW off my back when they know it is clearly illegal.

O'Hara Hearings, 283–285. Ms. Sandler's confidence in the law-abidingness of American employers is inspiring but hardly credible, since it is certain that she can see employers discriminating *against* blacks and women even though they know this is clearly illegal too.

If an employer knows he might be involved in costly adversary dealings with the government if he fails to meet his hiring goals and knows further that if the goals are accomplished the government will look the other way, he surely has a significant incentive to resort to (subtle) reverse discrimination if this is necessary to achieve the goals. Employers would be obtuse not to read the new Guidelines on Affirmative Action Appropriate Under Title VII, which seek to immunize employers against reverse discrimination suits when the employers give preferences pursuant to a bona fide affirmative action plan under E.O. 11246, as assurances not only that the government is not going to go after them for reverse discrimination but that the government is going to stop others from going after them as well. See below, Chapter Twelve.

CHAPTER TWELVE

1. The very language is included in the Revised Order at 60–2.20(a)(1).
2. 41 C.F.R. 60–60. 9, Section X, Subsection C:

> If discriminatory placement has occured you [this section is addressing the government investigator] must attempt to determine if and when the company has ceased discriminatory placement. Begin with a review of your analysis of new hire data, determining whether placement into departments and lines of progression has been oriented according to race or sex. If so, then all present minority and female incumbents of the units identified should be considered members of the affected class. If race or sex no longer appear to be factors in placement of new hires, further inquiry of the contractor must be made to determine when these factors ceased to be considerations in placement. Try to establish a definite date; all the incumbents of the units identified prior to that date will be identified as members of the affected class.

These instructions clearly indicate that the employer is to offer remedial benefits to those actually affected by his discrimination. Those blacks and women hired *after* the employer is no longer discriminating are excluded from the "affected class."
3. 41 C.F.R. 60–60.9, Section X, Subsection G:

> Could long-time affected class members possibly move up more than one job title immediately or with little extra training in order to obtain their *rightful place* in relationship to their company seniority?

(Emphasis added.)
4. The plan "may include the adoption of practices which will eliminate the. . . . effect of past discrimination by providing opportunities for members of groups which have been excluded, regardless of whether the persons benefited were themselves the victims. . . ." 44 *FR* 4427.
5. *The New York Times,* July 5, 1977, 13.
6. *EEOC* v. *American Telephone & Telegraph,* 13 FEP Cases 392 (1976).
7. It is common for the courts to give agreements arrived at through consent decrees the force of court orders.
8. 13 FEP Cases at 415.
9. In January 1979, the consent decree and the Model Plan expired. The government listed these employment gains at AT&T: women moved from 22.4% of management to 28.5% (in top-level management from 2.1% to 6.9%, in mid-level management from 11.2% to 20.7%); blacks moved from 10.6% overall to 12% and in management from 2.3% to 5.6%; Hispanics

moved from 2.5% overall to 3.9% and in management from 0.7% to 2.1%. *The Washington Post,* January 18, 1979, Al.

10. For example, in a consent decree signed in 1975 between the government and nine steel companies, hiring "goals" were set requiring half the openings in trade and craft jobs to be filled by minority and women employees. FEP 431: 125. See *United States* v. *Allegheny-Ludlum Industries.*

CHAPTER THIRTEEN

1. See Chapter Two where RTEC is defined and discussed.
2. Article XIV, Section 1, reads in full:

> All persons born or naturalized in the United States, and subject to the jurisdiction thereof, are citizens of the United States and of the State wherein they reside. No State shall make or enforce any law which shall abridge the privileges or immunities of citizens; nor shall any State deprive any person of life, liberty, or property, without due process of law; nor deny any person within its jurisdiction the equal protection of the laws.

The Amendment applied, thus, only to "State action," but this concept has been liberally construed by the Supreme Court, allowing the Amendment considerable reach. I shall leave aside the state action requirement in what follows.

3. At 559. See also his dissent in *Civil Rights Cases* (1883).
4. *United States* v. *Jefferson County Bd. of Education* at 876.
5. A leading case here is *Carter* v. *Gallagher;* another is *NAACP* v. *Allen. Carter* presents an interesting spectacle in the reverse discrimination case law. Initially, the *Carter* court struck down a lower court requiring the Minneapolis Fire Department to "give absolute preference in certification as firefighters . . . to twenty (20) Black, American-Indian, or Spanish-surnamed applicants who qualify for such positions" (*Carter* at 318). The court took the position that the Fourteenth Amendment forbade "any discrimination in employment based on race, whether the discrimination be against Whites or Blacks" and concluded that the required "absolute preference" for twenty minorities discriminated against whites. (*Carter* at 325.)

Having thus reversed the lower court, the *Carter* court accepted a petition for rehearing *en banc* and on rehearing reversed itself, ordering that "one out of every three persons hired by the Fire Department" be minority persons, until at least twenty such persons were hired (331). But though it reversed itself, the court did not make any serious effort to rebut its own previous argument against preferences! It attempted to make a distinction between the lower court's order of "absolute" preferences and its own order of ratio preferences, but it offered no argument that its order was nonpreferential and thus non-discriminatory. Instead, it attempted to defend the legitimacy of racial preferences by citing *without further comment* a precedent *(Swann* v. *Charlotte-Mecklenburg Board of Education)* which, in its initial decision it had claimed to be irrelevant to the question of the legitimacy of employment preferences! See the dissenting opinion of Justice Van Oosterhout, *Carter* at 332.

Carter would be amusing were it not for the fact that it is universally cited and relied upon by courts and government officials as authority that preferential hiring is constitutional. The arguments offered in *NAACP* v. *Allen* for the constitutionality of preferential hiring do not contradict themselves, but are unpersuasive, confused as they are about the relevance to the issue of being able accurately to measure qualifications.

6. Joseph Tussman and Jacobus tenBroek, "The Equal Protection of the Laws," *California Law Review,* 37 (September 1949), 343.

7. See Tussman and tenBroek, 344–346.

8. See *Lindsley* v. *Natural Carbonic Gas Co.,* and *Dunn* v. *Blumstein.*

9. See *New York City Transit Authority* v. *Beazer* at 4297, ftnt. 39.

10. Tussman and tenBroek, 348–349.

11. *McGowan* v. *Maryland* at 426.

12. *Vance* v. *Bradley* at 4177.

13. See *San Antonio* v. *Rodriguez.*

14. See *Kramer* v. *Union Free School District, Shapiro* v. *Thompson,* and *San Antonio* v. *Rodriguez.*

15. See *McLaughlin* v. *Florida* and *San Antonio* v. *Rodriguez.*

16. See *Griswold* v. *Connecticut, Roe* v. *Wade.*

17. *Shapiro* v. *Thompson* at 634:

any classification which serves to penalize the exercise of . . . [a constitutional] right, unless necessary to promote a *compelling* state interest, is unconstitutional.

18. Chief Justice Burger, dissenting in *Dunn* v. *Blumstein* at 363-364:

Some lines must be drawn. To challenge such lines by the "compelling state interest" standard is to condemn them all. So far as I am aware, no state law has ever satisfied this seemingly insurmountable standard, and I doubt one ever will, for it demands nothing less than perfection.

19. *Feinerman* at 257, 258. Note also a similar judgment by another court: "The 'right to be fairly considered for public employment', as the term is used by the plaintiff, clearly is not such a 'fundamental right'." *Koelfgen* v. *Jackson* at 250.

20. See *Massachusetts* v. *Feeney,* where the kind of argument made in *Feinerman* is characterized as "routine."

21. *Loving* v. *Virginia* at 9.

22. *NAACP* v. *Button* at 444.

23. *Brotherhood of R. R. Trainmen* v. *Virginia* at 8.

24. *McLaughlin* v. *Florida* at 192.
25. See *Weinberger* v. *Wiesenfeld, Frontiero* v. *Richardson, Reed* v. *Reed,* and *Craig* v. *Boren.*
26. See *McDaniel* v. *Barresi* and *Keyes* v. *School District.*
27. Such as a situation like that in *Korematsu* v. *United States.*
28. Such goals were found compelling by the Washington State Supreme Court in *DeFunis* v. *Odegaard.* When Marco DeFunis complained that he had been denied admission to the University of Washington School of Law on racial grounds when the School admitted several minority students with lower scores than his, the State Supreme Court held against him, finding "the state interest in eliminating racial imbalance in public legal education to be compelling" (*DeFunis* at 1182).
29. *Slaughterhouse Cases* at 81.
30. Arval A. Morris, "Constitutional Alternatives to Racial Preferences in Higher Education Admissions," *Santa Clara Law Review,* 17 (1977), 281, 290.
31. See *Frontiero* v. *Richardson* and *Reed* v. *Reed.*
32. See *Reynolds* v. *Sims* (one person, one vote imposed upon state governments).
33. See *Griffin* v. *Illinois* (state must provide indigent defendant with copy of transcript for appeal).
34. See Richard Kluger, *Simple Justice* (New York: Alfred A. Knopf, 1976), 618–641.
35. *McDonald* v. *Santa Fe Rail Transp. Corp.* at 296: "the 39th Congress was intent upon establishing in federal law a broader principle than would have been necessary to meet the particular and immediate plight of the newly freed Negro slaves." See also *Bakke* at 2750.
36. "The [equal protection] clause makes the concept of equality a test of legislation, but it does not stipulate any particular conception of that concept. Those who wrote the clause . . . outlawed whatever policies would violate equality, but left it to others to decide from time to time what that means." Ronald Dworkin, *Taking Rights Seriously* (Cambridge, Massachusetts: Harvard University Press, 1977), 226.
37. *United States* v. *Carolene Products Co.* at 152, ftnt. 4.
38. See *Shelley* v. *Kraemer* at 22 and *Missouri ex. rel. Gaines* v. *Canada* at 357.
39. However, Justice Marshall in his dissent in *Bakke* at 2805 rejected the idea that "Negroes cannot be afforded greater protection under the Fourteenth Amendment where it is necessary to remedy the effects of past discrimination." He claimed that we must still view blacks as the "special favorite" of the Amendment.
40. In two recent decisions, the Court spoke explicitly of "classifications which themselves supply a reason to infer antipathy," as if antipathy is the key factor in disqualifying the classification. See *Vance* v. *Bradley* at 4177 and *Massachusetts* v. *Feeney* at 4654.

CHAPTER FOURTEEN

1. Thomas Nagel, *Mortal Questions* (New York: Cambridge University Press, 1979), 113.
2. See Joseph Raz, "Principles of Equality," *Mind,* 88 (July 1978), 321–342, which very much influenced this section of Chapter Fourteen.
3. Ronald Dworkin, "Social Sciences and Constitutional Rights—The Consequences of Uncertainty," *Journal of Law & Education,* 6 (January 1977), 6, 11.
4. Kenneth Karst, "Foreword: Equal Citizenship Under the Fourteenth Amendment," *Harvard Law Review,* 91 (November 1977), 4.
5. See also Laurence H. Tribe, "Perspectives on *Bakke*: Equal Protection, Procedural Fairness, or Structural Justice?" *Harvard Law Review,* 92 (February 1979), 864–877.
6. A recent critic of reverse discrimination offers this version of RTEC:

As I understand the notion, equality of opportunity is a principle specifying the form that is to be followed in allocating access to schooling, jobs, promotions, elections, power, and the like. And the form to be followed is that no one should be denied access to competition for those things, for any reason, while those chosen should be chosen according to their ability to perform, and for no other reason.

Barry R. Gross, *Discrimination In Reverse: Is Turnabout Fair Play?* (New York: New York University Press, 1978), 105.

CHAPTER FIFTEEN

1. I have followed here some suggestions by David Lyons, in "Human Rights and the General Welfare," *Philosophy & Public Affairs,* 6 (Winter 1977), 113–129, and in "Rights, Utility, and Racial Discrimination," in Richard Bronaugh, ed., *Philosophical Law* (Westport, Connecticut: Greenwood Press, 1978), 74–83.
2. A person being put in his "rightful place" is being put in a position he *deserves* to be in.
3. Joel Dreyfuss and Charles Lawrence III, *The Bakke Case: The Politics of Inequality* (New York: Harcourt Brace Jovanovich, 1979), 87.

List of Cases

Albemarle Paper Company v. Moody, 422 U.S. 405 (1974).

Anthony v. Massachusetts, 415 F. Supp. 485 (1976).

Boston Chapter, NAACP v. Beecher, 371 F. Supp. 507 (1974).

Boston Chapter, NAACP v. Beecher, 504 F. 2d 1017 (1st Cir. 1974).

Bounds v. Smith, 97 S. Ct. 1491 (1977).

Bridgeport Guardians, Inc. v. Bridgeport Civil Service Commission, 354 F. Supp. 778 (1973).

Brotherhood of R. R. Trainmen v. Virginia, 377 U.S. 1 (1964).

Brown v. Board of Education, 347 U.S. 483 (1954).

Carter v. Gallagher, 452 F. 2d 315 (8th Cir. 1971).

Chance v. Board of Examiners, 534 F. 2d 993 (2nd Cir. 1976).

City of Los Angeles Department of Water v. Manhart, 98 S. Ct. 1370 (1978).

Civil Rights Cases, 109 U.S. 3 (1883).

Contractors Association of Eastern Pennsylvania v. Secretary of Labor, 442 F. 2d 159 (3rd Cir. 1971).

Craig v. Boren, 429 U.S. 190 (1976).

Cramer v. Virginia Commonwealth University, 415 F. Supp. 673 (1976).

DeFunis v. Odegaard, 507 P. 2d 1169 (1973).

DeFunis v. Odegaard, 416 U.S. 312 (1974).

Dunn v. Blumstein, 405 U.S. 330 (1972).

EEOC v. American Telephone & Telegraph Co., 13 FEP Cases 392 (1976).

Feinerman v. Jones, 356 F. Supp. 252 (1973).

Franks v. Bowman Transp. Company, 96 S. Ct. 1251 (1976).
Frontiero v. Richardson, 411 U.S. 677 (1973).
Germann v. Kipp, 429 F. Supp. 1323 (1977).
Glona v. American Guar. & Liab. Company, 391 U.S. 73 (1968).
Graham v. Richardson, 403 U.S. 65 (1971).
Griffin v. Illinois, 351 U.S. 12 (1956).
Griggs v. Duke Power Company, 401 U.S. 424 (1971).
Griswold v. Connecticut, 381 U.S. 479 (1965).
Harper v. Virginia Bd. of Elections, 383 U.S. 663 (1966).
Hernandez v. Texas, 347 U.S. 475 (1954).
In re Griffiths, 413 U.S. 717 (1973).
International Brotherhood of Teamsters v. United States, 431 U.S. 324 (1977).
Kaiser Aluminum & Chemical Corp. v. Weber, 47 LW 4851 (1979).
Keyes v. School District, 413 U.S. 189 (1973).
Koelfgen v. Jackson, 355 F. Supp. 243 (1972).
Korematsu v. United States, 323 U.S. 214 (1944).
Kotch v. Pilot Commissioners, 330 U.S. 552 (1947).
Kramer v. Union Free School District, 393 U.S. 818 (1969).
Levy v. Louisiana, 391 U.S. 68 (1968).
Lindsley v. National Carbonic Gas Co., 220 U.S. 61 (1911).
Louisiana v. United States, 380 U.S. 145 (1965).
Loving v. Virginia, 388 U.S. 1 (1967).
Massachusetts v. Feeney, 47 LW 4650 (1979).
McAleer v. American Telephone & Telegraph Co., 416 F. Supp. 435 (1976).
McDaniel v. Barresi, 402 U.S. 39 (1971).
McDonald v. Santa Fe Rail Transp. Corp., 427 U.S. 273 (1976).
McGowan v. Maryland, 366 U.S. 420 (1961).
Missouri ex. rel. Gaines v. Canada, 305 U.S. 337 (1938).
NAACP v. Allen, 493 F. 2d 614 (1974).
NAACP v. Button, 371 U.S. 415 (1963).
New York City Transit Authority v. Beazer, 47 LW 4291 (1979).
Patterson v. American Tobacco Company, 535 F. 2d 257 (4th Cir. 1976).
Plessy v. Ferguson, 163 U.S. 537 (1896).
Porcelli v. Titus, 302 F. Supp. 726 (1969).

Powell v. Texas, 392 U.S. 514 (1968).
Quarles v. Phillip Morris, Inc., 279 F. Supp. 505 (1968).
Reed v. Reed, 404 U.S. 71 (1971).
Regents of University of California v. Bakke, 98 S. Ct. 2733 (1978).
Reynolds v. Sims, 377 U.S. 533 (1964).
Rios v. Enterprise Association Steamfitters Local 638, 501 F. 2d 622 (2nd Cir. 1974).
Robinson v. Lorillard Corp., 444 F. 2d 791 (4th Cir. 1971).
Roe v. Wade, 410 U.S. 113 (1973).
San Antonio v. Rodriguez, 411 U.S. 1 (1973).
Shapiro v. Thompson, 394 U.S. 618 (1969).
Shelley v. Kraemer, 334 U.S. 1 (1948).
Skinner, v. Oklahoma ex. rel. Williamson, 316 U.S. 535 (1942).
Sugarman v. Dougall, 413 U.S. 634 (1973).
Swann v. Charlotte-Mecklenburg Board of Education, 402 U.S. 1 (1971).
The Slaughterhouse Cases, 16 Wall 36 (1873).
United Jewish Organization of Willamsburgh, Inc. v. Carey, 97 S. Ct. 996 (1976).
United States v. Allegheny-Ludlum Steel Corp., 11 FEP Cases 167 (1975).
United States v. Bethlehem Steel Corp., 446 F. 2d 652 (2nd Cir. 1971).
United States v. Carolene Products Co., 304 U.S. 144 (1938).
United States v. Chesapeake and Ohio Ry., 471 F. 2d 582 (4th Cir. 1972).
United States v. Guest, 383 U.S. 745 (1966).
United States v. Jefferson County Bd. of Education, 372 F. 2d 836 (5th Cir. 1967).
United States v. N. L. Industries, Inc., 479 F. 2d 354 (8th Cir. 1973).
United States v. St. Louis-San Francisco Railway Co., 464 F. 2d 301 (8th Cir. 1972).
Vance v. Bradley, 47 LW 4176 (1979).
Washington v. Davis, 96 S. Ct. 2040 (1976).
Weber v. Kaiser Aluminum & Chemical Corp., 563 F. 2d 216 (5th Cir. 1977).
Weinberger v. Wiesenfeld, 420 U.S. 636 (1975).

Bibliography and References

Items cited in the text or notes are preceded by an asterisk.

Adelson, Joseph. "Living With Quotas." *Commentary,* 65 (May 1978), 23–29.

*Alexander, George J. "Symposium—*Bakke* v. *Board of Regents:* Foreword." *Santa Clara Law Review,* 17 (1977), 271–278.

Amdur, Robert. "Compensatory Justice: The Question of Costs." *Political Theory,* 7 (May 1979), 229–244.

*Auer, Andreas. "Public School Desegregation and the Color-Blind Constitution." *Southwestern Law Journal,* 27 (August 1973), 454–489.

Axelsen, Diana. "With All Deliberate Delay: On Justifying Preferential Policies in Education and Employment." *Philosophical Forum,* 9 (Winter–Spring 1977–1978), 264–288.

*Babcock, Barbara, and Ann Freedman, Eleanor Norton, and Susan Ross. *Sex Discrimination and the Law: Causes and Remedies.* Boston: Little, Brown and Company, 1975.

Balabkins, Nicholas. *West German Reparations to Israel.* New Brunswick, New Jersey: Rutgers University Press, 1971.

*Barnett, Marguerite Ross. "A Theoretical Perspective on American Racial Policy." *Public Policy for the Black Community: Strategies and Perspectives.* Eds. Marguerite Ross Barnett and James A. Hefner. Port Washington, New York: Alfred Publishing Company, 1976, 1–54.

Bayles, Michael. "Compensatory Reverse Discrimination in Hiring." *Social Theory and Practice,* 2 (Spring 1973), 301–312.

*————. "Reparations to Wronged Groups." *Analysis*, 33 (June 1973), 182–184.

*Becker, Gary. *The Economic Approach to Human Behavior.* Chicago: University of Chicago Press, 1976.

*Bedau, Hugo Adam. "Compensatory Justice and the Black Manifesto." *The Monist*, 56 (January 1972), 20–42.

Bell, Derrick A., Jr. "Bakke, Minority Admissions, and the Usual Price of Racial Remedies." *California Law Review*, 67 (January 1979), 3–19.

————. "Book Review: *Affirmative Discrimination: Ethnic Inequality and Public Policy*, by Nathan Glazer." *Emory Law Journal*, 25 (Fall 1976), 879–898.

————. "Introduction: Awakening After *Bakke*." *Harvard Civil Rights—Civil Liberties Law Review*, 14 (Spring 1979), 1–6.

————. "Racial Remediation: An Historical Perspective on Current Conditions." *Notre Dame Lawyer*, 52 (October 1976), 5–29.

Bennett, William J. and Terry Eastland. "Why Bakke Won't End Reverse Discrimination." *Commentary*, 66 (September 1978), 29–35.

*Bittker, Boris I. *The Case for Black Reparations.* New York: Vintage Books, 1973.

*Black, Virginia. "The Erosion of Legal Principles in Creation of Legal Policies." *Ethics*, 84 (January 1974), 93–115.

Blackstone, William T. "An Assessment of the Ethical Pros and Cons of Reverse Discrimination." *Philosophy and Public Policy.* Ed. Donnie J. Self. Norfolk, Virginia: Teagle & Little, Inc., 1977, 53–67.

————. "Compensatory Justice and Affirmative Action." *Proceedings of the American Catholic Philosophical Association*, 69 (1975), 218–229.

————. "Reverse Discrimination and Compensatory Justice." *Social Theory and Practice*, 3 (Spring 1975), 253–288.

————, and Robert Heslep, eds. *Social Justice and Preferential Treatment.* Athens, Georgia: University of Georgia Press, 1977.

Blasi, Vincent. "*Bakke* as Precedent: Does Mr. Justice Powell Have a Theory?" *California Law Review*, 67 (January 1979), 21–68.

*Block, N. J., and Gerald Dworkin, eds. *The I. Q. Controversy.* New York: Pantheon Books, 1976.

*Blumrosen, Alfred. "Quotas, Common Sense, and Law in Labor Relations: Three Dimensions of Equal Opportunity." *Rutgers Law Review*, 27 (Spring 1974), 675–703.

Boxill, Bernard. "The Morality of Preferential Hiring." *Philosophy & Public Affairs*, 7 (Spring 1978), 246–268.

*———. "The Morality of Reparations." *Today's Moral Problems*. Ed. Richard Wasserstrom. New York: Macmillan Publishing Company, 1975, 209–217.

Bracy, Warren. "The Questionable Legality of Affirmative Action: A Response." *Journal of Urban Law*, 51 (February 1974), 421–431.

———. "The Questionable Legality of Affirmative Action: A Response to Rejoinder." *Journal of Urban Law*, 52 (November 1974), 273–276.

*Browne, Robert S., and Robert Vernon. *Should the U. S. Be Partitioned Into Separate and Independent Nations—One a Homeland for White Americans and Another a Homeland for Black Americans?* New York: Merit Publishers, 1968.

Bundy, McGeorge. "The Issue Before the Court: Who Gets Ahead in America?" *The Atlantic*, 240 (November 1977), 41–54.

Bunzel, John H. "Bakke v. University of California." *Commentary*, 63 (March 1977), 59–64.

Cadei, Raymond M. "Hiring Goals, California State Government, and Title VII: Is This Numbers Game Legal?" *Pacific Law Journal*, 8 (January 1977), 49–72.

Calabresi, Guido. "*Bakke* as Pseudo-Tragedy." *Catholic University Law Review*, 28 (Spring 1979), 427–444.

*Campbell, T. D. "Equality of Opportunity." *Proceedings of the Aristotelian Society*, 75 (1974–1975), 51–68.

Cohen, Carl. "The DeFunis Case: Race and the Constitution." *The Nation*, 220 (February 8, 1975), 135–145.

———. "Why Racial Preference Is Illegal and Immoral." *Commentary*, 67 (June 1979), 40–52.

Cohen, Marshall, and Thomas Nagel and Thomas Scanlon, eds. *Equality and Preferential Treatment*. Princeton, New Jersey: Princeton University Press, 1977.

Coleman, Jules L. "Justice and Preferential Hiring." *Journal of Critical Analysis*, 5 (July–October 1973), 27–30.

280   *Bibliography and References*

*Copp, David. "Collective Actions and Secondary Actions." *American Philosophical Quarterly*, 16 (July 1979), 177–186.

*Coser, Rose Laub. "Affirmative Action: Letter to a Worried Colleague." *Dissent*, 22 (Fall 1975), 366–369.

Cowan, J. L. "Inverse Discrimination." *Analysis*, 33 (October 1972), 10–12.

Cox, Archibald. "Foreword: Constitutional Adjudication and the Promotion of Human Rights." *Harvard Law Review*, 80 (November 1966), 91–122.

———. *The Role of the Supreme Court in American Government*. New York: Oxford University Press, 1976.

Crocker, Lawrence. "Preferential Treatment." *Feminism and Philosophy*. Eds. Mary Vetterling-Braggin, Frederick A. Elliston, and Jane English. Totowa, New Jersey: Littlefield, Adams and Company, 1977, 190–209.

*Davidson, Kenneth. "Preferential Treatment and Equal Opportunity." *Oregon Law Review*, 55 (1976), 53–83.

"Developments in the Law—Employment Discrimination and Title VII of the Civil Rights Act of 1964." *Harvard Law Review*, 84 (March 1971), 1109–1316.

"Developments in the Law—Equal Protection." *Harvard Law Review*, 82 (March 1969), 1065–1192.

Dixon, Robert G., Jr. *"Bakke: A Constitutional Analysis." California Law Review*, 67 (January 1979), 69–86.

———. "The Supreme Court and Equality: Legislative Classification, Desegregation, and Reverse Discrimination." *Cornell Law Review*, 62 (March 1977), 494–562.

*Dreyfuss, Joel, and Charles Lawrence. *The Bakke Case: The Politics of Inequality*. New York: Harcourt Brace Jovanovich, 1979.

*Dworkin, Ronald. "How to Read the Civil Rights Act." *New York Review of Books*, 26 (December 20, 1979), 37–43.

*———. "Social Sciences and Constitutional Rights—The Consequences of Uncertainty." *Journal of Law and Education*, 6 (January 1977), 3–12.

*———. *Taking Rights Seriously*. Cambridge, Massachusetts: Harvard University Press, 1977.

———. "The Bakke Decision: Did It Decide Anything?" *New York Review of Books*, 25 (August 17, 1978), 20–25.

————. "Why Bakke Has No Case." *New York Review of Books,* 24 (November 10, 1977), 11–15.

Edwards, Harry T. "Race Discrimination in Employment: What Price Equality?" *University of Illinois Law Forum,* 1976 (1976), 572–626.

————, and Barry L. Zaretsky. "Preferential Remedies for Employment Discrimination." *Michigan Law Review,* 74 (November 1975), 1–48.

Elshtain, Jean Bethke. "The Feminist Movement and the Question of Equality." *Polity,* 7 (Summer 1975), 452–477.

Ely, John Hart. "The Constitutionality of Reverse Racial Discrimination." *University of Chicago Law Review,* 41 (Summer 1974), 723–741.

Ezorsky, Gertrude. "On 'Groups and Justice'." *Ethics,* 87 (January 1977), 182–185.

Federal Higher Educations Programs Institutional Eligibility. Hearings Before the Special Subcommittee on Education. United States House of Representatives, 93rd Congress, 2nd Session, August-September 1974. Washington, D. C.: Government Printing Office, 1974.

*Feinberg, Joel. *Social Philosophy.* Englewood Cliffs, New Jersey: Prentice-Hall, Inc., 1973.

Fiss, Owen. "A Theory of Fair Employment Laws." *University of Chicago Law Review,* 38 (Winter 1971), 235–314.

————. "Groups and the Equal Protection Clause." *Philosophy & Public Affairs,* 5 (Winter 1976), 107–177.

————. "The Fate of An Idea Whose Time Has Come: Antidiscrimination Law in the Second Decade After *Brown* v. *Board of Education.*" *University of Chicago Law Review,* 41 (Summer 1974), 742–773.

Fontham, Michael R. "The Proposed EEOC Guidelines: Legalization of Employment Discrimination Against White Males." *Journal of Intergroup Relations,* 6 (December 1978), 30–39.

*Frankel, Charles. "Equality of Opportunity." *Ethics,* 81 (April 1971), 191–211.

Freeman, Richard B. "The New Job Market for Black Academicians." *Industrial and Labor Relations Review,* 30 (January 1977), 161–174.

Fried, Marlene Gerber. "In Defense of Preferential Hiring." *Philosophical Forum*, 5 (Fall-Winter 1973–1974), 309–319.

*French, Peter A. "The Corporation as a Moral Person." *American Philosophical Quarterly*, 16 (July 1979), 207–215.

*French, Stanley, and Andreas Gutman. "The Principle of National Self-Determination." *Philosophy, Morality, and International Affairs*. Eds. Virginia Held, Sidney Morgenbesser, and Thomas Nagel. New York: Oxford University Press, 1974, 138–153.

*Fullinwider, Robert K. "On Preferential Hiring." *Feminism and Philosophy*. Eds. Mary Vetterling-Braggin, Frederick A. Elliston, and Jane English. Totowa, New Jersey: Littlefield, Adams and Company, 1977, 210–224.

*———. "Preferential Hiring and Compensation." *Social Theory and Practice*, 3 (Spring 1975), 307–320.

Galloway, Russell W., Jr., and Henry Hewitt. "*Bakke* Below: A Constitutional Fallacy." *Santa Clara Law Review*, 17 (1977), 385–404.

Gellhorn, Ernest, and D. Brock Hornby. "Constitutional Limitations on Admissions Procedures and Standards—Beyond Affirmative Action." *Virginia Law Review*, 60 (October 1974), 975–1011.

*Glazer, Nathan. *Affirmative Discrimination: Ethnic Inequality and Public Policy*. New York: Basic Books, 1975.

———. "Why Bakke Won't End Reverse Discrimination." *Commentary*, 66 (September 1978), 36–41.

Goff, Edwin L. "Affirmative Action, John Rawls, and a Partial Compliance Theory of Justice." *Cultural Hermeneutics*, 4 (November 1976), 43–59.

Goldman, Alan H. "Affirmative Action." *Philosophy & Public Affairs*, 5 (Winter 1976), 178–195.

———. "Justice and Hiring by Competence." *American Philosophical Quarterly*, 14 (January 1977), 17–28.

———. *Justice and Reverse Discrimination*. Princeton, New Jersey: Princeton University Press, 1979.

———. "Limits to the Justification of Reverse Discrimination." *Social Theory and Practice*, 3 (Spring 1975), 289–306.

*———. "Reparations to Individuals or Groups?" *Analysis*, 35 (April 1975), 168–170.

————. "Reply to Jagger." *Social Theory and Practice,* 4 (Spring 1977), 235–237.

*Golightly, Cornelius. "Justice and 'Discrimination For' in Higher Education." *Philosophic Exchange,* 1 (Summer 1974), 5–14.

*Gottlieb, Gidon. "Comment." *Is the Law Dead?* Ed. Eugene V. Rostow. New York: Simon and Schuster, 1971, 194–208.

Graglia, Lino A. *Disaster By Decree: The Supreme Court Decisions on Race and the Schools.* Ithaca, New York: Cornell University Press, 1976.

Graubard, Allen. "Is There an Alternative to 'Reverse Discrimination'?" *Working Papers for a New Society* (May-June 1978), 11–13.

*Greely, Hank. "The Equality of Allocation By Lot." *Harvard Civil Rights—Civil Liberties Law Review,* 12 (Winter 1977), 113–141.

Green, Mark. "Reparations for Blacks." *Commonweal,* 90 (June 1969), 359–362.

Greenawalt, Kent. "Judicial Scrutiny of 'Benign' Racial Preferences in Law School Admissions." *Columbia Law Review,* 75 (April 1975), 559–602.

————. "The Unresolved Problems of Reverse Discrimination." *California Law Review,* 67 (January 1979), 87–129.

Griswold, Erwin N. "Some Observations on the *DeFunis* Case." *Columbia Law Review,* 75 (April 1975), 512–519.

*Gruner, Rolf. "On the Action of Social Groups." *Inquiry,* 19 (Winter 1976), 443–454.

*Gross, Barry R. *Discrimination in Reverse: Is Turnabout Fair Play?* New York: New York University Press, 1978.

*————, ed. *Reverse Discrimination.* Buffalo, New York: Prometheus Press, 1977.

*Guinier, Ewart. "Review: *The Case for Black Reparations* by Boris I. Bittker." *Yale Law Journal,* 82 (July 1973), 1719–1724.

Hall, James H., Jr. "A Case for Reverse Discrimination." *Philosophy and Public Policy.* Ed. Donnie J. Self. Norfolk, Virginia: Teagle & Little, Inc., 1977, 68–73.

Harder, Martha B. "How They Get Us With Subtle Discrimination." *Context,* 12 (Spring 1978), 21–23.

Harrington, Michael, and Arnold Kaufman. "Black Reparations—

Two Views." *Dissent,* 16 (July-August 1969), 317–320.

*Harvey, William. "Some Different Thoughts About Bakke." *National Review,* 30 (February 3, 1978), 151–152, 171.

*Hayek, Friedrich A. *The Constitution of Liberty.* Chicago: Henry Regnery and Company, 1972.

Hebert, Stanley, and Charles Reischel. "Title VII and the Multiple Approaches to Eliminating Employment Discrimination." *New York University Law Review,* 46 (May 1971), 449–485.

Held, Virginia. "Reasonable Progress and Self-Respect." *The Monist,* 57 (January 1973), 13–27.

Henkin, Louis. "*DeFunis:* An Introduction." *Columbia Law Review,* 75 (April 1975), 483–494.

———. "What of the Right to Practice a Profession?" *California Law Review,* 67 (January 1979), 131–141.

Hill, James. "What Justice Requires: Some Comments on Professor Schoeman's Views on Compensatory Justice." *Personalist,* 56 (Winter 1975), 96–103.

Hill, Herbert. "The New Judicial Perception of Employment Discrimination: Litigation Under Title VII of the Civil Rights Act of 1964." *University of Colorado Law Review,* 43 (March 1972), 243–268.

*Hook, Sidney. "Discrimination, Color Blindness, and the Quota System." *Reverse Discrimination.* Ed. Barry Gross. Buffalo, New York: Prometheus Books, 1977, 84–87.

Horowitz, Donald L. "Are the Courts Going Too Far?" *Commentary,* 63 (January 1977), 37–44.

Horowitz, Harold W., and Kenneth L. Karst. *Law, Lawyers and Social Change.* Indianapolis, Indiana: Bobbs-Merrill, Inc., 1969.

*Hughes, Graham. *The Conscience of the Courts: Law and Morals in American Life.* Garden City, New York: Anchor/Doubleday, 1975.

Jacobson, Julius. "Notes on the Bakkelash." *New Politics,* 12 (Winter 1978), 3, 66–68.

Jagger, Alison. "Relaxing the Limits of Preferential Treatment." *Social Theory and Practice,* 4 (Spring 1977), 227–235.

Jones, Hardy. "Fairness, Meritocracy, and Reverse Discrimination." *Social Theory and Practice,* 4 (Spring 1977), 211–226.

*Karst, Kenneth L. "Foreword: Equal Citizenship Under the Fourteenth Amendment." *Harvard Law Review*, 91 (November 1977), 1–68.

———, and Harold W. Horowitz. "Affirmative Action and Equal Protection." *Virginia Law Review*, 60 (October 1974), 955–974.

———. "The *Bakke* Opinions and Equal Protection Doctrine." *Harvard Civil Rights—Civil Liberties Law Review*, 14 (Spring 1979), 7–29.

Katzner, Louis. "Is the Favoring of Women and Blacks in Employment and Educational Opportunities Justified?" *Philosophy of Law*. Eds. Joel Feinberg and Hyman Gross. Encino, California: Dickenson Publishing Company, 1975, 291–296.

*Ketchum, Sara Ann, and Christine Pierce. "Implicit Racism." *Analysis*, 36 (January 1976), 91–95.

Kirp, David L. "Law, Politics, and Equal Educational Opportunity: The Limits of Judicial Involvement." *Harvard Educational Review*, 47 (May 1977), 117–137.

Kleinberg, Stanley S. "Woodruff on Discrimination." *Analysis*, 37 (October 1976), 46–48.

*Kluger, Richard. *Simple Justice*. New York: Alfred A. Knopf, 1976.

Lavinsky, Larry M. "*DeFunis* v. *Odegaard:* The 'Non-Decision' With a Message." *Columbia Law Review*, 75 (April 1975), 520–533.

Levin, Betsy, and Willis D. Hawley, eds. *The Courts, Social Science, and School Desegregation*. New Brunswick, New Jersey: Transaction Books, 1977.

*Longwood, Merle. "Justice and Reparations: The Black Manifesto Reconsidered." *Lutheran Quarterly*, 27 (August 1975), 203–213.

Lorch, Barbara R. "Reverse Discrimination in Hiring in Sociology Departments: A Preliminary Report." *American Sociologist*, 8 (August 1973), 116–170.

*Lyons, David. "Human Rights and the General Welfare." *Philosophy & Public Affairs*, 6 (Winter 1977), 113–129.

*———. "Rights, Utility, and Racial Discrimination." *Philosophical Law*. Ed. Richard Bronaugh. Westport, Connecticut: Greenwood Press, 1978, 74–83.

MacGuigan, Mark R. "Reverse Discrimination Reversed." *Philosophical Law.* Ed. Richard Bronaugh. Westport, Connecticut: Greenwood Press, 1978, 84–92.

Martin, Michael. "Pedagogical Arguments for Preferential Hiring and Tenuring of Women Teachers in the University." *Philosophical Forum,* 5 (Fall–Winter 1973–1974), 325–333.

McGary, Howard, Jr. "Justice and Reparations." *Philosophical Forum,* 9 (Winter–Spring 1977–1978), 250–263.

Meltzer, Bernard D. "Labor Arbitration and Overlapping and Conflicting Remedies for Employment Discrimination." *University of Chicago Law Review,* 39 (Fall 1971), 30–50.

*Morris, Arval A. "Constitutional Alternatives to Racial Preferences in Higher Education Admissions." *Santa Clara Law Review,* 17 (1977), 279–327.

Moulton, Janice. "The Preferential Hiring Issue." *Philosophy and Public Policy.* Ed. Donnie J. Self. Norfolk, Virginia: Teagle & Little, Inc., 1977, 41–52.

Munzer, Stephen. "Review: Nathan Glazer, *Affirmative Discrimination: Ethnic Inequality and Public Policy.*" *Theory and Decision,* 7 (October 1976), 331–334.

*Nagel, Thomas. "Equal Treatment and Compensatory Discrimination." *Philosophy & Public Affairs,* 2 (Summer 1973), 348–363.

*———. *Mortal Questions.* New York: Cambridge University Press, 1979.

Navasky, Victor. "The Greening of Griffin Bell." *The New York Times Magazine,* February 27, 1977, 41–44, 50.

Newton, Lisa. "Reverse Discrimination as Unjustified." *Ethics,* 83 (July 1973), 308–312.

Nickel, James W. "Classification by Race in Compensatory Programs." *Ethics,* 84 (January 1974), 146–150.

———. "Discrimination and Morally Relevant Characteristics." *Analysis,* 32 (March 1972), 113–114.

———. "Preferential Policies in Hiring and Admissions: A Jurisprudential Approach." *Columbia Law Review,* 75 (April 1975), 534–558.

———. "Should Reparations Be to Individuals or to Groups?" *Analysis,* 34 (April 1974), 154–160.

Noonan, Richard D. "Semantics of Equality of Educational Opportunity." *Teachers College Record,* 76 (September 1974), 63–88.

Note. "Proportional Representation By Race: The Constitutionality of Benign Racial Redistricting." *Michigan Law Review,* 74 (March 1976), 820–841.

Note. "*Weber* v. *Kaiser Aluminum & Chemical Corp.:* The Challenge to Voluntary Compliance Under Title VII." *Columbia Journal of Law and Social Problems,* 14 (1978), 123–187.

Nunn, William A. "Reverse Discrimination." *Analysis,* 34 (April 1974), 151–154.

O'Neil, Robert M. "*Bakke* in Balance: Some Preliminary Thoughts." *California Law Review,* 67 (January 1979), 143–170.

*———. *Discriminating Against Discrimination: Preferential Admissions and the DeFunis Case.* Bloomington, Indiana: Indiana University Press, 1975.

———. "Racial Preference and Higher Education: The Larger Context." *Virginia Law Review,* 60 (October 1974), 925–954.

*O'Neill, Onora. "Efficiency and Equal Opportunity." Unpublished.

*———. "How Do We Know When Opportunities Are Equal?" *Feminism and Philosophy.* Eds. Mary Vetterling-Braggin, Frederick A. Elliston, and Jane English. Totowa, New Jersey: Littlefield, Adams and Company, 1977, 177–189.

*———. "Opportunities, Inequalities and Education." *Theory and Decision,* 7 (October 1976), 275–295.

Oshinsky, David. "Unshaded Opinions: Reviews of Robert M. O'Neil, *Discriminating Against Discrimination: Preferential Admissions and the DeFunis Case,* and Nathan Glazer, *Affirmative Discrimination: Ethnic Inequality and Public Policy,*" *Change,* 8 (May 1976), 58–60.

Pemberton, John deJ., Jr., ed. *Equal Employment Opportunity— Responsibilities, Rights, Remedies.* New York: Practicing Law Institute, 1975.

Pollack, Louis H. "*DeFunis* Non Est Disputantum." *Columbia Law Review,* 75 (April 1975), 495–511.

Poplin, Caroline. "Fair Employment in a Depressed Economy: The Layoff Problem." *UCLA Law Review,* 23 (December 1975), 177–234.

Posner, Richard. "The *Bakke* Case and the Future of 'Affirmative

Action'." *California Law Review*, 67 (January 1979), 171–189.

———. "The *DeFunis* Case and the Constitutionality of Preferential Treatment of Racial Minorities." *The Supreme Court Review*. Ed. Philip Kurland. Chicago: University of Chicago Press, 1975, 1–32.

*Pottinger, Stanley. "The Drive Toward Equality." *Sex Discrimination and the Law*. Barbara Babcock, et al. Boston: Little, Brown and Company, 1975, 514–518.

*Rawls, John. *A Theory of Justice*. Cambridge, Massachusetts: Harvard University Press, 1971.

*———. "Justice as Fairness." *Philosophical Review*, 67 (April 1958), 164–194.

*Raz, Joseph. "Principles of Equality." *Mind*, 88 (July 1978), 321–342.

Redish, Martin H. "Preferential Law School Admissions and the Equal Protection Clause: An Analysis of the Competing Arguments." *UCLA Law Review*, 22 (December 1974), 343–400.

Richards, David A. J. "Equal Opportunity and School Financing: Towards a Moral Theory of Constitutional Adjudication." *University of Chicago Law Review*, 41 (Fall 1973), 32–71.

———. *The Moral Criticism of the Law*. Encino, California: Dickenson Publishing Company, 1977.

*Richardson, Henry J. III. "Black People, Technocracy, and Legal Process: Thoughts, Fears, and Goals." *Public Policy for the Black Community: Strategies and Perspectives*. Eds. Marguerite Ross Barnett and James A. Hefner. Port Washington, New York: Alfred Publishing Company, 1976, 157–190.

Rossum, Ralph A. "Ameliorative Racial Preference and the Fourteenth Amendment: Some Constitutional Problems." *Journal of Politics*, 38 (May 1976), 346–366.

*St. Antoine, Theodore. "Affirmative Action, A 'Heroic' Measure." *The New York Times*, November 26, 1976, Op-Ed page.

*———. "Affirmative Action: Hypocritical Euphemism or Noble Mandate?" *University of Michigan Journal of Law Reform*, 10 (Fall 1976), 28–43.

Samford, Frank P. "Towards a Constitutional Definition of Racial Discrimination." *Emory Law Journal*, 25 (Summer 1976), 509–578.

Sandalow, Terrance. "Judicial Protection of Minorities." *Michigan Law Review*, 75 (April–May 1977), 1162–1195.

———. "Racial Preferences in Higher Education: Political Responsibility and the Judicial Role." *University of Chicago Law Review*, 42 (Summer 1975), 653–703.

*Sasseen, Robert F. "Affirmative Action and the Principle of Equality." *Studies in Philosophy and Education*, 9 (Spring 1976), 275–295.

Schoeman, Ferdinand. "When Is It Just to Discriminate?" *Personalist*, 56 (Spring 1975), 170–177.

Schwerin, Kurt. "German Compensation for Victims of Nazi Persecution." *Northwestern University Law Review*, 67 (September–October 1972), 479–527.

Sedler, Robert Allen. "Beyond *Bakke:* The Constitution and Redressing the Social History of Racism." *Harvard Civil Rights—Civil Liberties Law Review*, 14 (Spring 1979), 133–171.

———. "Racial Preference, Reality, and the Constitution: *Bakke* v. *Regents of University of California." Santa Clara Law Review*, 17 (1977), 329–384.

Seligman, Daniel. "How 'Equal Opportunity' Turned Into Employment Quotas." *Fortune*, 87 (March 1973), 160–174.

*Sher, George, "Justifying Reverse Discrimination in Employment." *Philosophy & Public Affairs*, 4 (Winter 1975), 159–170.

*———. "Groups and Justice." *Ethics*, 87 (January 1977), 174–181.

Sherain, Howard, "The Questionable Legality of Affirmative Action." *Journal of Urban Law*, 51 (August 1973), 25–47.

———. "The Questionable Legality of Affirmative Action: A Rejoinder." *Journal of Urban Law*, 52 (November 1974), 267–271.

Sherman, Malcolm, J. "Affirmative Action and the AAUP." *AAUP Bulletin*, 61 (Winter 1975), 293–303.

———. "Anti-Intellectualism and Civil Rights." *Change*, 8 (Winter 1976), 34–40.

Shiner, Roger A. "Individuals, Groups and Inverse Discrimination." *Analysis*, 33 (June 1973), 185–187.

Silvestri, Philip. "The Justification of Inverse Discrimination." *Analysis*, 34 (October 1973), 31.

Simon, Robert L. "Equality, Merit, and the Determination of Our

Gifts." *Social Research,* 41 (Autumn 1974), 492–514.

*———. "Preferential Hiring: A Reply to Judith Jarvis Thomson." *Philosophy & Public Affairs,* 3 (Spring 1974), 312–320.

———. "Statistical Justification of Discrimination." *Analysis,* 38 (January 1978), 37–42.

*Simpson, Evan. "Discrimination as an Example of Moral Irrationality." *Fact, Value and Perception: Essays in Honor of Charles A. Baylis.* Ed. Paul Welsh. Durham, North Carolina: Duke University Press, 1975, 107–122.

Sindler, Allan P. "The Court's Three Decisions." *Regulation,* 2 (September-October 1978), 15–23.

*Solomon, Lewis D., and Judith S. Heeter. "Affirmative Action in Higher Education: Towards a Rationale for Preference." *Notre Dame Lawyer,* 52 (October 1976), 41–76.

Sowell, Thomas. " 'Affirmative Action' Reconsidered." *Public Interest,* 42 (Winter 1976), 47–65.

Steele, Claude, and Stephen Greer. "Affirmative Action and Academic Hiring: A Case Study of a Value Conflict." *Journal of Higher Education,* 47 (July–August 1976), 413–435.

*Strike, Kenneth A. "Justice and Reverse Discrimination." *University of Chicago School Review,* 84 (August 1976), 516–537.

Taylor, Paul. "Reverse Discrimination and Compensatory Justice." *Analysis,* 33 (June 1973), 177–182.

Tenzer, Morton J., and Rose Laub Coser. "A Debate on Affirmative Action." *Dissent,* 23 (Spring 1976), 207–210.

*Thalberg, Irving. "Reverse Discrimination and the Future." *Philosophical Forum,* 5 (Fall–Winter 1973–1974), 294–308.

Thomas, D. A. Lloyd. "Competitive Equality of Opportunity." *Mind,* 86 (July 1977), 388–404.

*Thomson, Judith Jarvis. "Preferential Hiring." *Philosophy & Public Affairs,* 2 (Summer 1973), 364–384.

Tillar, Darrell Long. "Setting the Record Straight About Affirmative Action." *Context,* 11 (Spring 1977), 12–14.

*Tollett, Kenneth. "What Led to Bakke." *The Center Magazine,* 11 (January-February 1978), 2–10.

*Tribe, Laurence H. "Perspectives on Bakke: Equal Protection, Procedural Fairness, or Structural Justice?" *Harvard Law Review,* 92 (February 1979), 864–877.

*Tussman, Joseph, and Jacobus tenBroek. "The Equal Protection of the Laws." *California Law Review*, 37 (September 1949), 341–381.

*Vetterling, Mary K. "Some Common Sense Notes on Preferential Hiring." *Philosophical Forum*, 5 (Fall–Winter 1973–1974), 320–324.

Wade, Francis C. "Preferential Treatment of Blacks." *Social Theory and Practice*, 4 (Spring 1978), 445–470.

Warren, Mary Anne. "Secondary Sexism and Quota Hiring." *Philosophy & Public Affairs*, 6 (Spring 1977), 240–261.

*Wasserstrom, Richard A. "Racism, Sexism, and Preferential Treatment: An Approach to the Topics." *UCLA Law Review*, 24 (February 1977), 581–622.

———. "The University and the Case for Preferential Treatment." *American Philosophical Quarterly*, 13 (April 1976), 165–170.

Welch, Finis. "Employment Quotas for Minorities." *Journal of Political Economy*, 84 (August 1976), 5105–5139.

Wolff, Robert Paul. "The Concept of Social Injustice." *From Contract to Community: Political Theory at the Crossroads*. Ed. Fred R. Dallmayr. New York: Marcel Dekker, Inc., 1978, 65–79.

Woodruff, Paul. "What's Wrong With Discrimination?" *Analysis*, 36 (March 1976), 158–160.

Zimmer, Michael J. "Beyond Defunis: Disproportionate Impact Analysis and Mandated 'Preferences' in Law School Admissions." *North Carolina Law Review*, 54 (February 1976), 317–388.

Index